REEL LOVE

REEL LOVE

THE COMPLETE COLLECTION

by
OWEN MICHAEL JOHNSON

LETTERED BY
COLIN BELL & PYE PARR

Unbound

This edition first published in 2019

Acts One and Two previously self-published
by Dogooder Comics and Changeling Studios respectively

Unbound
6th Floor Mutual House, 70 Conduit Street, London W1S 2GF

www.unbound.com

Supported using public funding by ARTS COUNCIL ENGLAND

The Lakes International Comic Art Festival

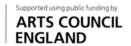

A CIP record for this book is available from the British Library

ISBN 978-1-78352-733-5 (trade hbk)
ISBN 978-1-78352-735-9 (ebook)

Printed in Slovenia by DZS Group

1 3 5 7 9 8 6 4 2

For my mother

ACT ONE
PROJECTIONS

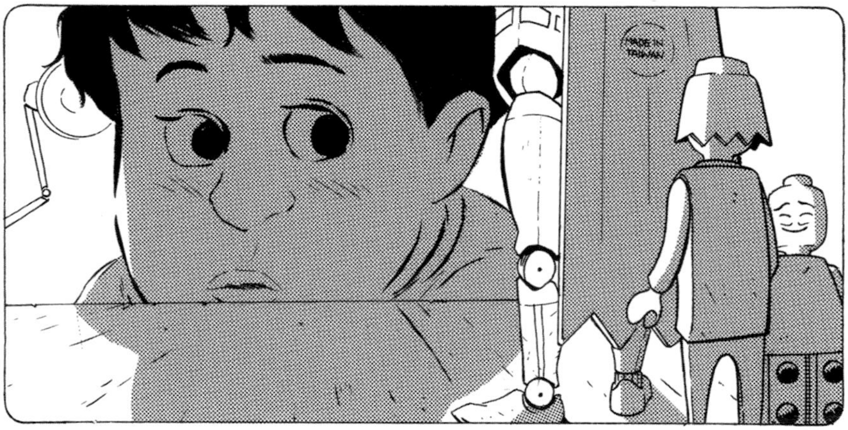
MADE IN TAIWAN

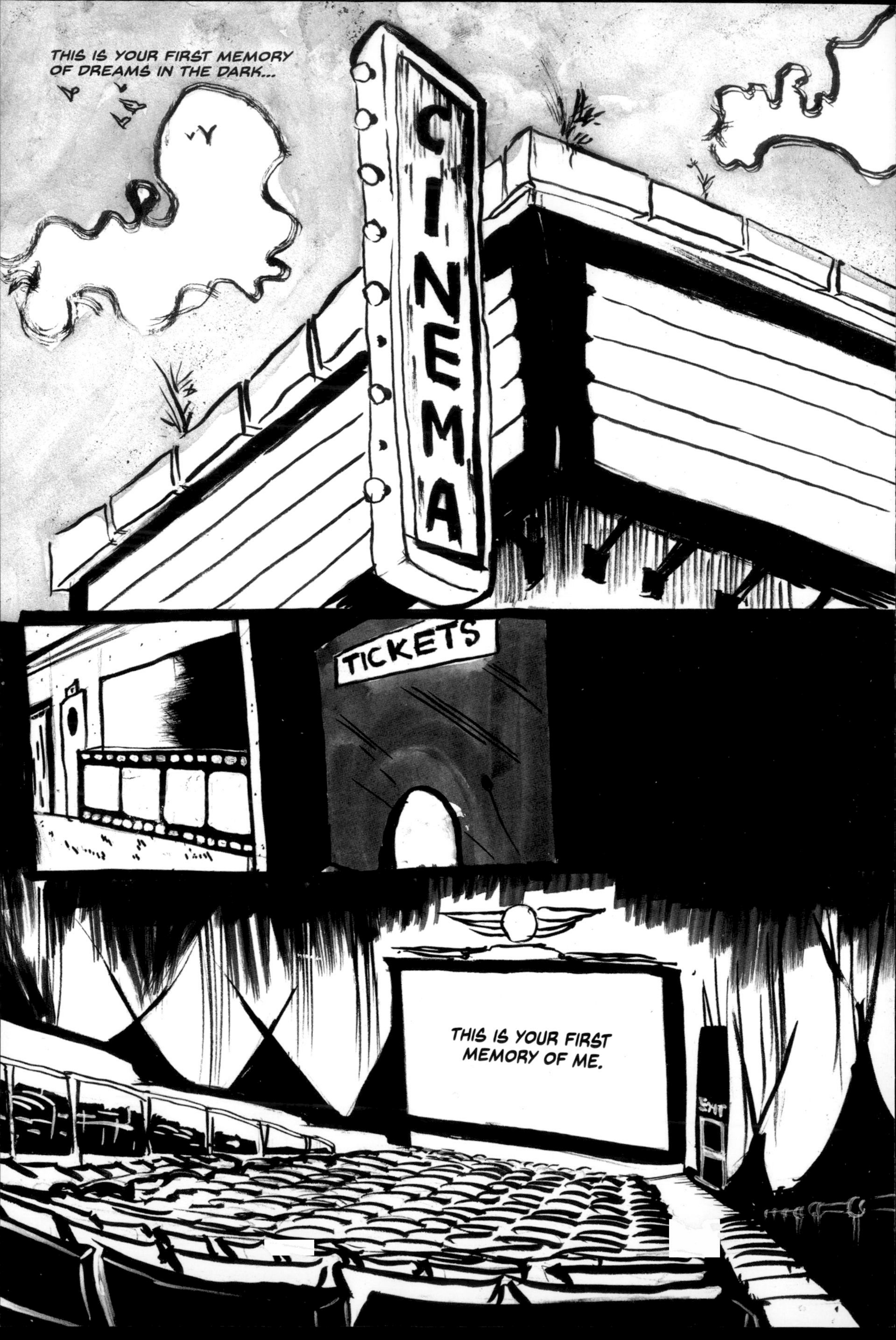
THIS IS YOUR FIRST MEMORY OF DREAMS IN THE DARK...
CINEMA
TICKETS
THIS IS YOUR FIRST MEMORY OF ME.

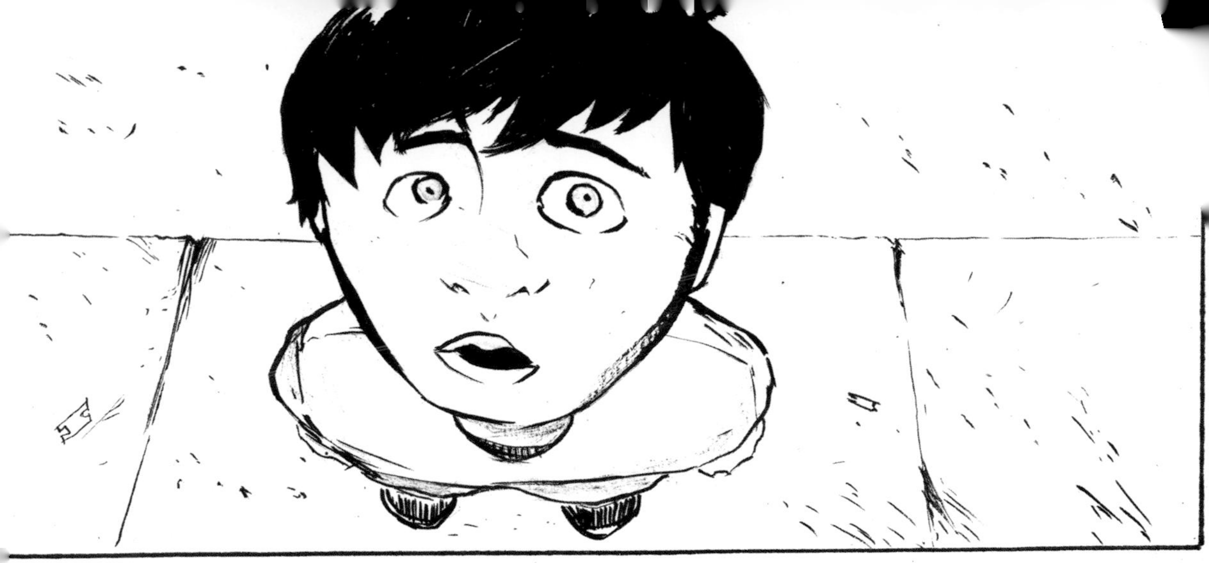

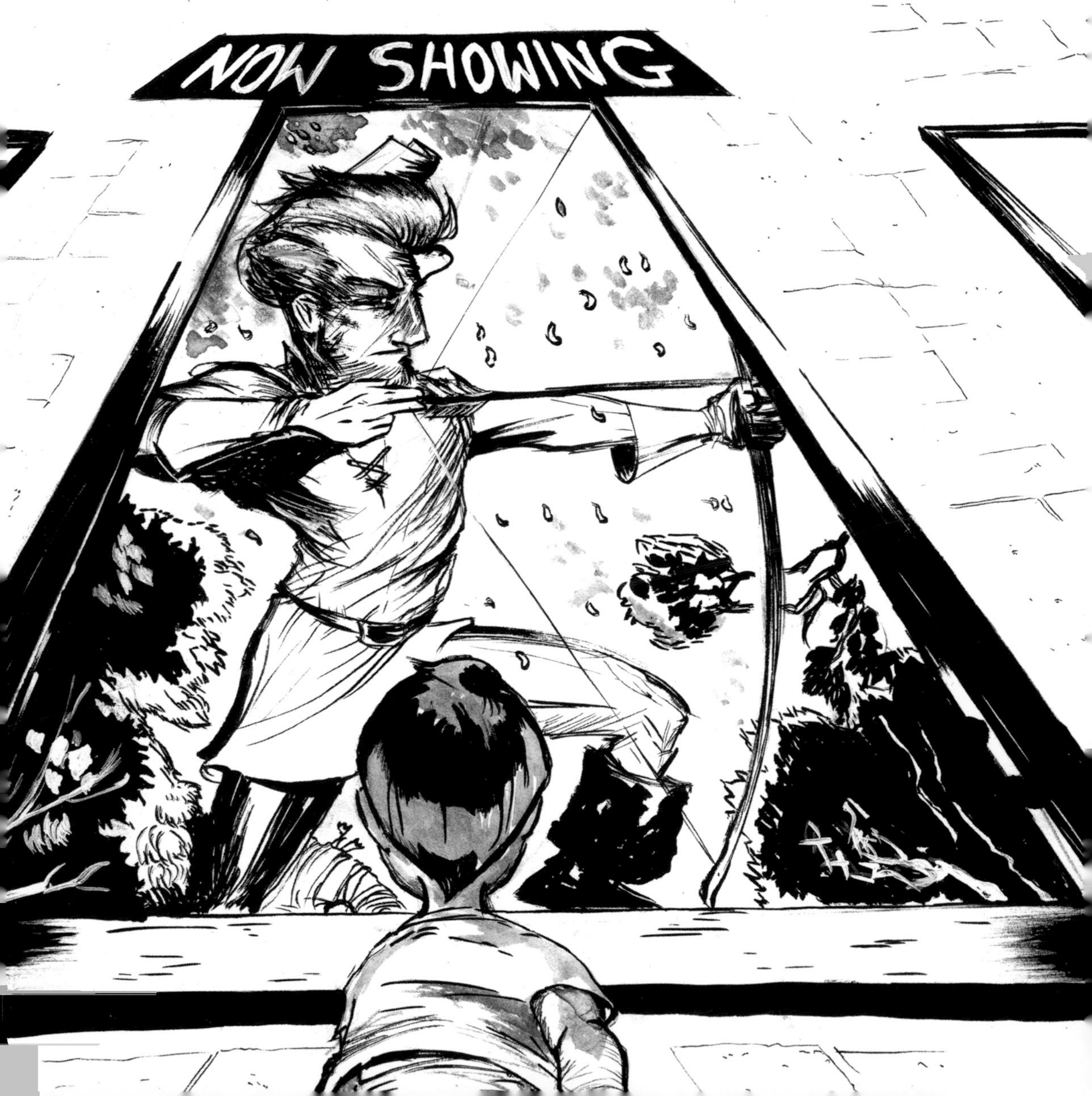
NOW SHOWING

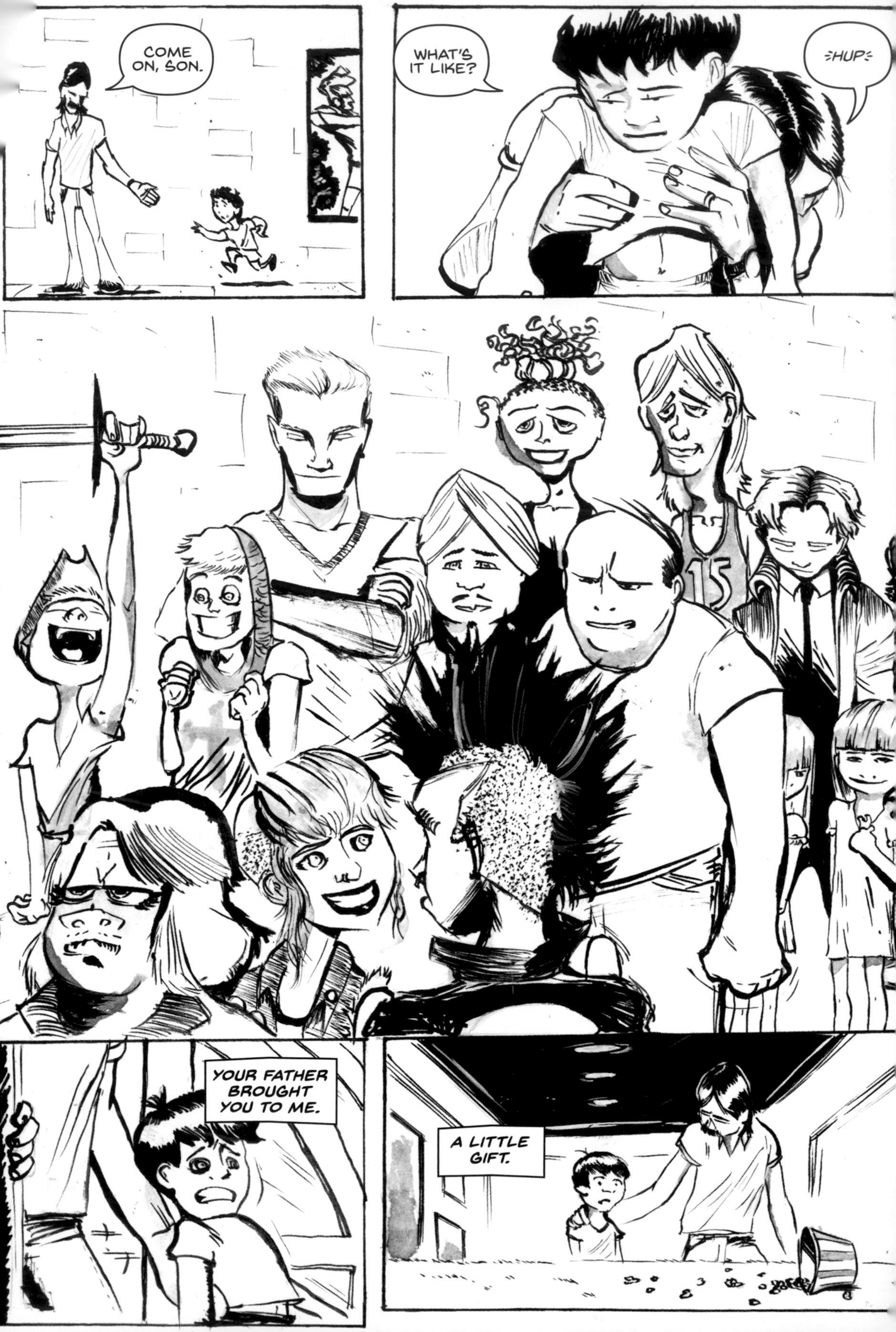
COME ON, SON.
WHAT'S IT LIKE?
HUP
YOUR FATHER BROUGHT YOU TO ME.
A LITTLE GIFT.

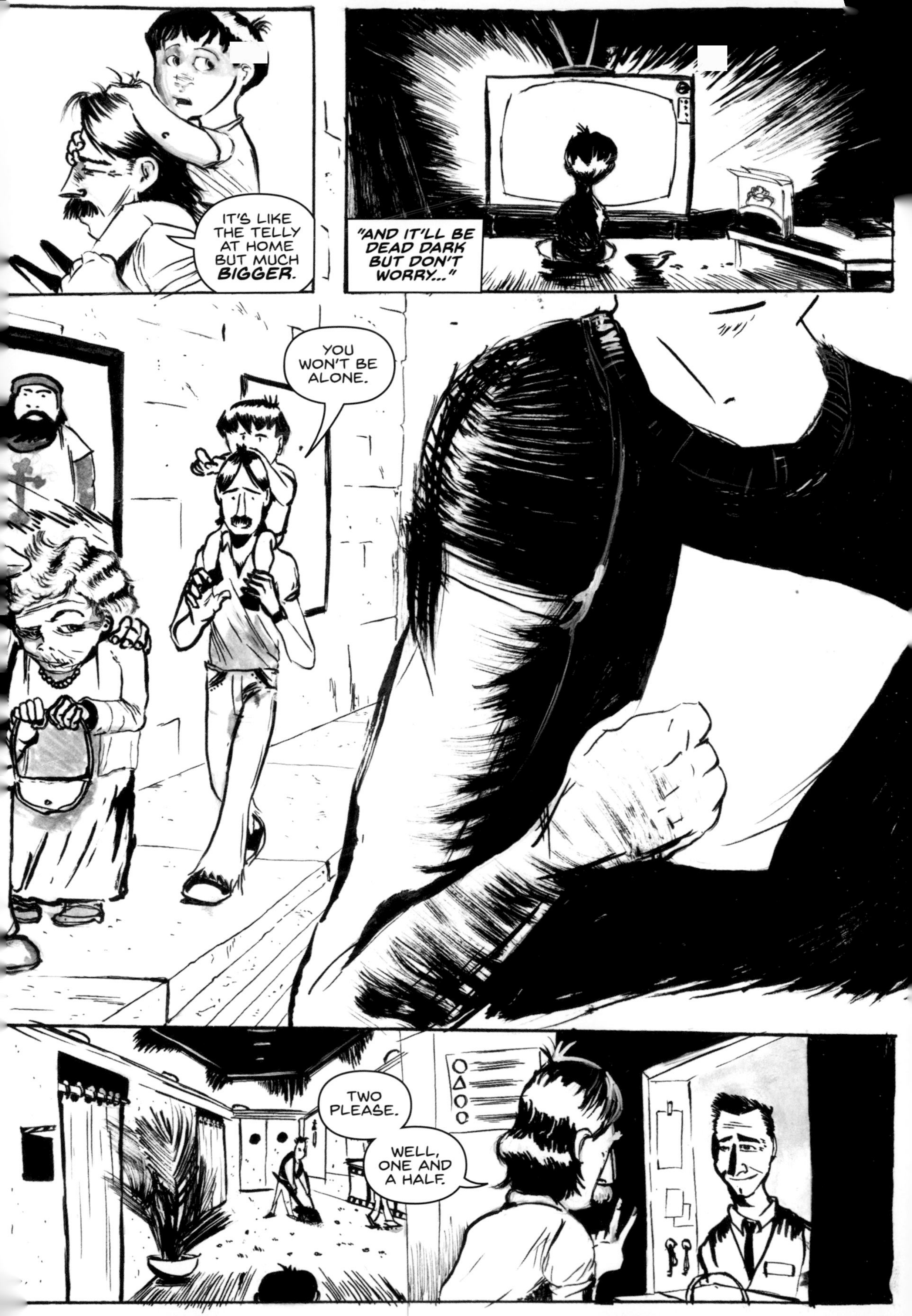
IT'S LIKE THE TELLY AT HOME BUT MUCH BIGGER.
"AND IT'LL BE DEAD DARK BUT DON'T WORRY..."
YOU WON'T BE ALONE.
TWO PLEASE.
WELL, ONE AND A HALF.

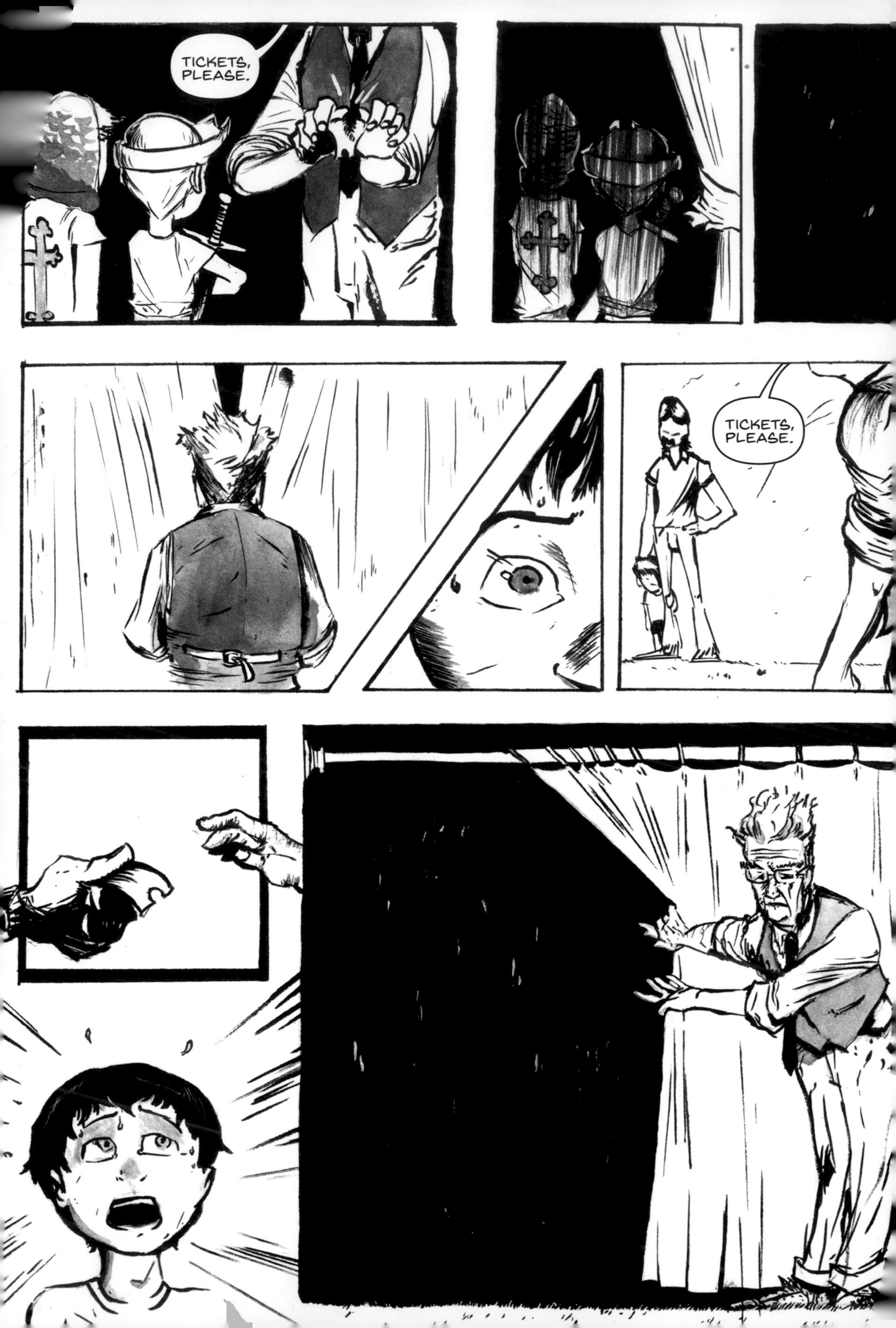
TICKETS, PLEASE.
TICKETS, PLEASE.

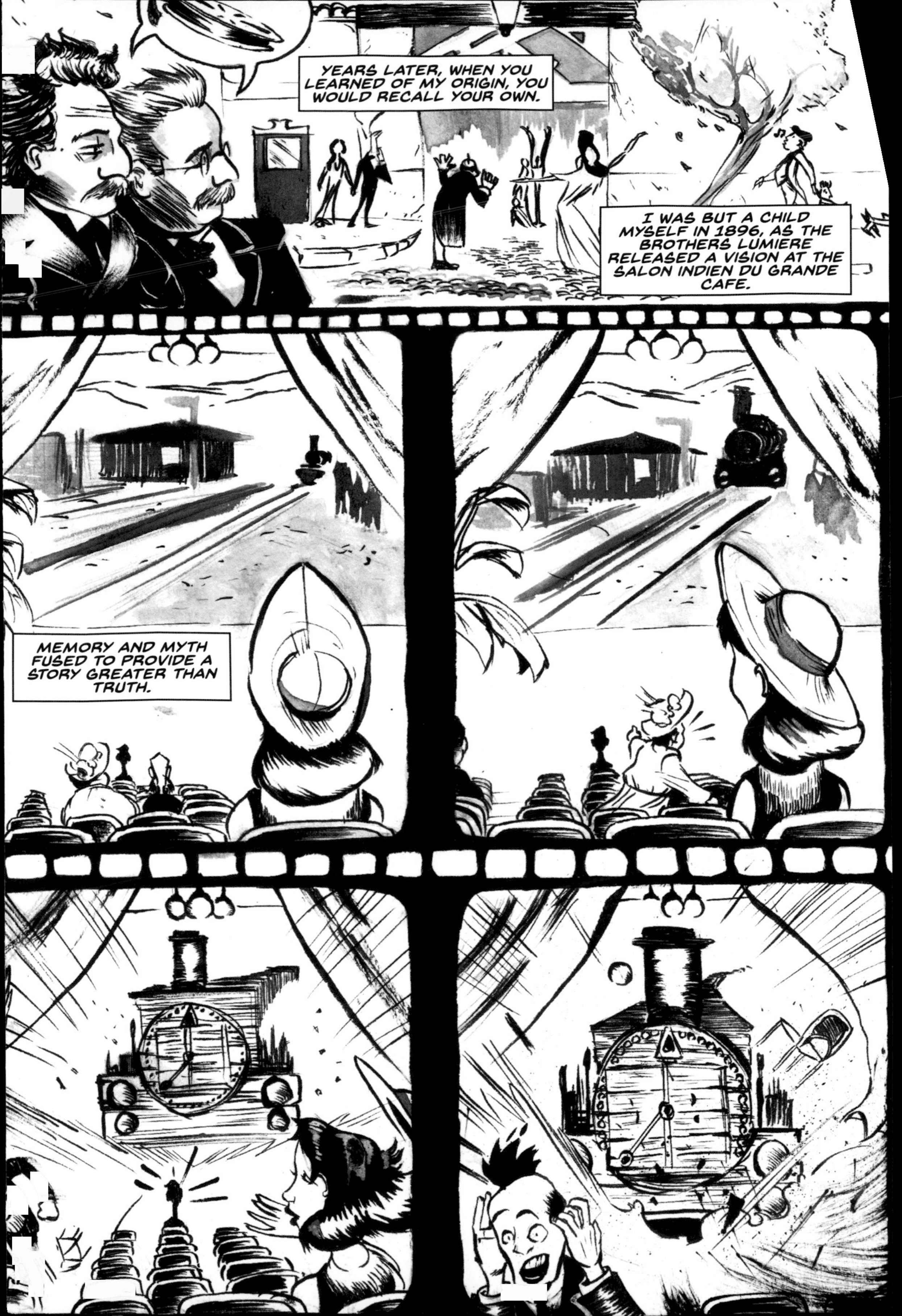
YEARS LATER, WHEN YOU LEARNED OF MY ORIGIN, YOU WOULD RECALL YOUR OWN.
I WAS BUT A CHILD MYSELF IN 1896, AS THE BROTHERS LUMIERE RELEASED A VISION AT THE SALON INDIEN DU GRANDE CAFE.
MEMORY AND MYTH FUSED TO PROVIDE A STORY GREATER THAN TRUTH.

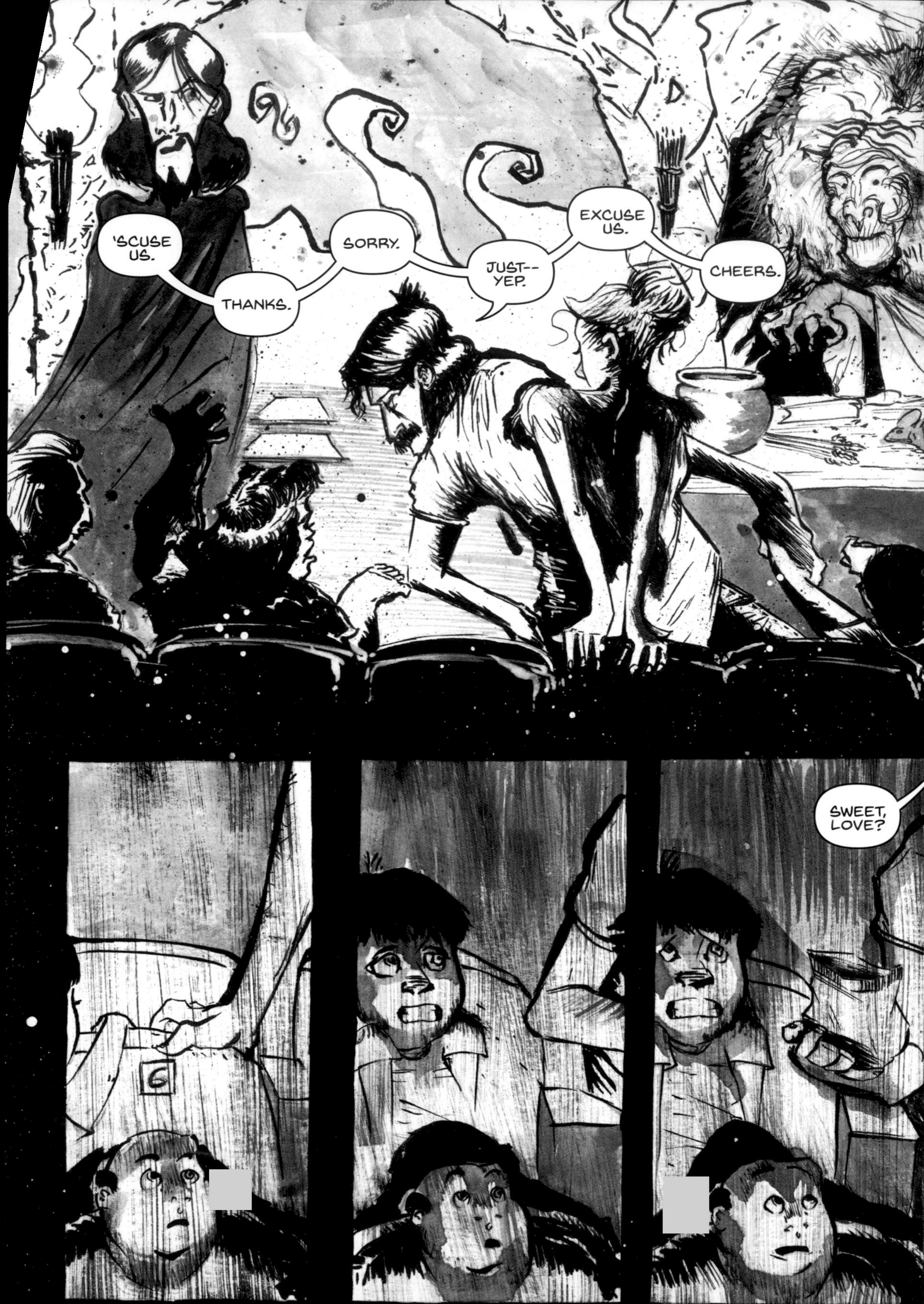
'SCUSE US.
THANKS.
SORRY.
JUST-- YEP.
EXCUSE US.
CHEERS.
SWEET, LOVE?

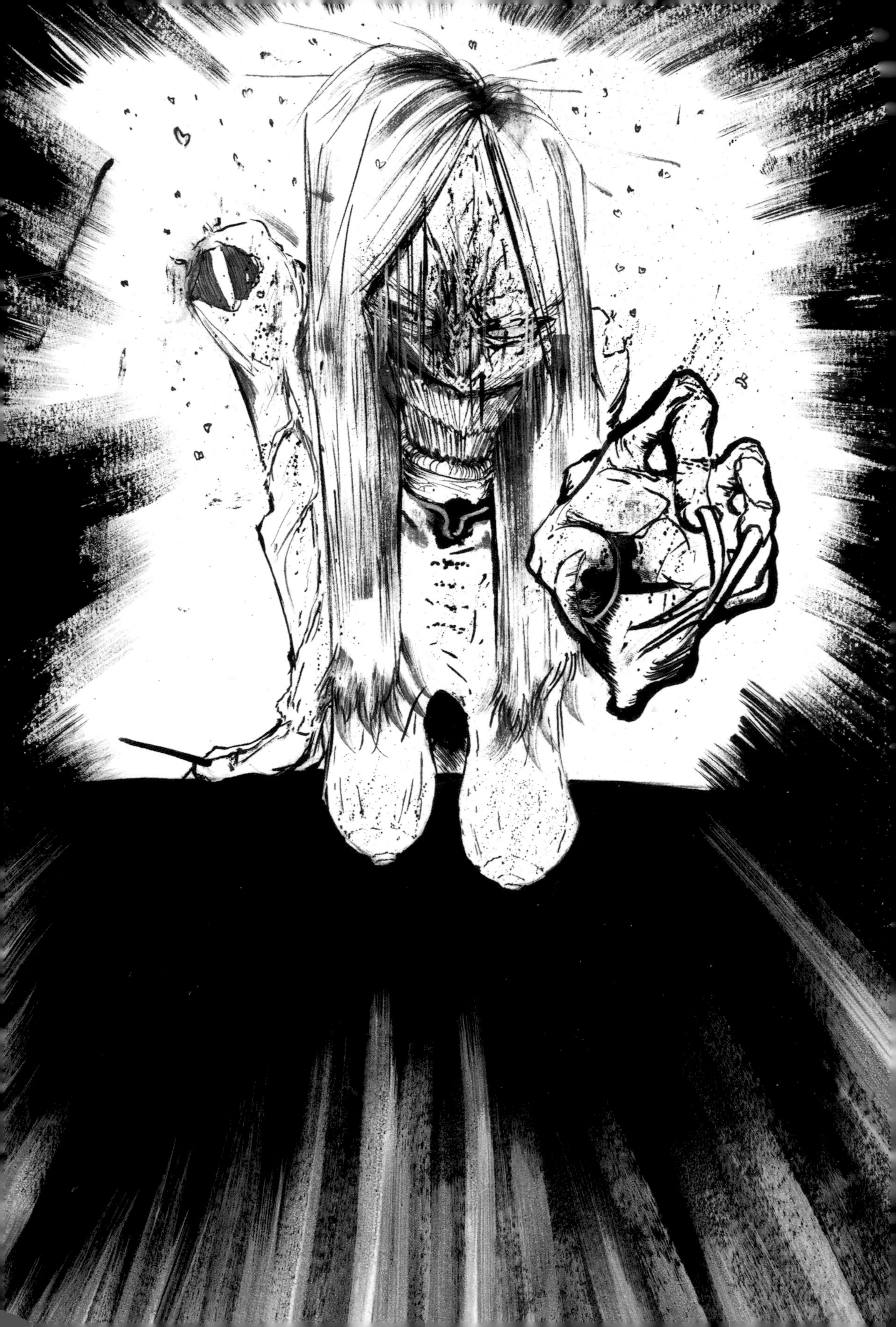

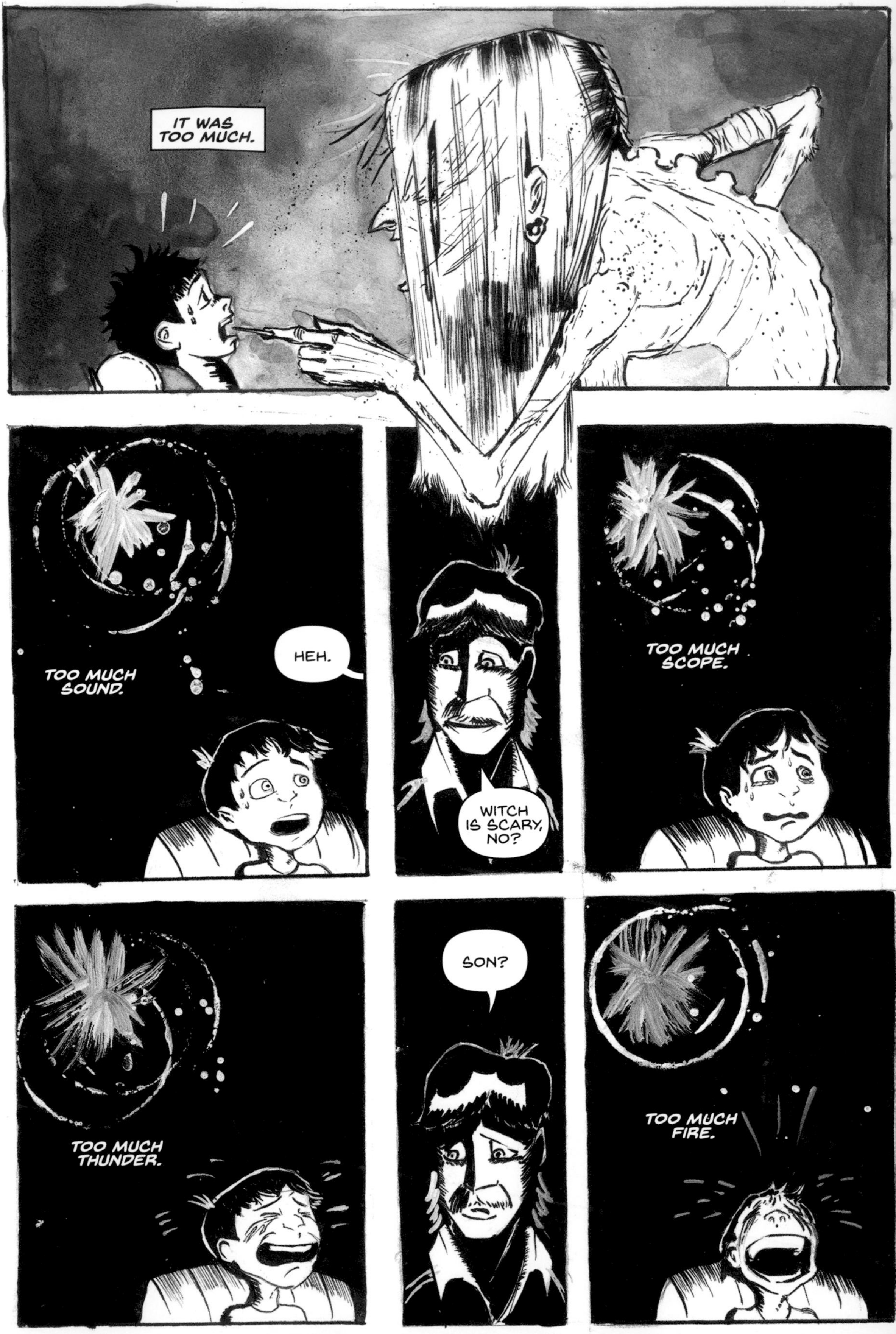
IT WAS TOO MUCH.
TOO MUCH SOUND.
HEH.
WITCH IS SCARY, NO?
TOO MUCH SCOPE.
TOO MUCH THUNDER.
SON?
TOO MUCH FIRE.

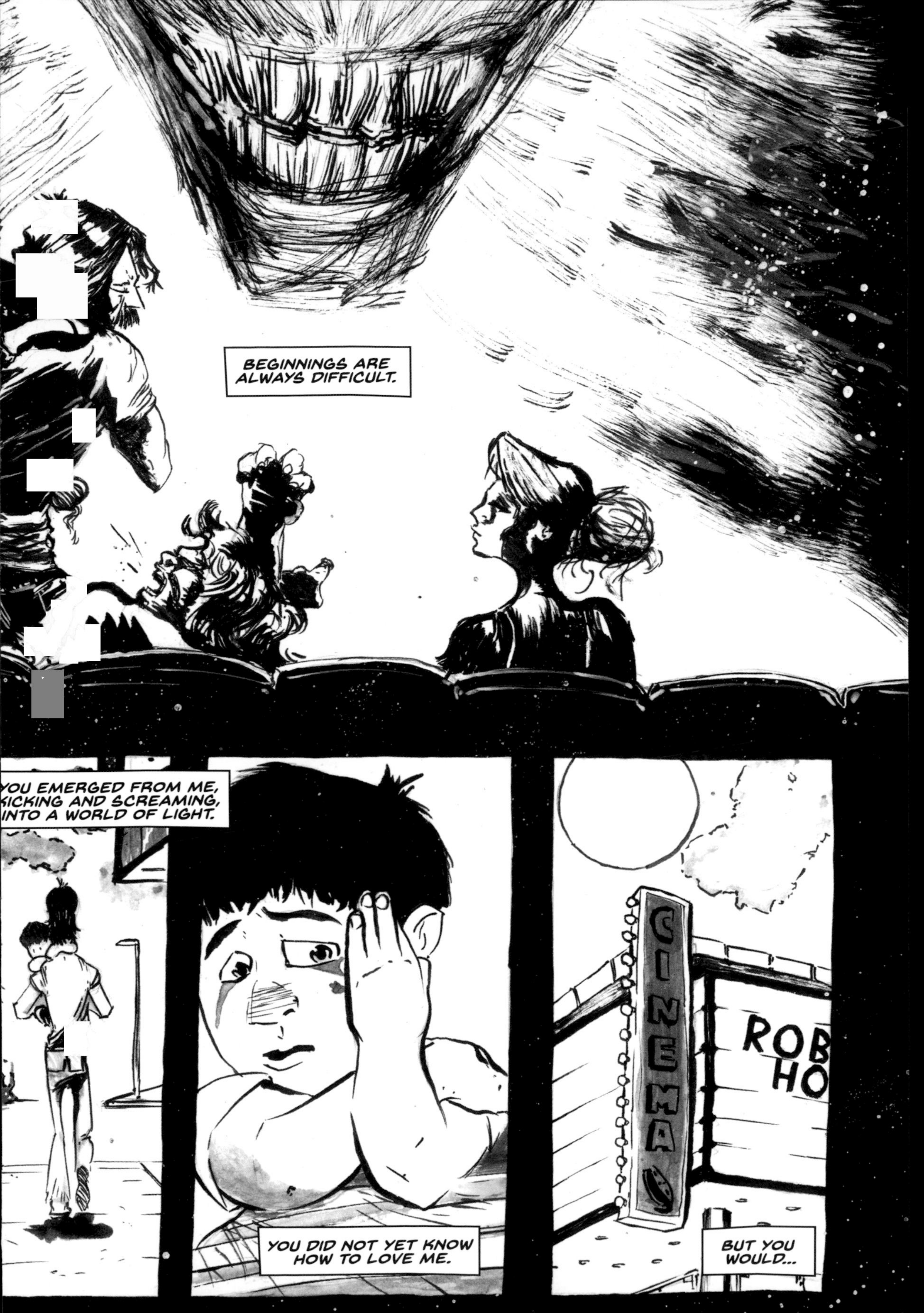
BEGINNINGS ARE ALWAYS DIFFICULT.
YOU EMERGED FROM ME, KICKING AND SCREAMING, INTO A WORLD OF LIGHT.
YOU DID NOT YET KNOW HOW TO LOVE ME.
CINEMA
ROB
HO
BUT YOU WOULD...

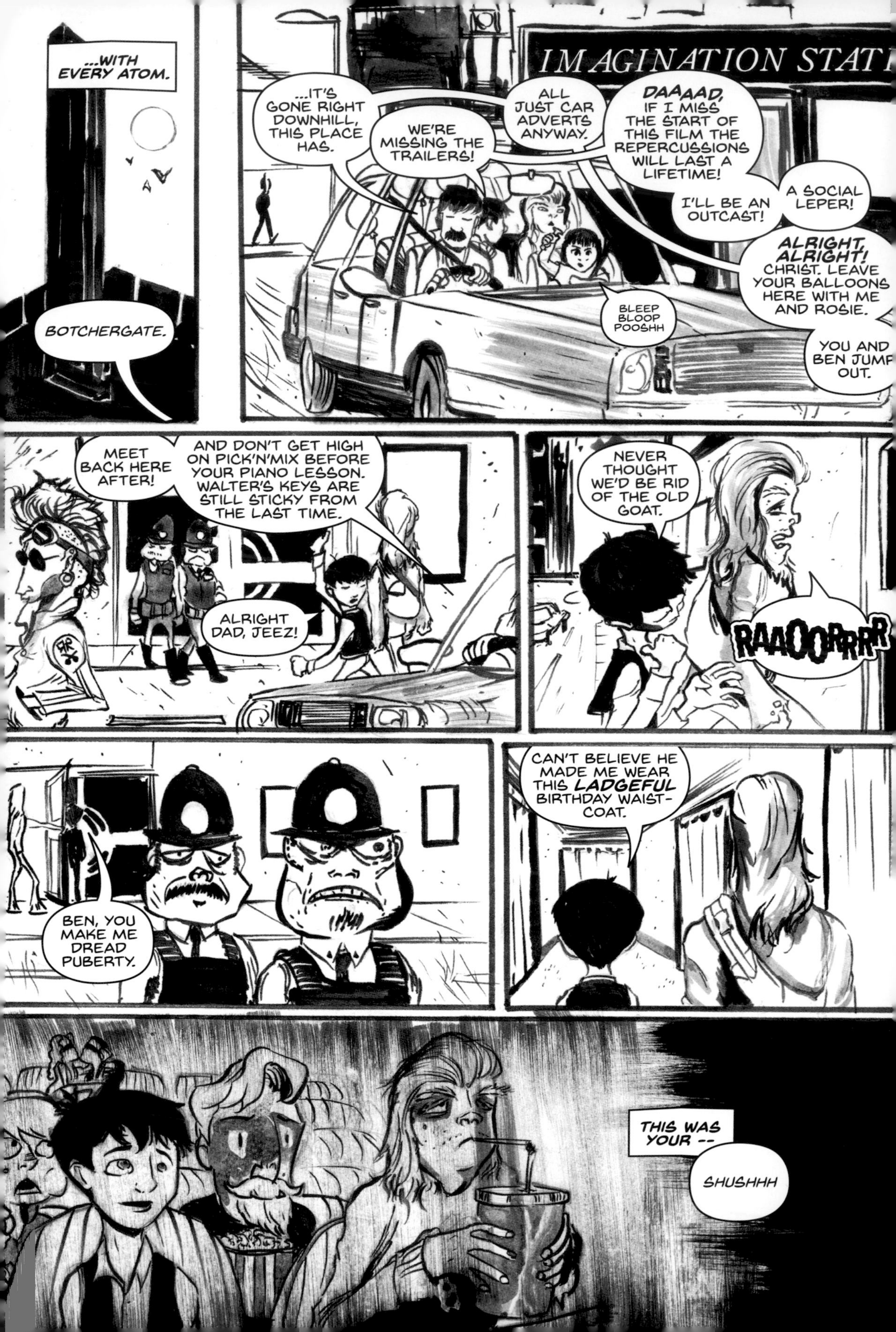
...WITH EVERY ATOM.
IMAGINATION STATI
...IT'S GONE RIGHT DOWNHILL, THIS PLACE HAS.
WE'RE MISSING THE TRAILERS!
ALL JUST CAR ADVERTS ANYWAY.
DAAAAD, IF I MISS THE START OF THIS FILM THE REPERCUSSIONS WILL LAST A LIFETIME!
I'LL BE AN OUTCAST!
A SOCIAL LEPER!
ALRIGHT, ALRIGHT! CHRIST. LEAVE YOUR BALLOONS HERE WITH ME AND ROSIE.
BLEEP BLOOP POOSHH
YOU AND BEN JUMP OUT.
BOTCHERGATE.
MEET BACK HERE AFTER!
AND DON'T GET HIGH ON PICK'N'MIX BEFORE YOUR PIANO LESSON. WALTER'S KEYS ARE STILL STICKY FROM THE LAST TIME.
ALRIGHT DAD, JEEZ!
NEVER THOUGHT WE'D BE RID OF THE OLD GOAT.
RAAOORRRR
BEN, YOU MAKE ME DREAD PUBERTY.
CAN'T BELIEVE HE MADE ME WEAR THIS LADGEFUL BIRTHDAY WAIST-COAT.
THIS WAS YOUR --
SHUSHHH

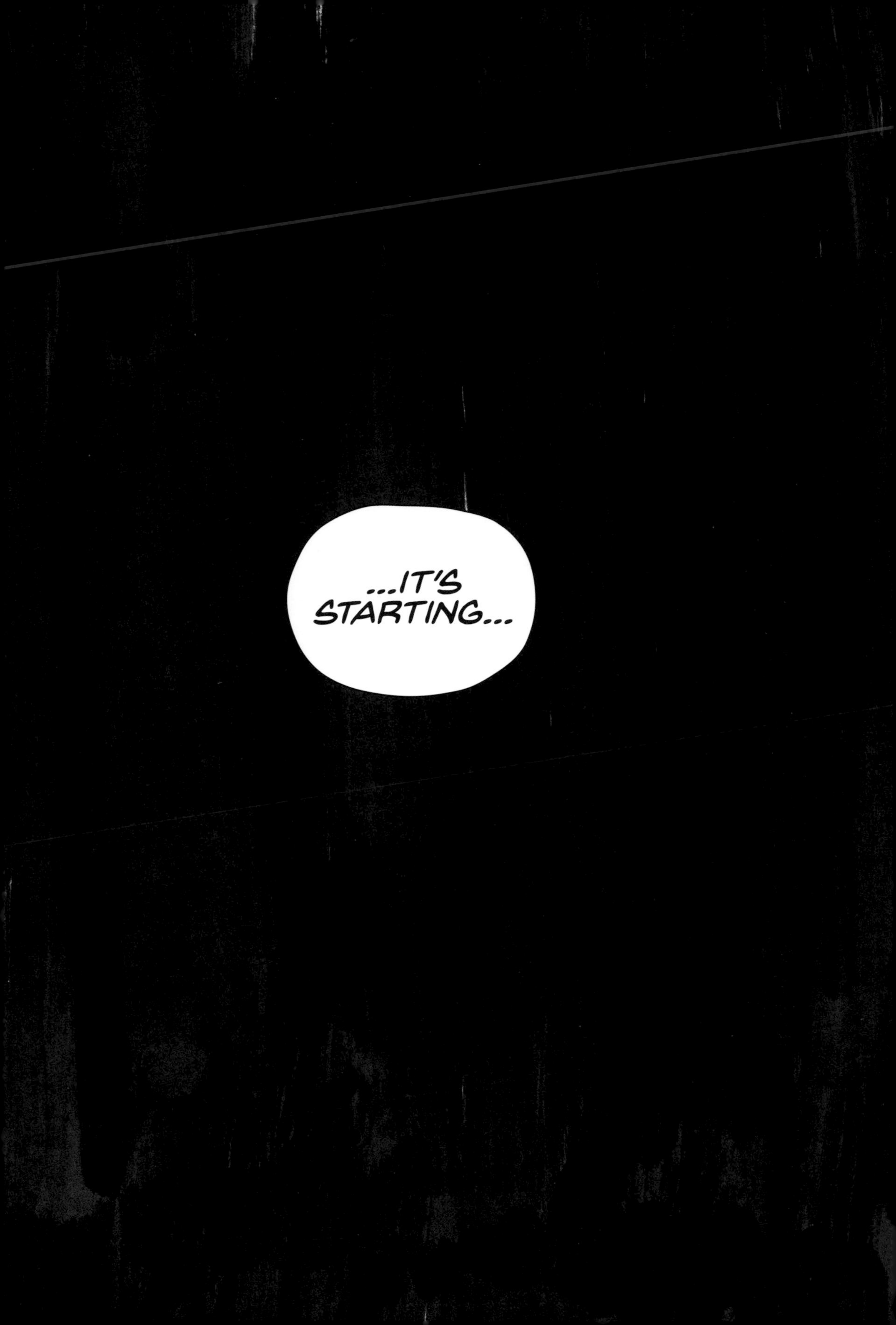
...IT'S STARTING...

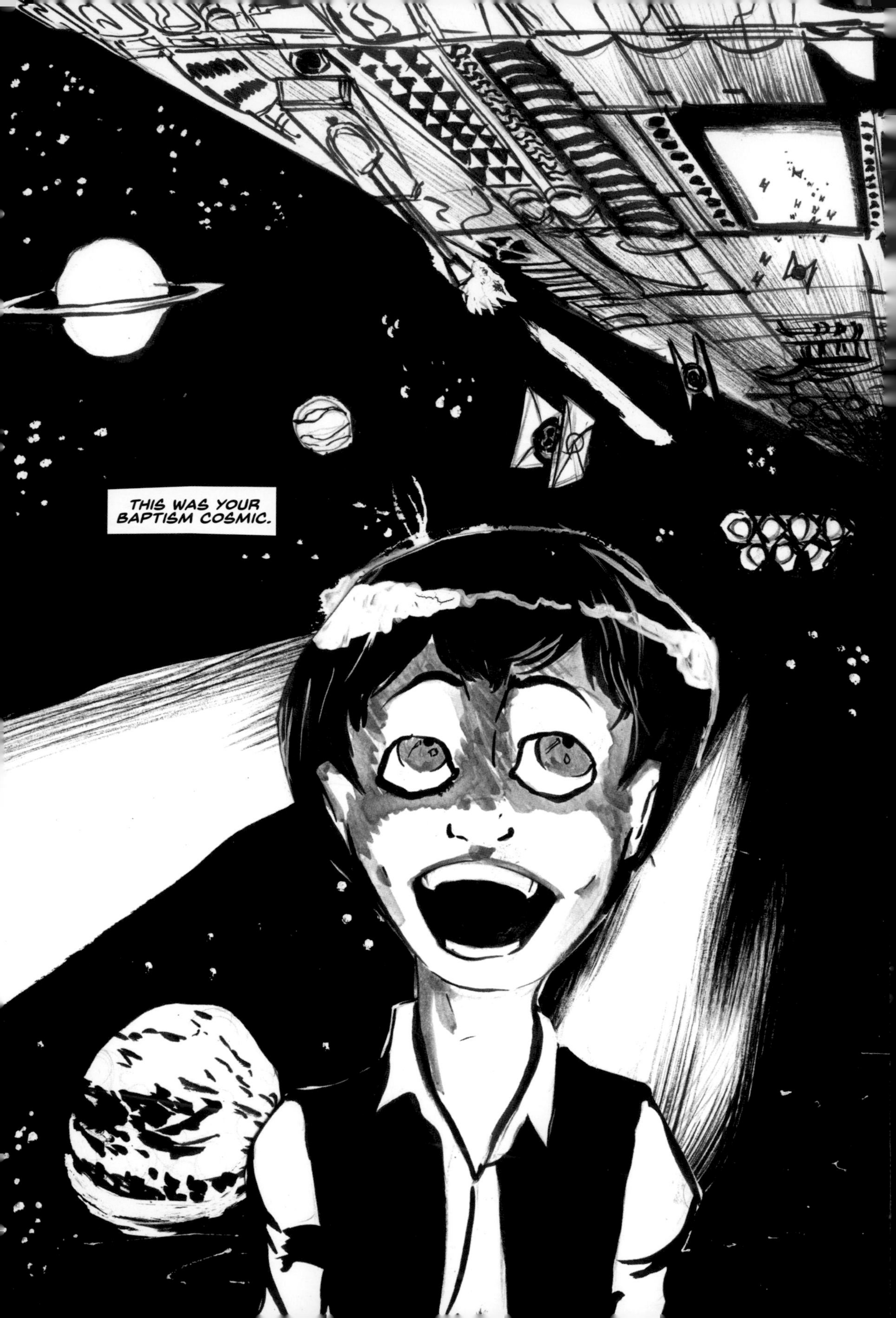
THIS WAS YOUR BAPTISM COSMIC.

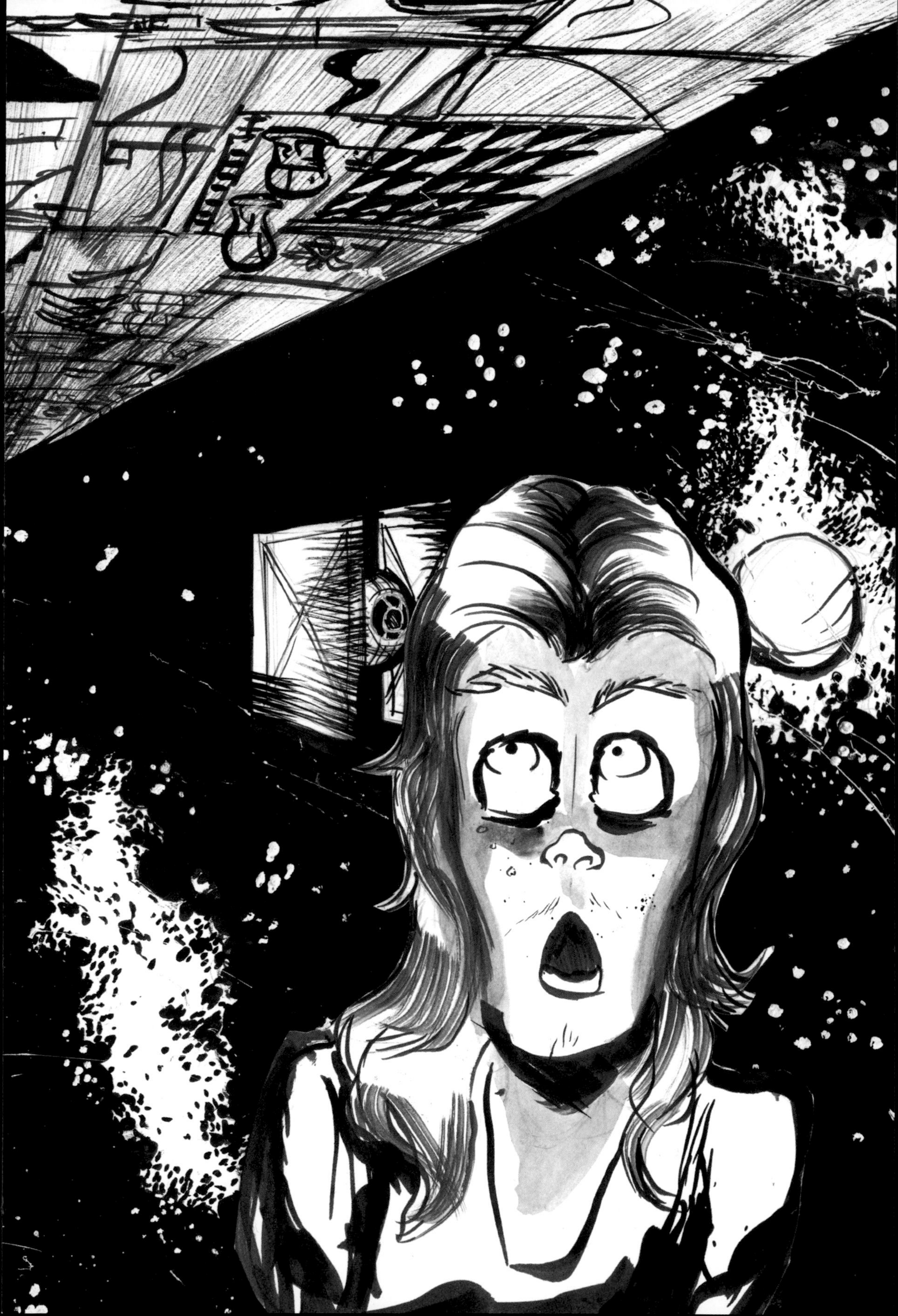

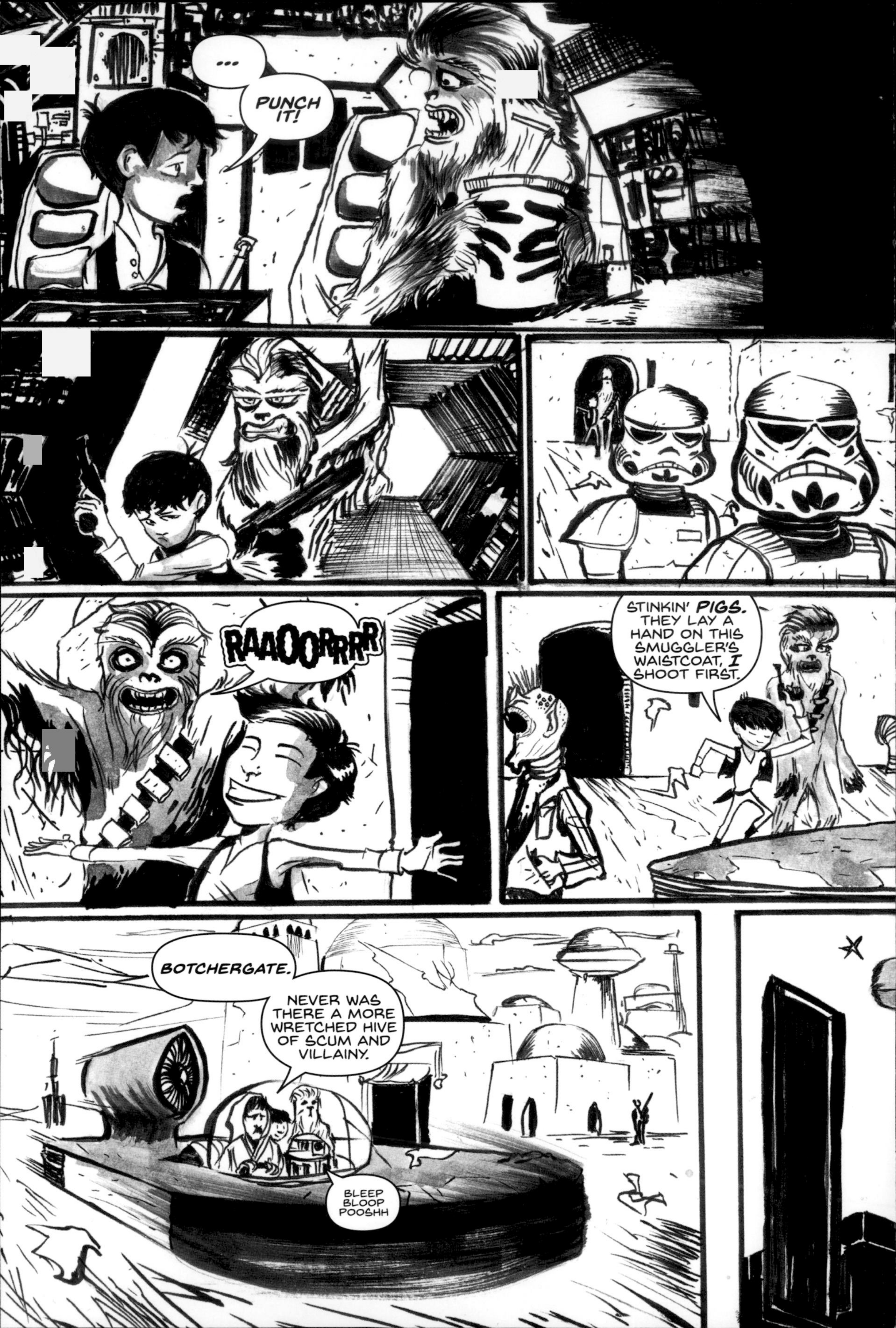
...
PUNCH IT!
RAAOORRRR
STINKIN' PIGS. THEY LAY A HAND ON THIS SMUGGLER'S WAISTCOAT, I SHOOT FIRST.
BOTCHERGATE.
NEVER WAS THERE A MORE WRETCHED HIVE OF SCUM AND VILLAINY.
BLEEP BLOOP POOSHH

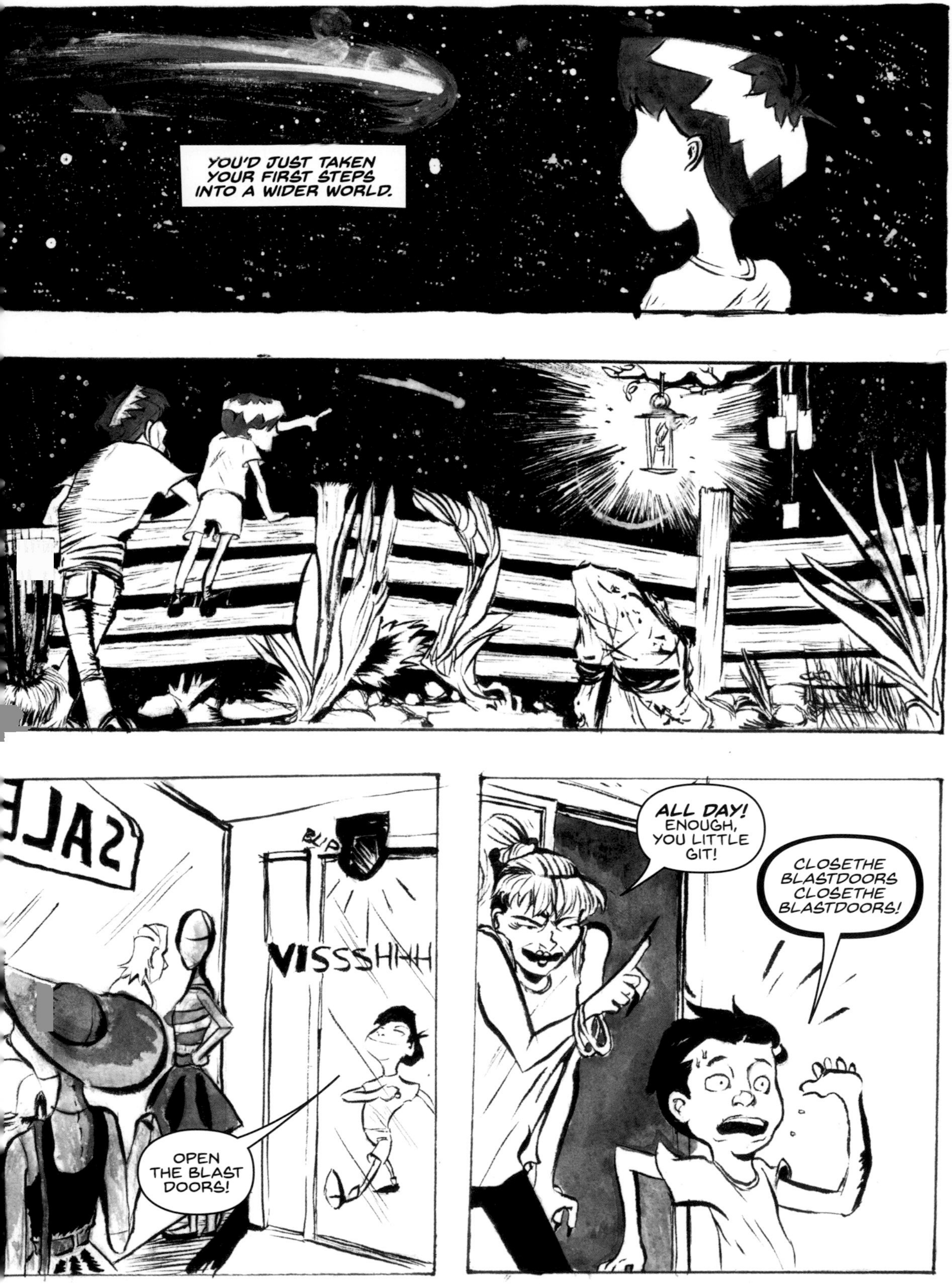
YOU'D JUST TAKEN YOUR FIRST STEPS INTO A WIDER WORLD.
SALE
BLIP
VISSSHHH
OPEN THE BLAST DOORS!
ALL DAY! ENOUGH, YOU LITTLE GIT!
CLOSETHE BLASTDOORS CLOSETHE BLASTDOORS!

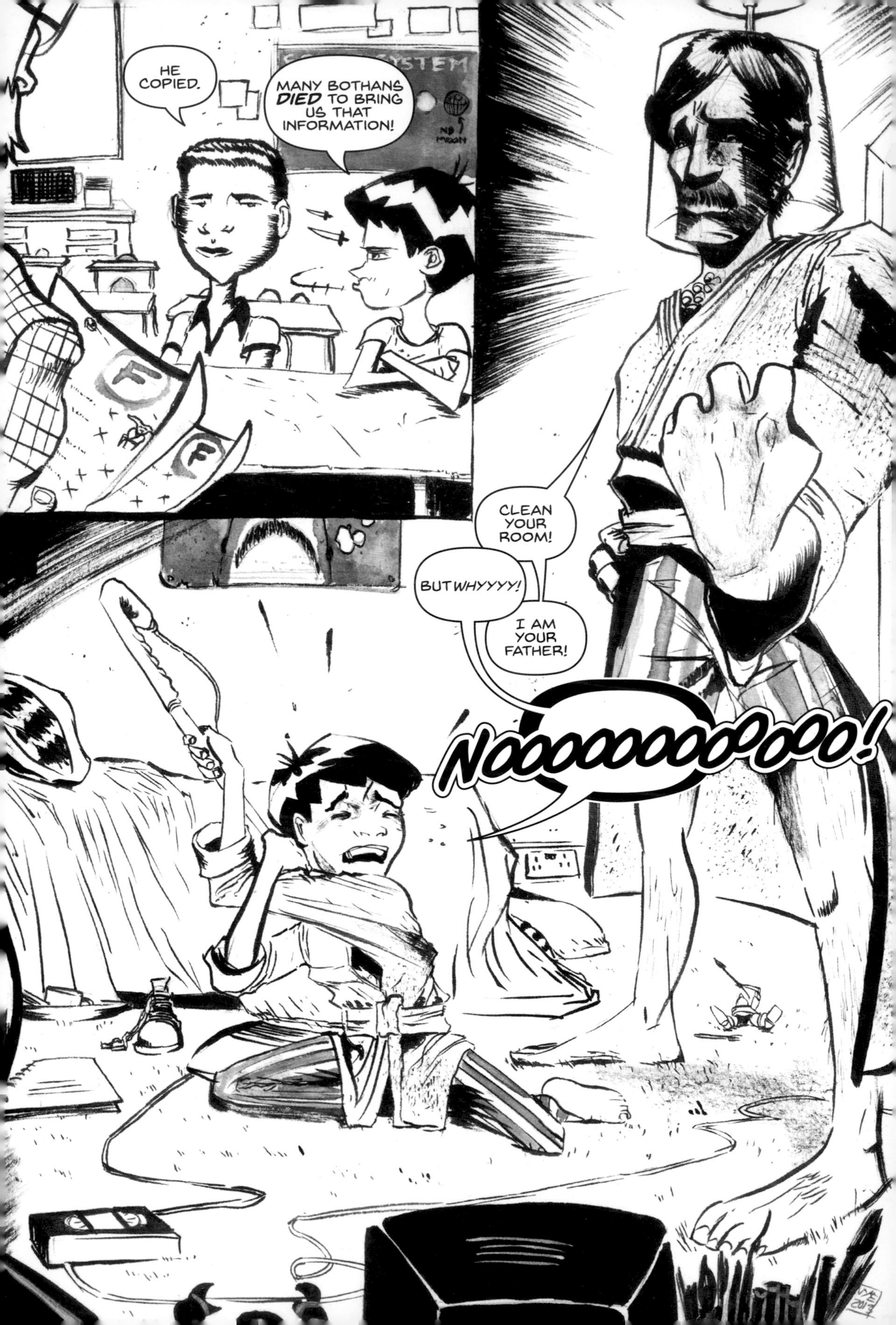
HE COPIED.
MANY BOTHANS *DIED* TO BRING US THAT INFORMATION!
CLEAN YOUR ROOM!
BUT WHYYYY!
I AM YOUR FATHER!
NOOOOOOOOOOOO!

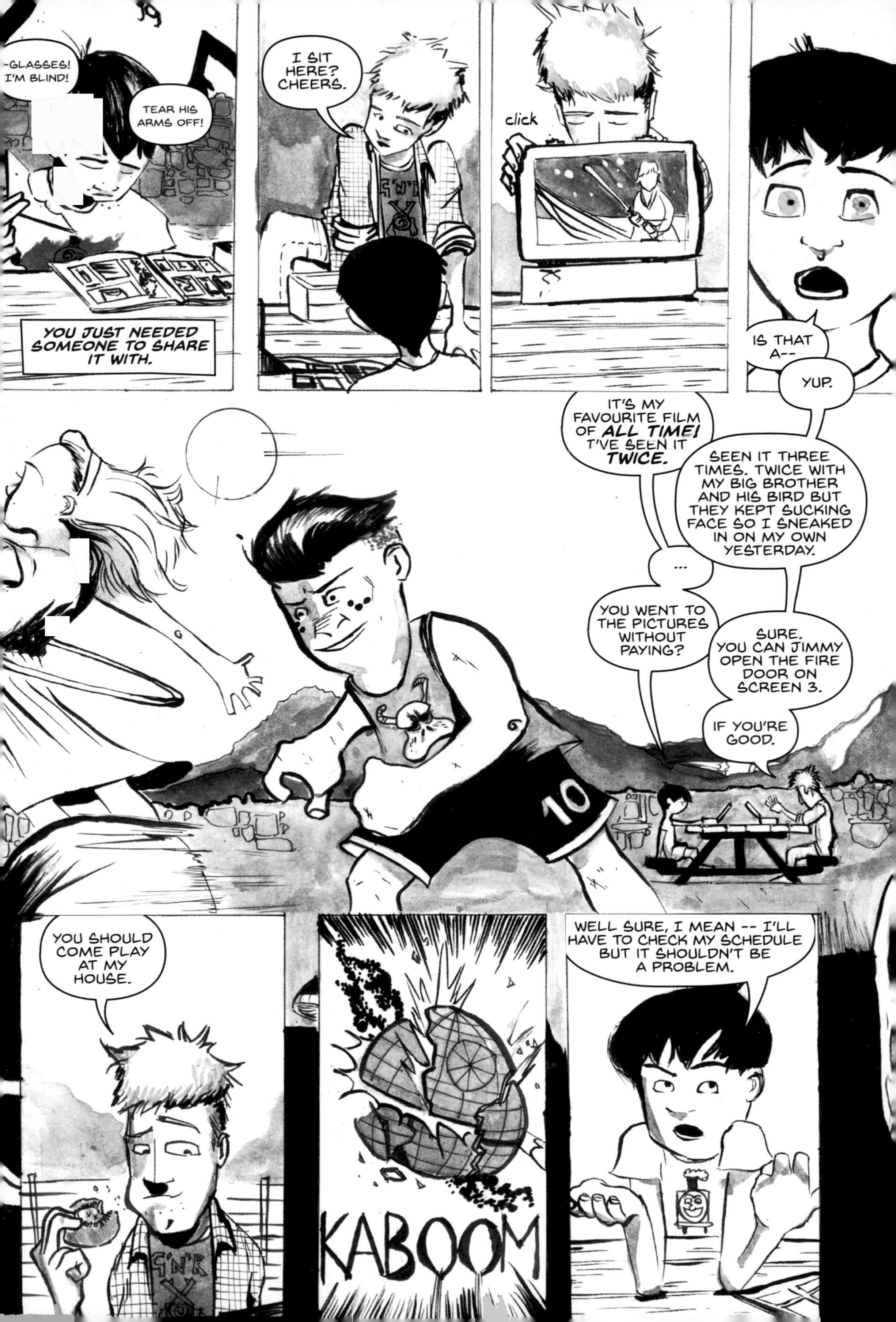

-GLASSES! I'M BLIND!
TEAR HIS ARMS OFF!
YOU JUST NEEDED SOMEONE TO SHARE IT WITH.
I SIT HERE? CHEERS.
click
IS THAT A--
YUP.
IT'S MY FAVOURITE FILM OF ALL TIME! I'VE SEEN IT TWICE.
SEEN IT THREE TIMES. TWICE WITH MY BIG BROTHER AND HIS BIRD BUT THEY KEPT SUCKING FACE SO I SNEAKED IN ON MY OWN YESTERDAY.
...
YOU WENT TO THE PICTURES WITHOUT PAYING?
SURE. YOU CAN JIMMY OPEN THE FIRE DOOR ON SCREEN 3.
IF YOU'RE GOOD.
10
YOU SHOULD COME PLAY AT MY HOUSE.
KABOOM
WELL SURE, I MEAN -- I'LL HAVE TO CHECK MY SCHEDULE BUT IT SHOULDN'T BE A PROBLEM.

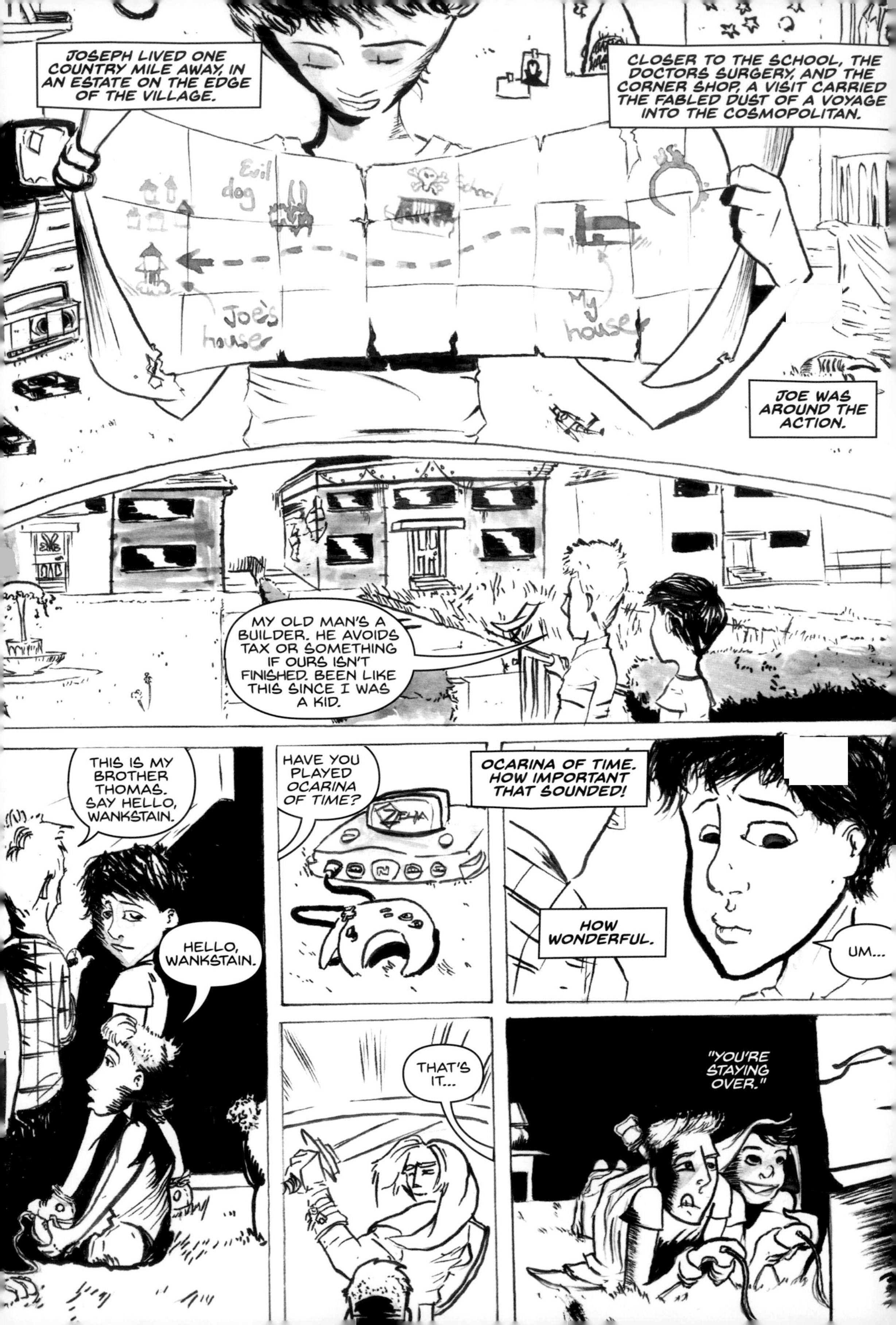
JOSEPH LIVED ONE COUNTRY MILE AWAY, IN AN ESTATE ON THE EDGE OF THE VILLAGE.
CLOSER TO THE SCHOOL, THE DOCTORS SURGERY, AND THE CORNER SHOP, A VISIT CARRIED THE FABLED DUST OF A VOYAGE INTO THE COSMOPOLITAN.
Evil dog
School
Joe's house
My house
JOE WAS AROUND THE ACTION.
MY OLD MAN'S A BUILDER. HE AVOIDS TAX OR SOMETHING IF OURS ISN'T FINISHED. BEEN LIKE THIS SINCE I WAS A KID.
THIS IS MY BROTHER THOMAS. SAY HELLO, WANKSTAIN.
HELLO, WANKSTAIN.
HAVE YOU PLAYED OCARINA OF TIME?
OCARINA OF TIME. HOW IMPORTANT THAT SOUNDED!
HOW WONDERFUL.
UM...
THAT'S IT...
"YOU'RE STAYING OVER."

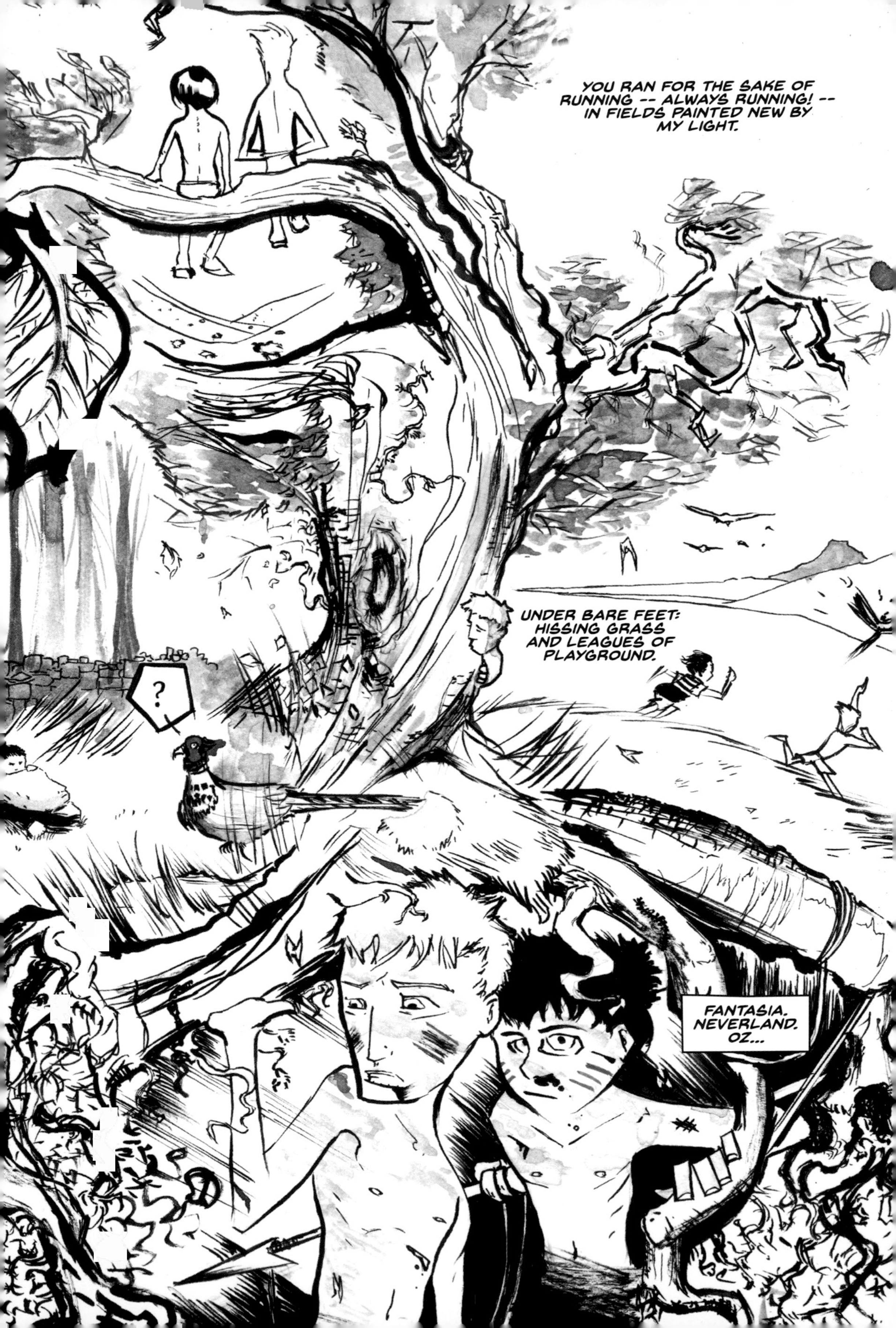
YOU RAN FOR THE SAKE OF RUNNING -- ALWAYS RUNNING! -- IN FIELDS PAINTED NEW BY MY LIGHT.
UNDER BARE FEET: HISSING GRASS AND LEAGUES OF PLAYGROUND.
?
FANTASIA. NEVERLAND. OZ...

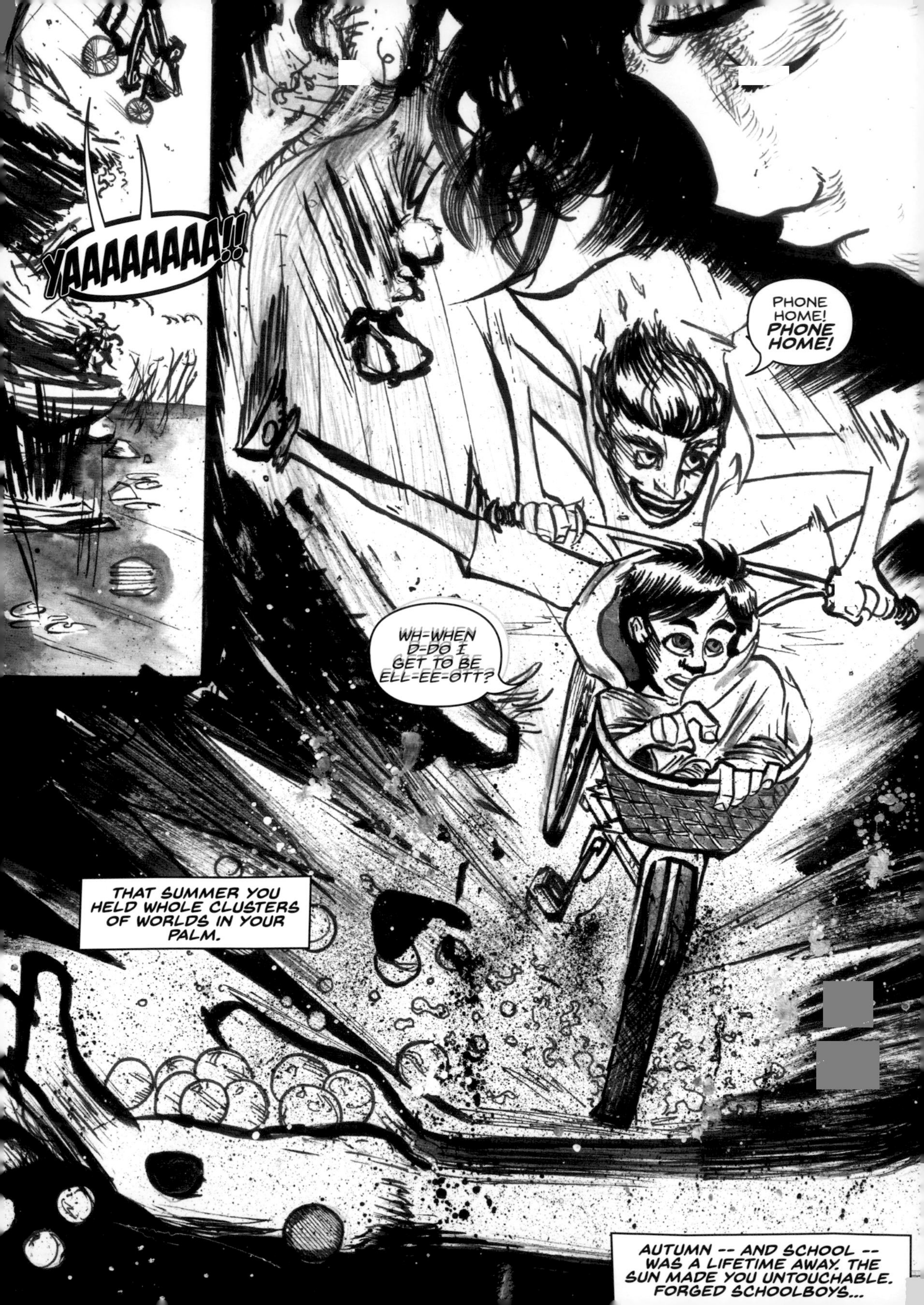
YAAAAAAA!!
PHONE HOME! PHONE HOME!
WH-WHEN D-DO I GET TO BE ELL-EE-OTT?
THAT SUMMER YOU HELD WHOLE CLUSTERS OF WORLDS IN YOUR PALM.
AUTUMN -- AND SCHOOL -- WAS A LIFETIME AWAY. THE SUN MADE YOU UNTOUCHABLE. FORGED SCHOOLBOYS...

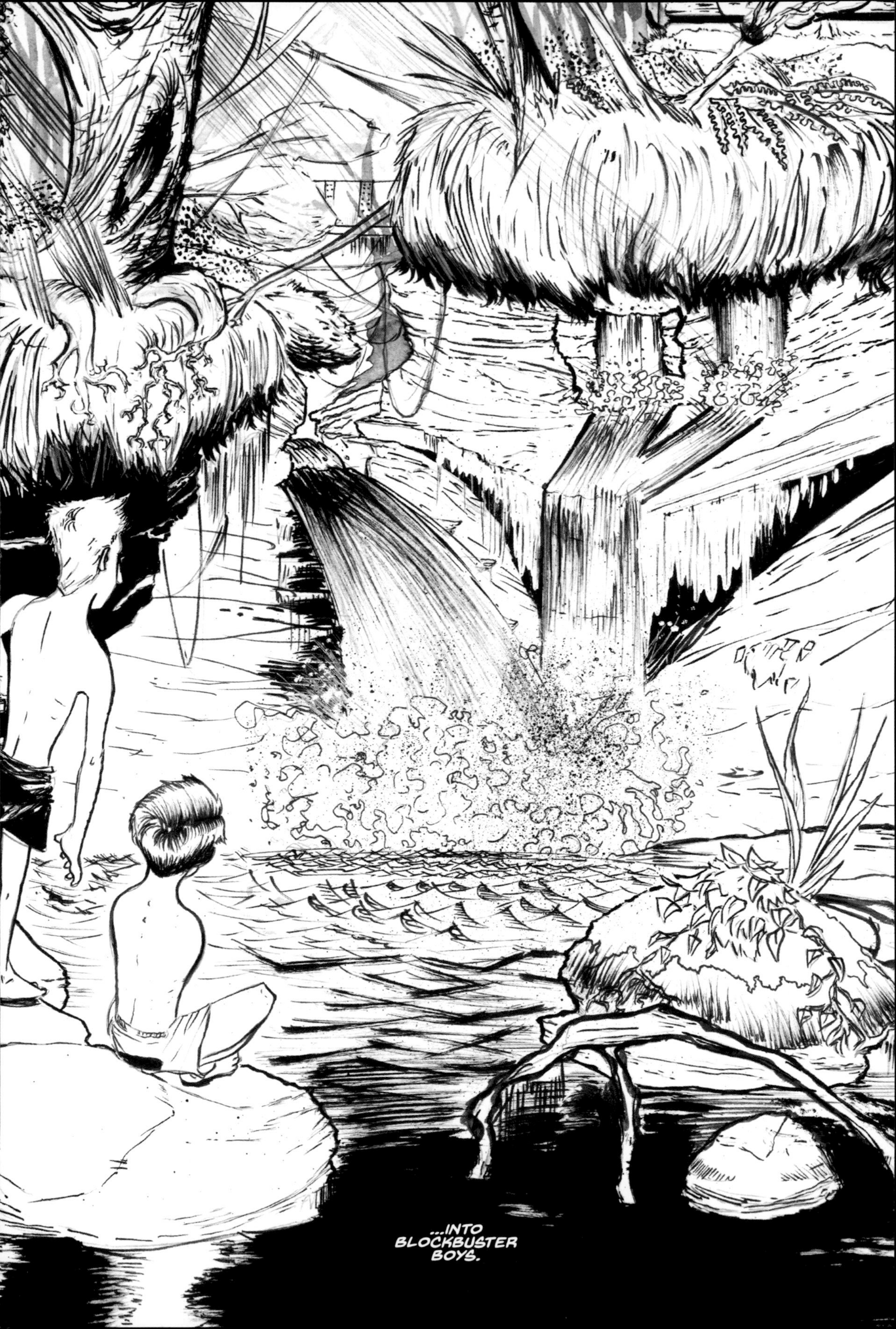
...INTO
BLOCKBUSTER
BOYS.

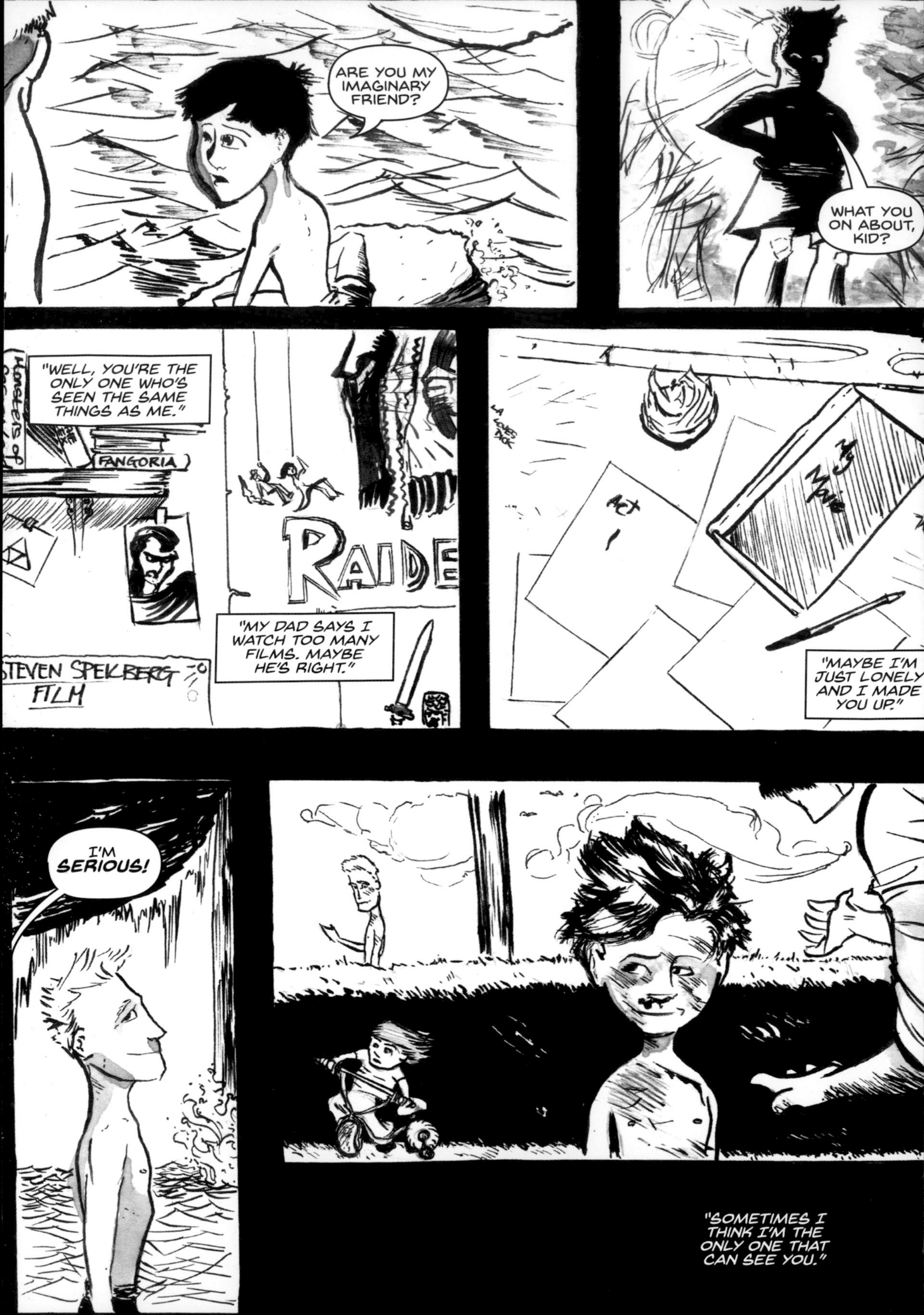

ARE YOU MY IMAGINARY FRIEND?
WHAT YOU ON ABOUT, KID?
"WELL, YOU'RE THE ONLY ONE WHO'S SEEN THE SAME THINGS AS ME."
FANGORIA
RAIDE
STEVEN SPEKBERG FILM
"MY DAD SAYS I WATCH TOO MANY FILMS. MAYBE HE'S RIGHT."
Act 1
"MAYBE I'M JUST LONELY AND I MADE YOU UP."
I'M **SERIOUS!**
"SOMETIMES I THINK I'M THE ONLY ONE THAT CAN SEE YOU."

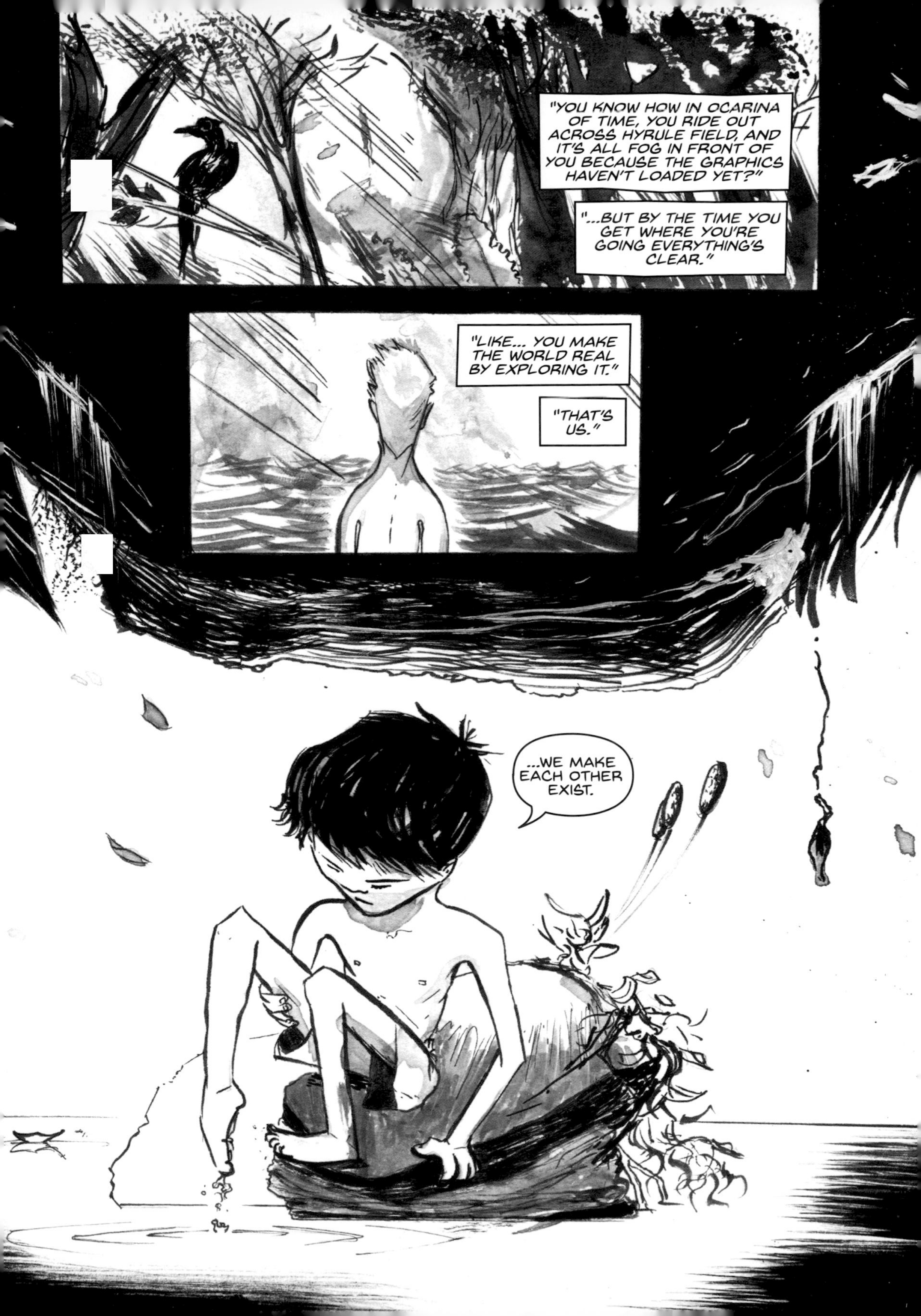
"YOU KNOW HOW IN OCARINA OF TIME, YOU RIDE OUT ACROSS HYRULE FIELD, AND IT'S ALL FOG IN FRONT OF YOU BECAUSE THE GRAPHICS HAVEN'T LOADED YET?"
"...BUT BY THE TIME YOU GET WHERE YOU'RE GOING EVERYTHING'S CLEAR."
"LIKE... YOU MAKE THE WORLD REAL BY EXPLORING IT."
"THAT'S US."
...WE MAKE EACH OTHER EXIST.

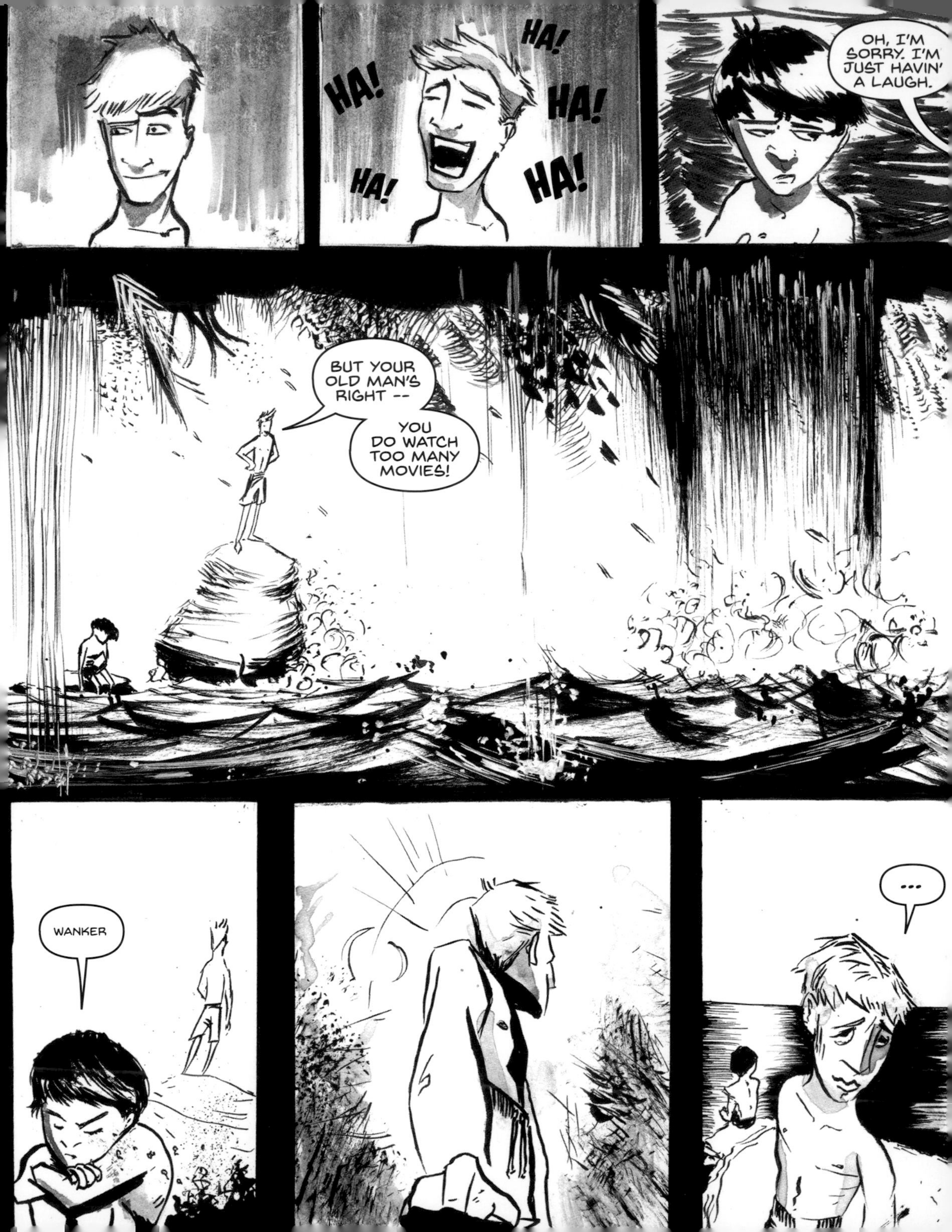
HA!
HA!
HA!
HA!
HA!
OH, I'M SORRY. I'M JUST HAVIN' A LAUGH.
BUT YOUR OLD MAN'S RIGHT --
YOU DO WATCH TOO MANY MOVIES!
WANKER
...

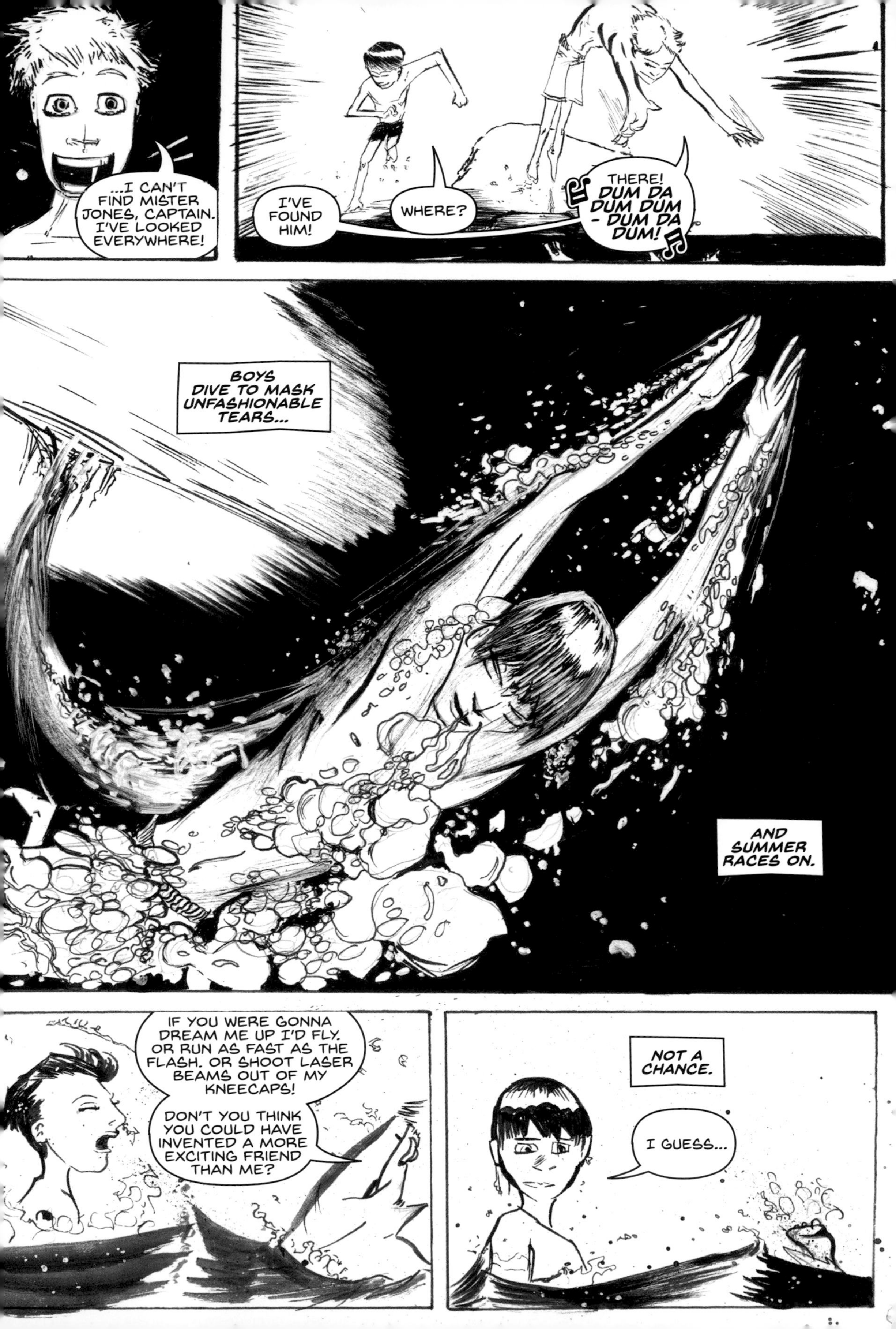
...I CAN'T FIND MISTER JONES, CAPTAIN. I'VE LOOKED EVERYWHERE!
I'VE FOUND HIM!
WHERE?
THERE! DUM DA DUM DUM - DUM DA DUM!
BOYS DIVE TO MASK UNFASHIONABLE TEARS...
AND SUMMER RACES ON.
IF YOU WERE GONNA DREAM ME UP I'D FLY. OR RUN AS FAST AS THE FLASH. OR SHOOT LASER BEAMS OUT OF MY KNEECAPS!
DON'T YOU THINK YOU COULD HAVE INVENTED A MORE EXCITING FRIEND THAN ME?
NOT A CHANCE.
I GUESS...

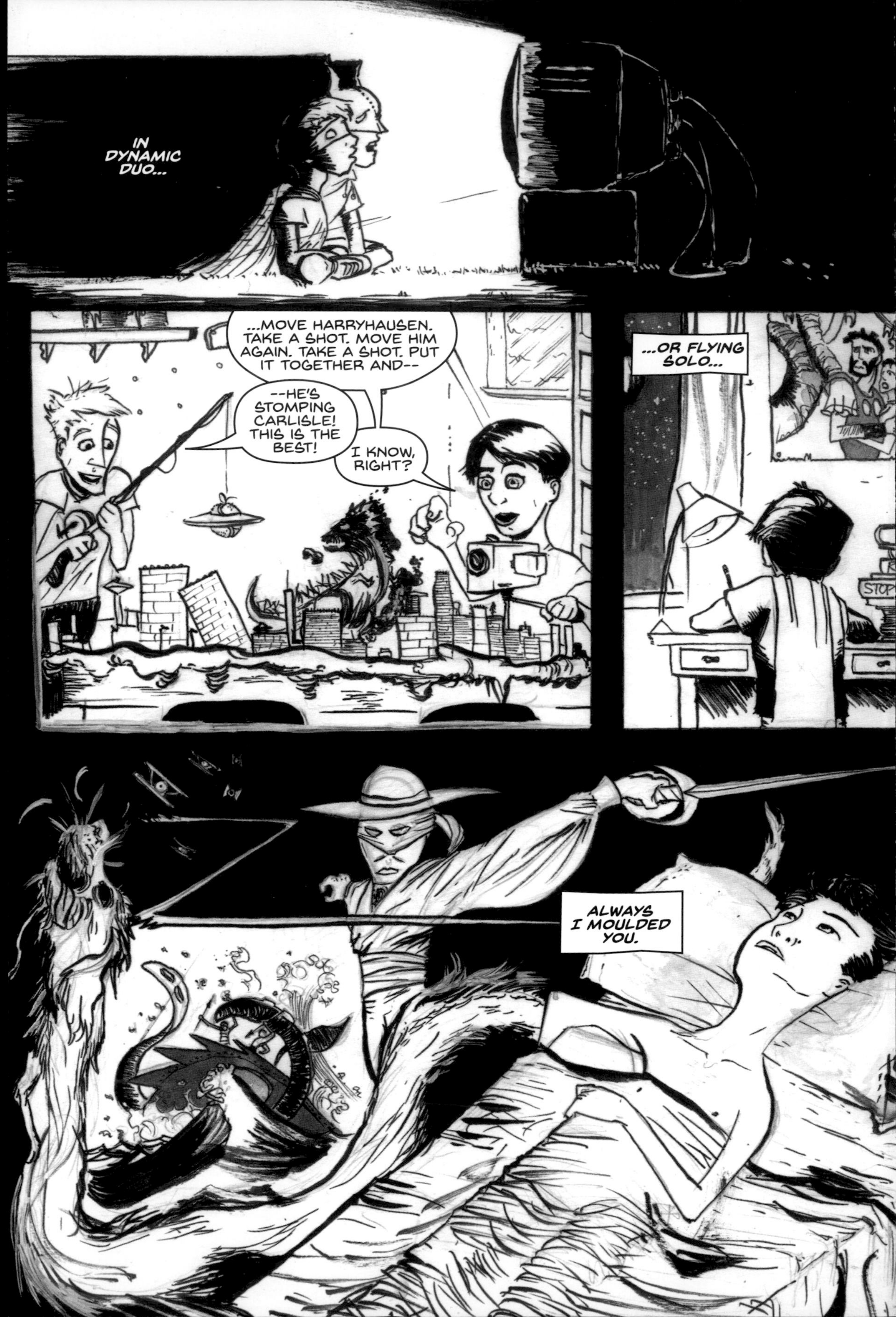
IN DYNAMIC DUO...
...MOVE HARRYHAUSEN. TAKE A SHOT. MOVE HIM AGAIN. TAKE A SHOT. PUT IT TOGETHER AND--
--HE'S STOMPING CARLISLE! THIS IS THE BEST!
I KNOW, RIGHT?
...OR FLYING SOLO...
STOP
ALWAYS I MOULDED YOU.

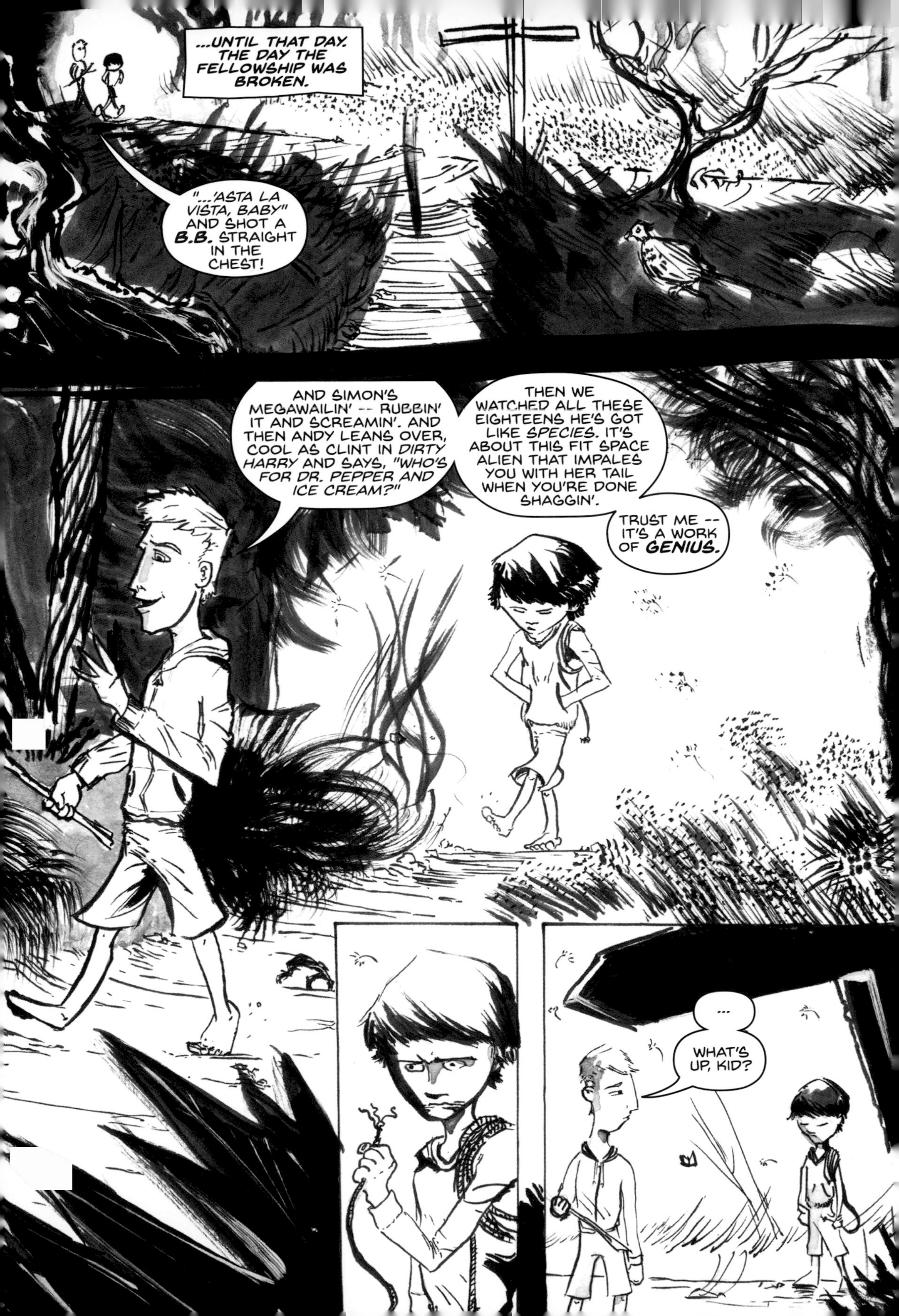
...UNTIL THAT DAY. THE DAY THE FELLOWSHIP WAS BROKEN.
"...'ASTA LA VISTA, BABY" AND SHOT A B.B. STRAIGHT IN THE CHEST!
AND SIMON'S MEGAWAILIN' -- RUBBIN' IT AND SCREAMIN'. AND THEN ANDY LEANS OVER, COOL AS CLINT IN DIRTY HARRY AND SAYS, "WHO'S FOR DR. PEPPER AND ICE CREAM?"
THEN WE WATCHED ALL THESE EIGHTEENS HE'S GOT LIKE SPECIES. IT'S ABOUT THIS FIT SPACE ALIEN THAT IMPALES YOU WITH HER TAIL WHEN YOU'RE DONE SHAGGIN'.
TRUST ME -- IT'S A WORK OF GENIUS.
...
WHAT'S UP, KID?

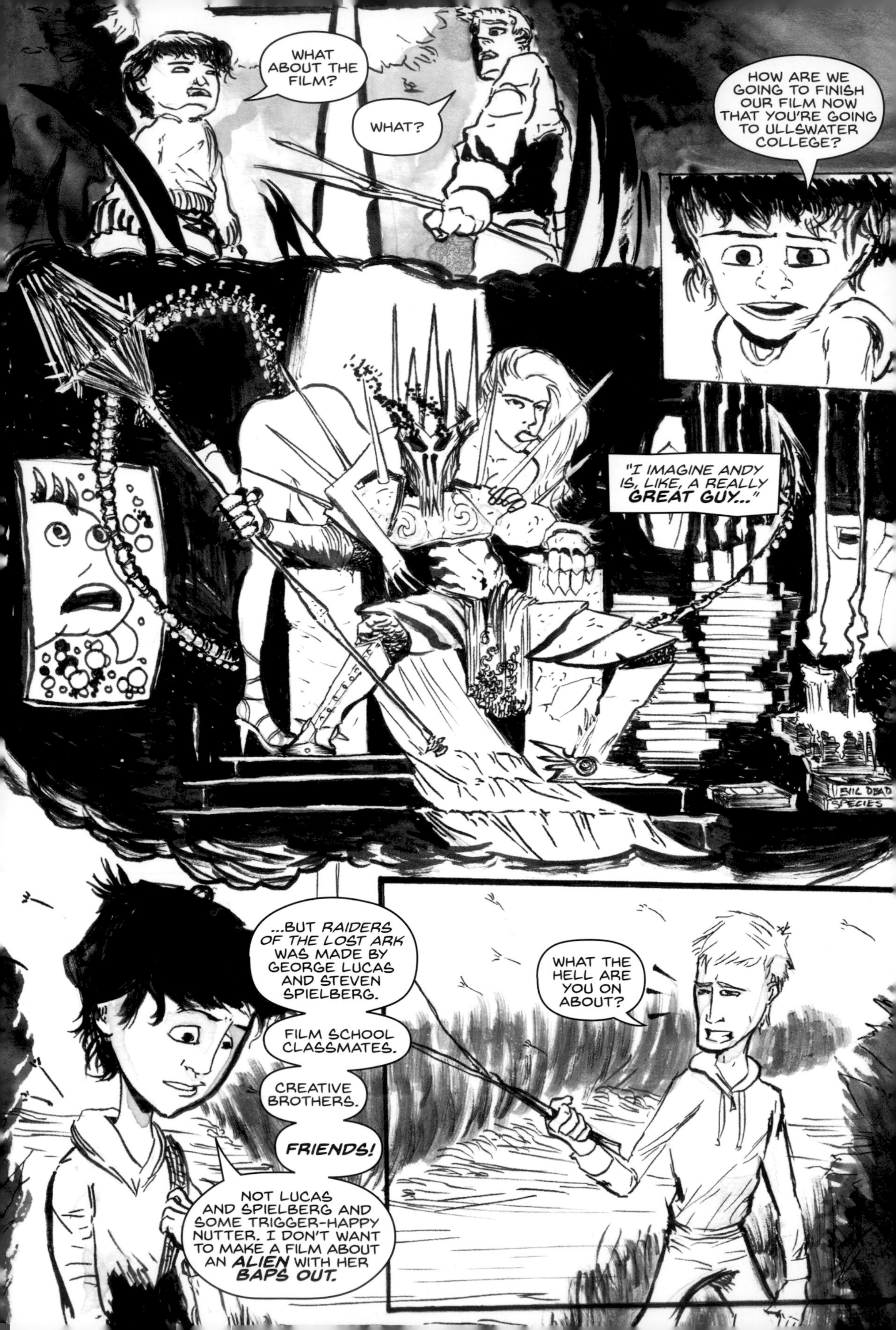
WHAT ABOUT THE FILM?
WHAT?
HOW ARE WE GOING TO FINISH OUR FILM NOW THAT YOU'RE GOING TO ULLSWATER COLLEGE?
"I IMAGINE ANDY IS, LIKE, A REALLY GREAT GUY..."
EVIL DEAD
SPECIES
...BUT RAIDERS OF THE LOST ARK WAS MADE BY GEORGE LUCAS AND STEVEN SPIELBERG.
FILM SCHOOL CLASSMATES.
CREATIVE BROTHERS.
FRIENDS!
WHAT THE HELL ARE YOU ON ABOUT?
NOT LUCAS AND SPIELBERG AND SOME TRIGGER-HAPPY NUTTER. I DON'T WANT TO MAKE A FILM ABOUT AN ALIEN WITH HER BAPS OUT.

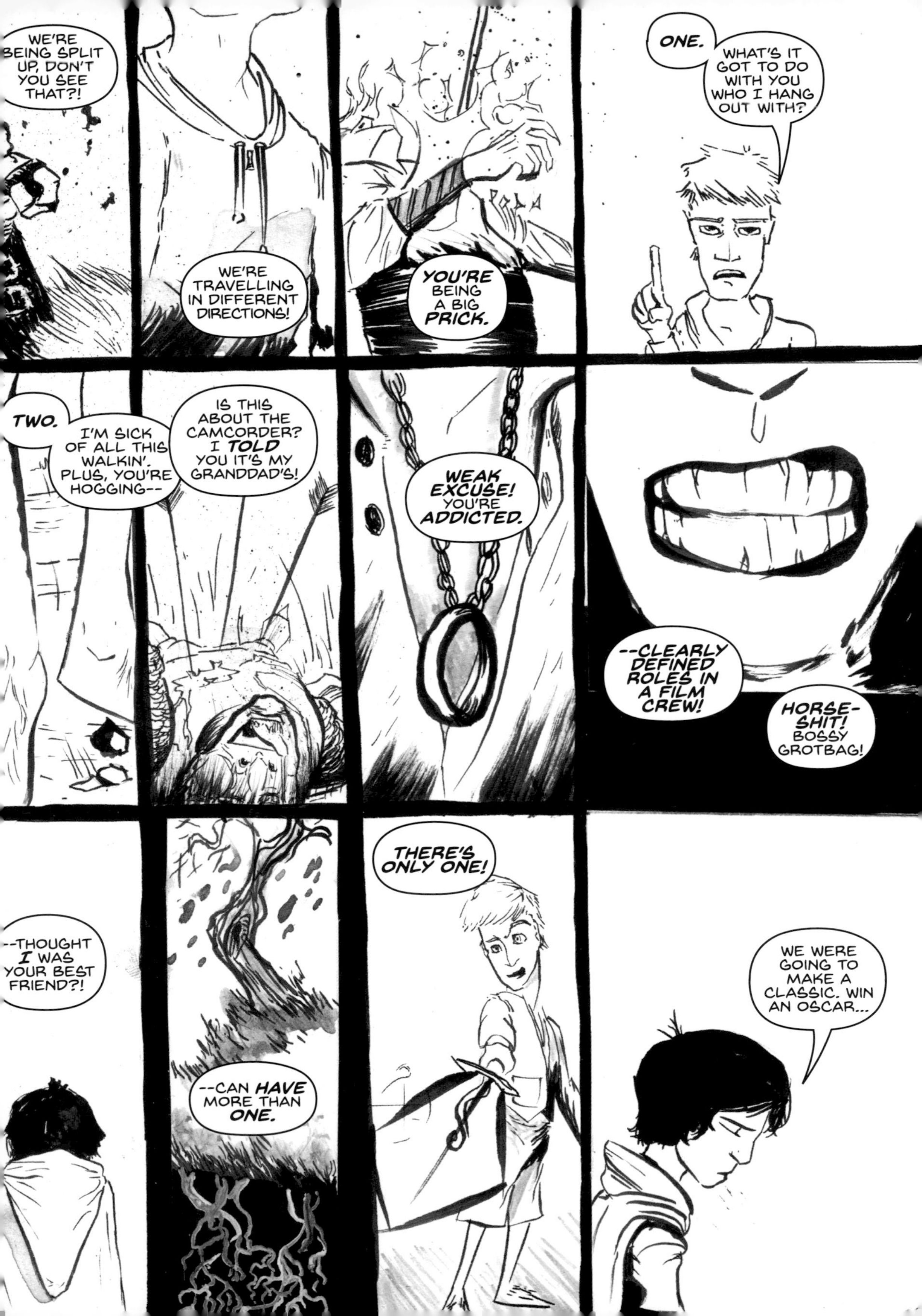
WE'RE BEING SPLIT UP, DON'T YOU SEE THAT?!
WE'RE TRAVELLING IN DIFFERENT DIRECTIONS!
YOU'RE BEING A BIG PRICK.
ONE.
WHAT'S IT GOT TO DO WITH YOU WHO I HANG OUT WITH?
TWO.
I'M SICK OF ALL THIS WALKIN'. PLUS, YOU'RE HOGGING--
IS THIS ABOUT THE CAMCORDER? I TOLD YOU IT'S MY GRANDDAD'S!
WEAK EXCUSE! YOU'RE ADDICTED.
--CLEARLY DEFINED ROLES IN A FILM CREW!
HORSE-SHIT! BOSSY GROTBAG!
--THOUGHT I WAS YOUR BEST FRIEND?!
--CAN HAVE MORE THAN ONE.
THERE'S ONLY ONE!
WE WERE GOING TO MAKE A CLASSIC. WIN AN OSCAR...

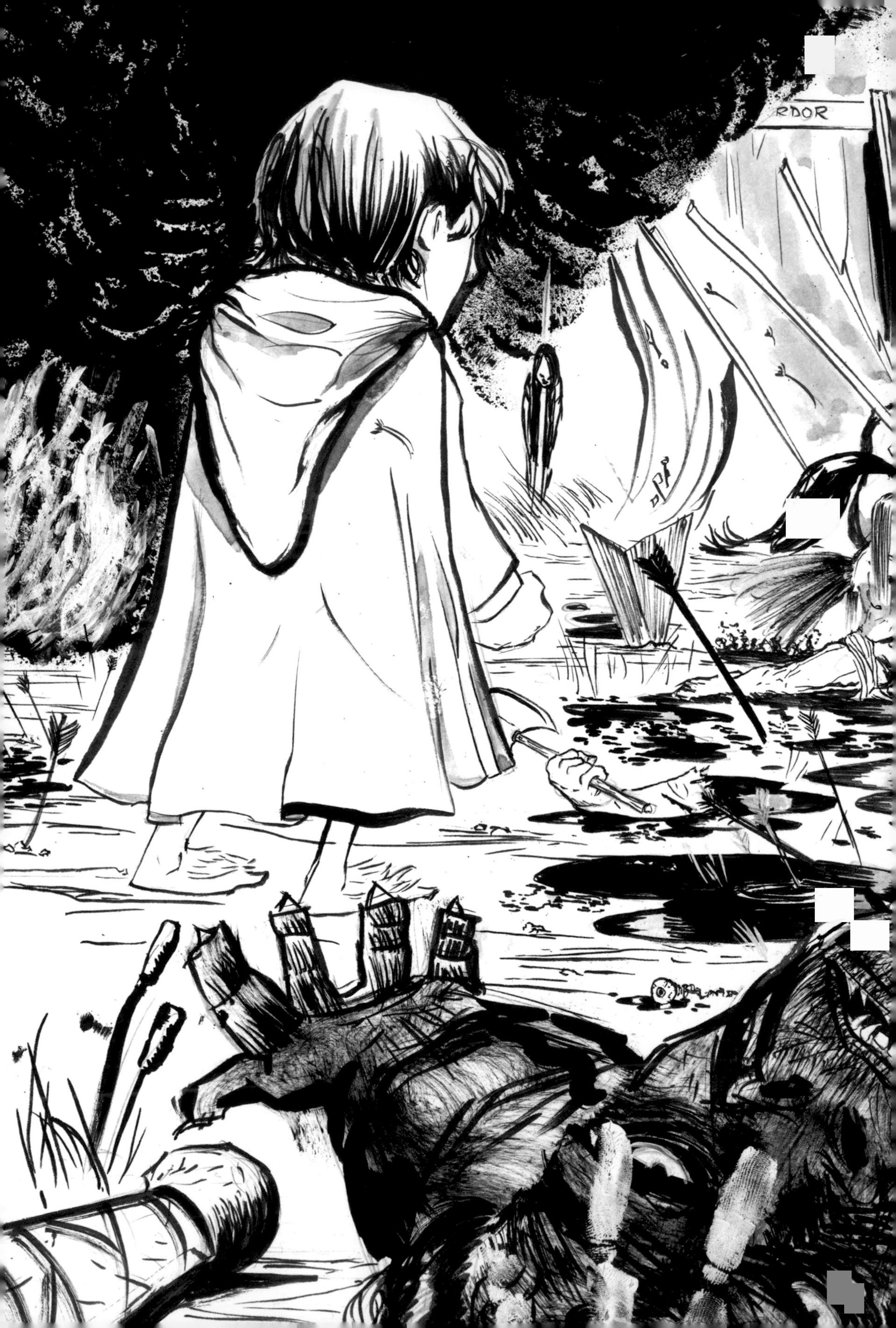
RDOR

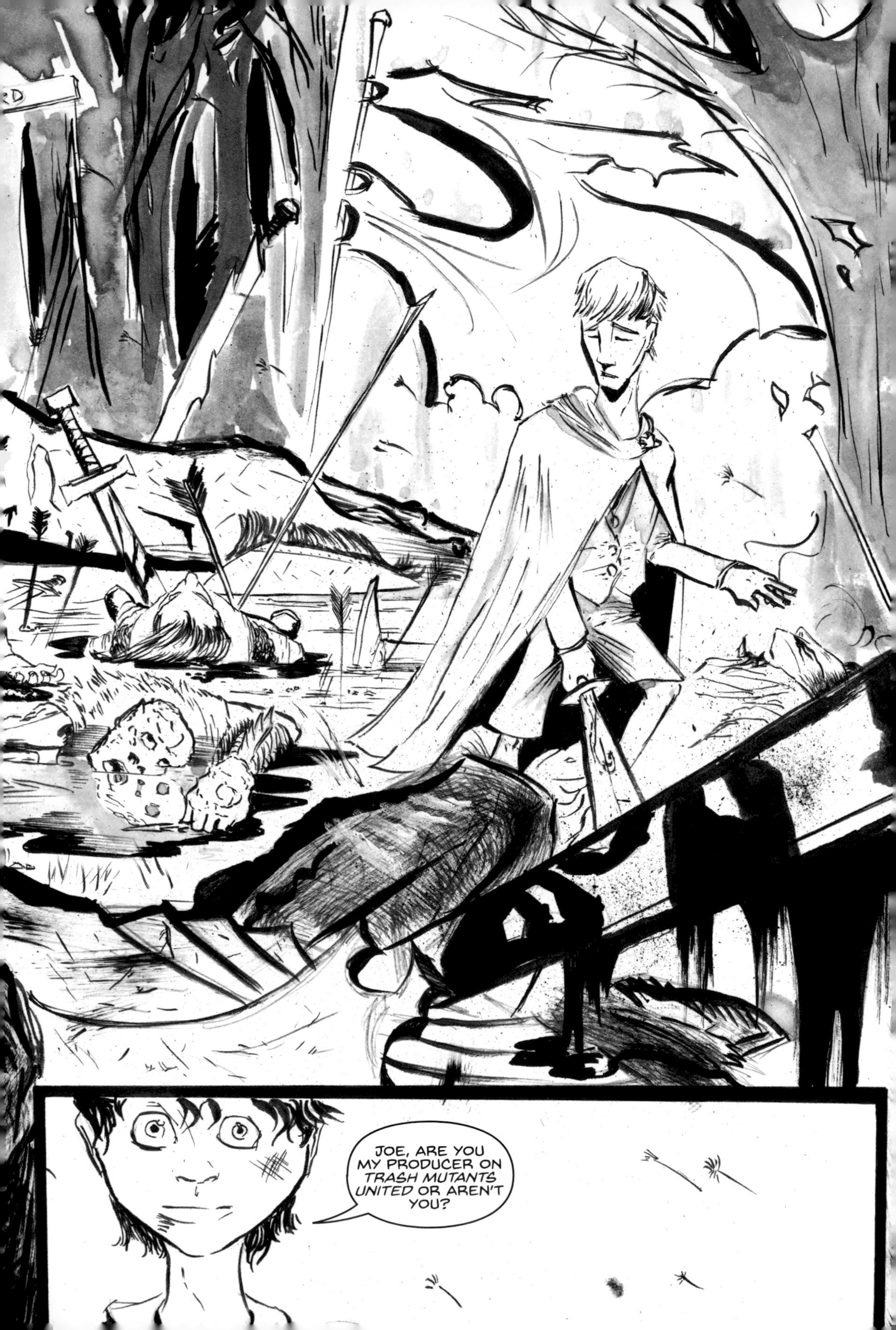
JOE, ARE YOU MY PRODUCER ON *TRASH MUTANTS UNITED* OR AREN'T YOU?

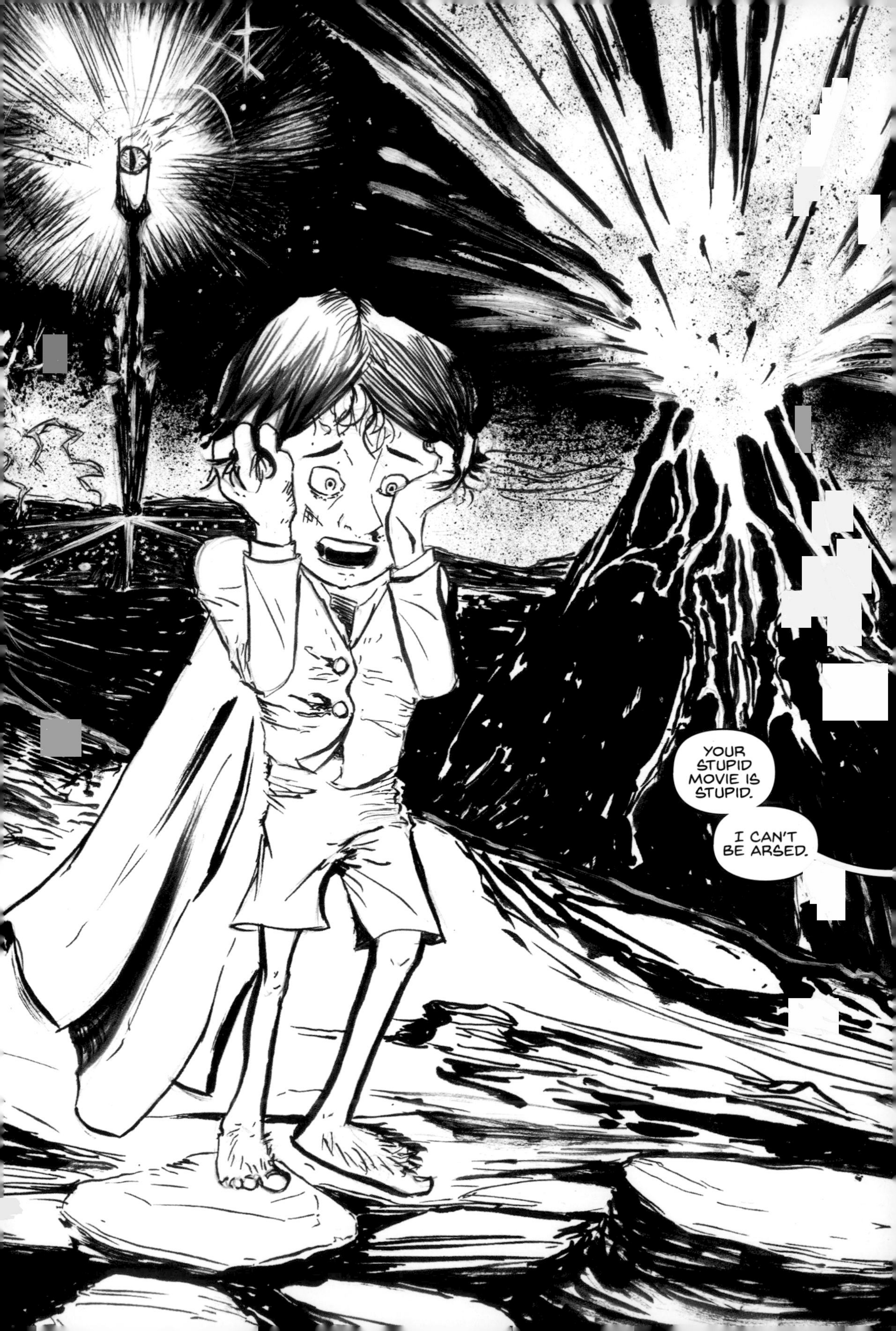
YOUR STUPID MOVIE IS STUPID.
I CAN'T BE ARSED.

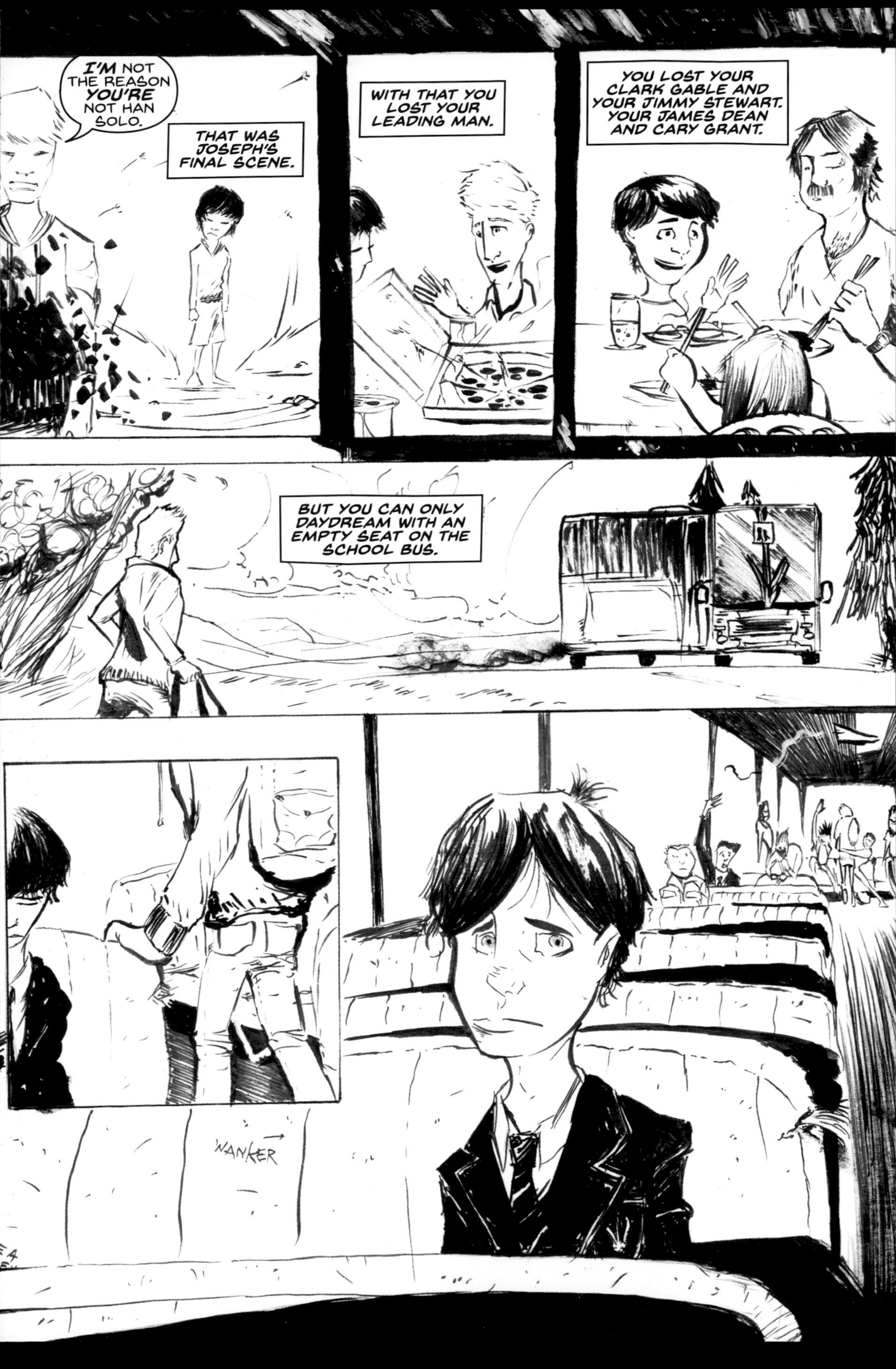
I'M NOT THE REASON YOU'RE NOT HAN SOLO.
THAT WAS JOSEPH'S FINAL SCENE.
WITH THAT YOU LOST YOUR LEADING MAN.
YOU LOST YOUR CLARK GABLE AND YOUR JIMMY STEWART. YOUR JAMES DEAN AND CARY GRANT.
BUT YOU CAN ONLY DAYDREAM WITH AN EMPTY SEAT ON THE SCHOOL BUS.
WANKER

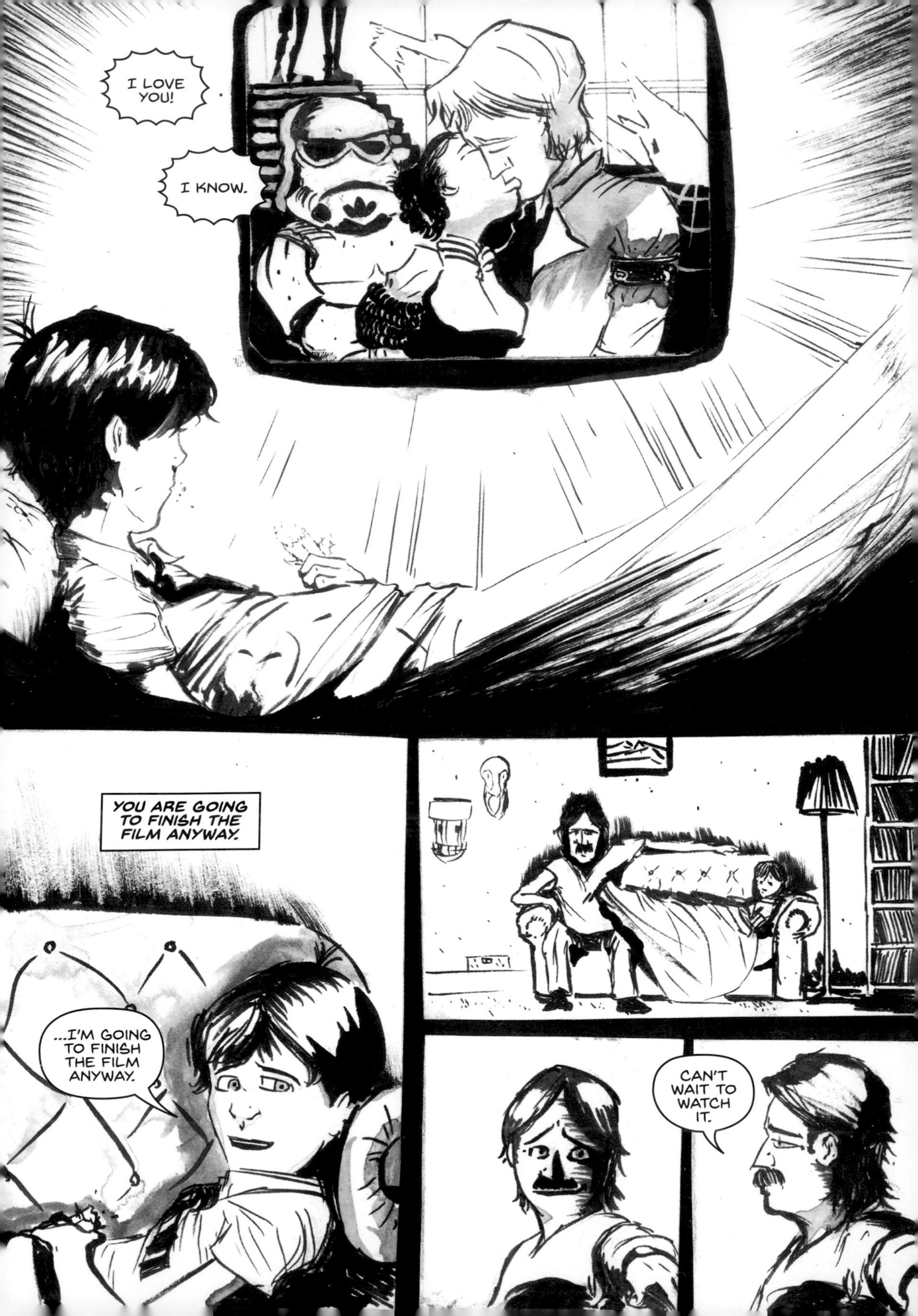
I LOVE YOU!
I KNOW.
YOU ARE GOING TO FINISH THE FILM ANYWAY.
...I'M GOING TO FINISH THE FILM ANYWAY.
CAN'T WAIT TO WATCH IT.

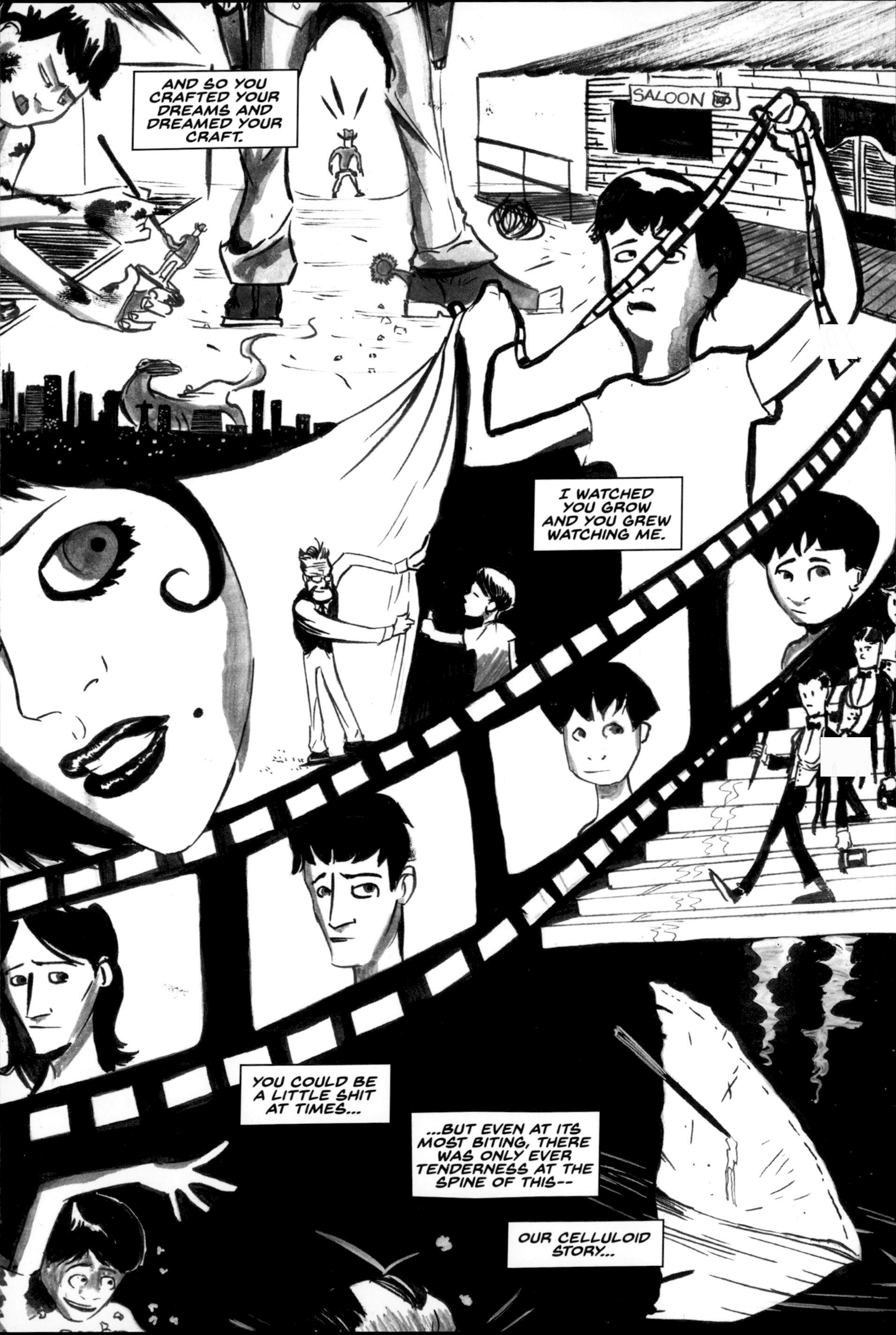
AND SO YOU CRAFTED YOUR DREAMS AND DREAMED YOUR CRAFT.
SALOON
I WATCHED YOU GROW AND YOU GREW WATCHING ME.
YOU COULD BE A LITTLE SHIT AT TIMES...
...BUT EVEN AT ITS MOST BITING, THERE WAS ONLY EVER TENDERNESS AT THE SPINE OF THIS--
OUR CELLULOID STORY...

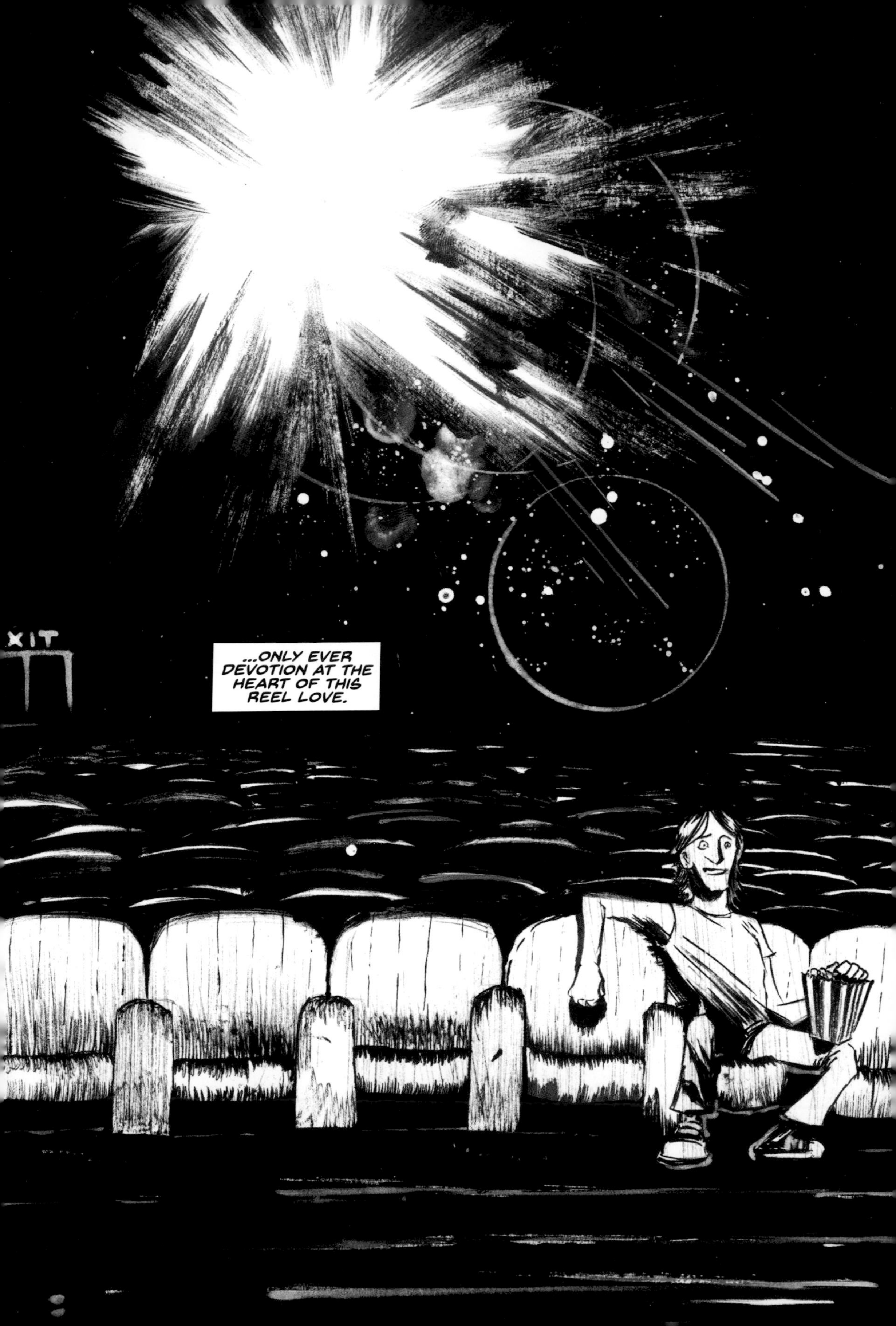

XIT
...ONLY EVER DEVOTION AT THE HEART OF THIS REEL LOVE.

ACT TWO
CONCESSIONS

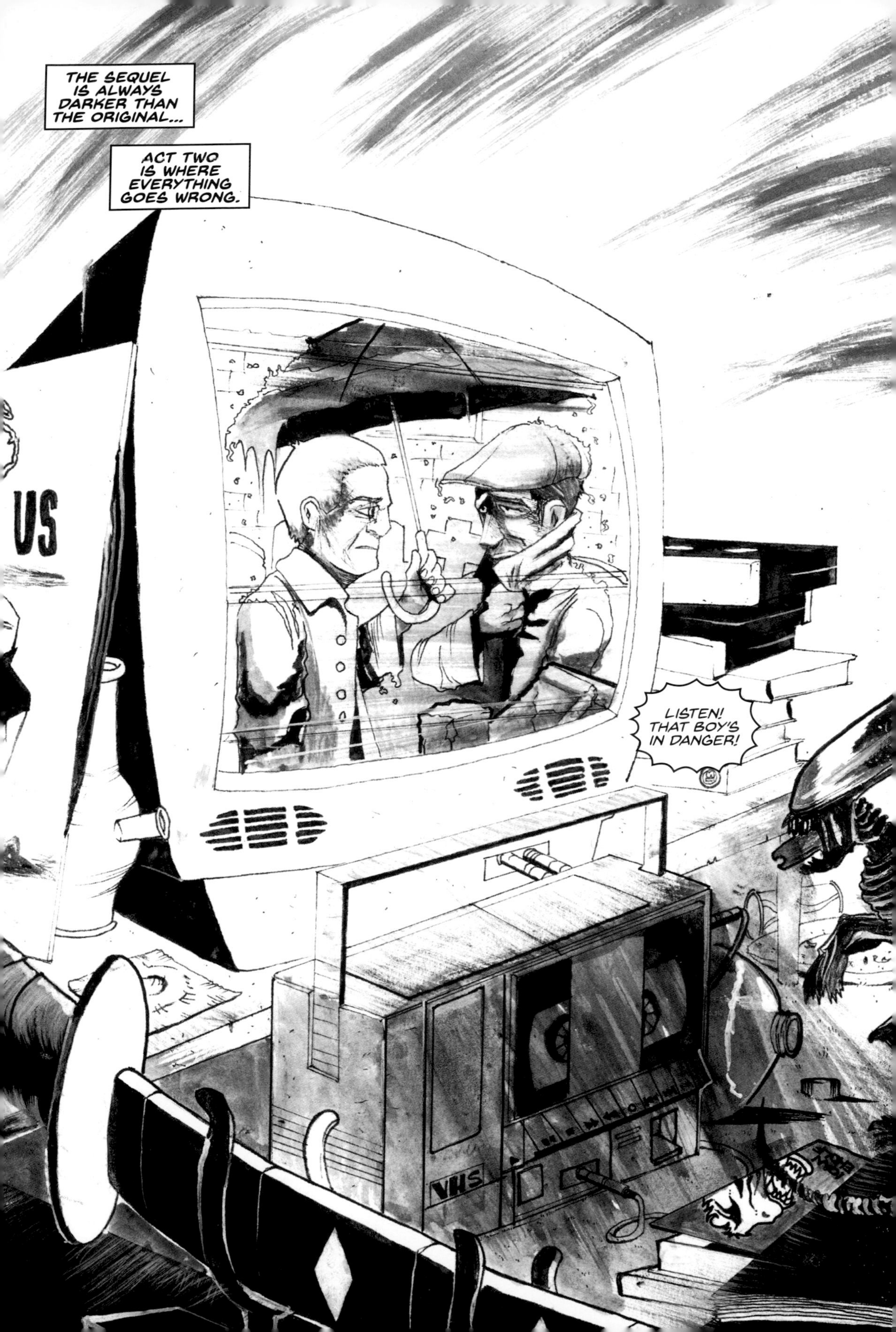
THE SEQUEL IS ALWAYS DARKER THAN THE ORIGINAL...
ACT TWO IS WHERE EVERYTHING GOES WRONG.
LISTEN! THAT BOY'S IN DANGER!
VHS

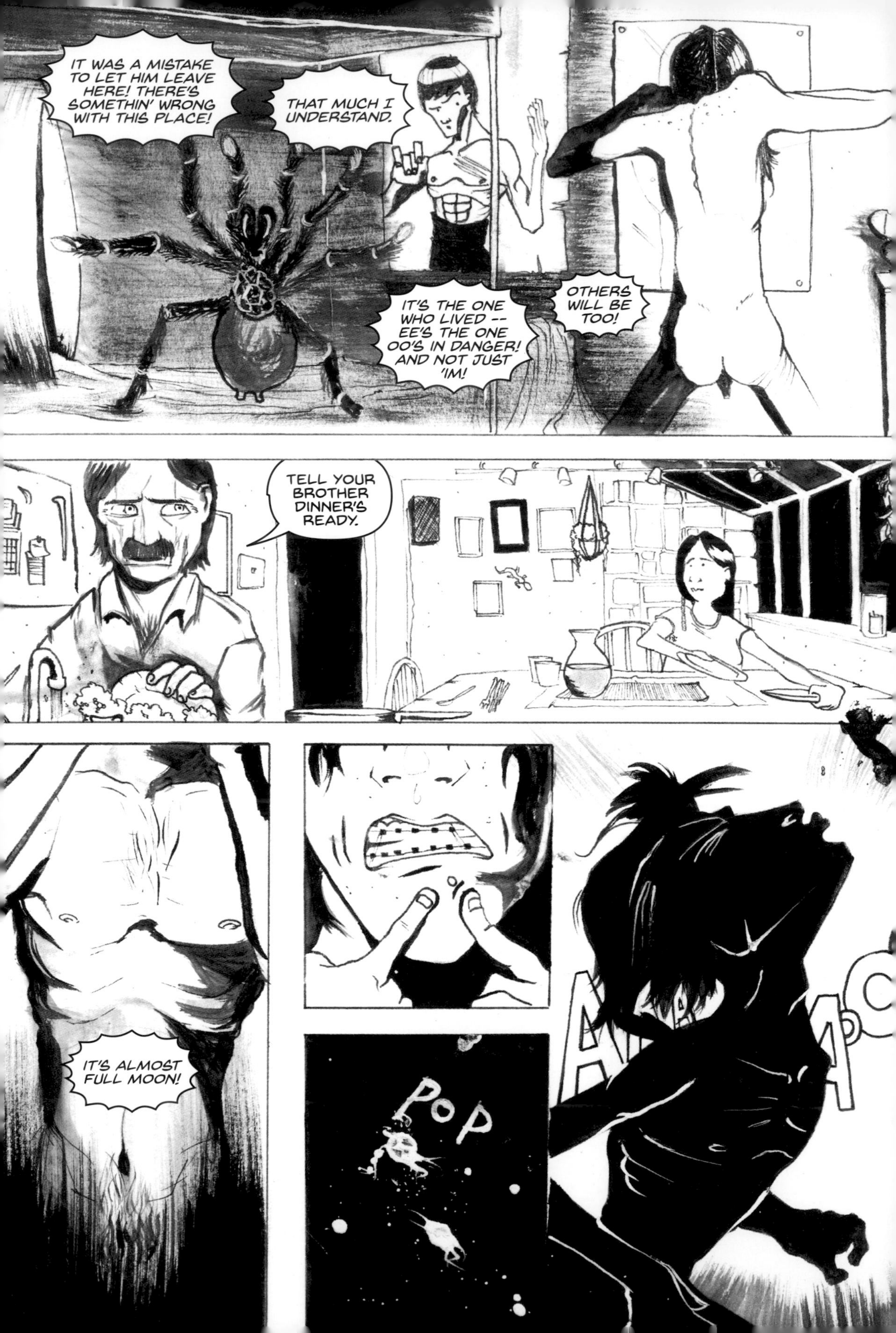
IT WAS A MISTAKE TO LET HIM LEAVE HERE! THERE'S SOMETHIN' WRONG WITH THIS PLACE!
THAT MUCH I UNDERSTAND.
IT'S THE ONE WHO LIVED -- EE'S THE ONE OO'S IN DANGER! AND NOT JUST 'IM!
OTHERS WILL BE TOO!
TELL YOUR BROTHER DINNER'S READY.
IT'S ALMOST FULL MOON!
POP

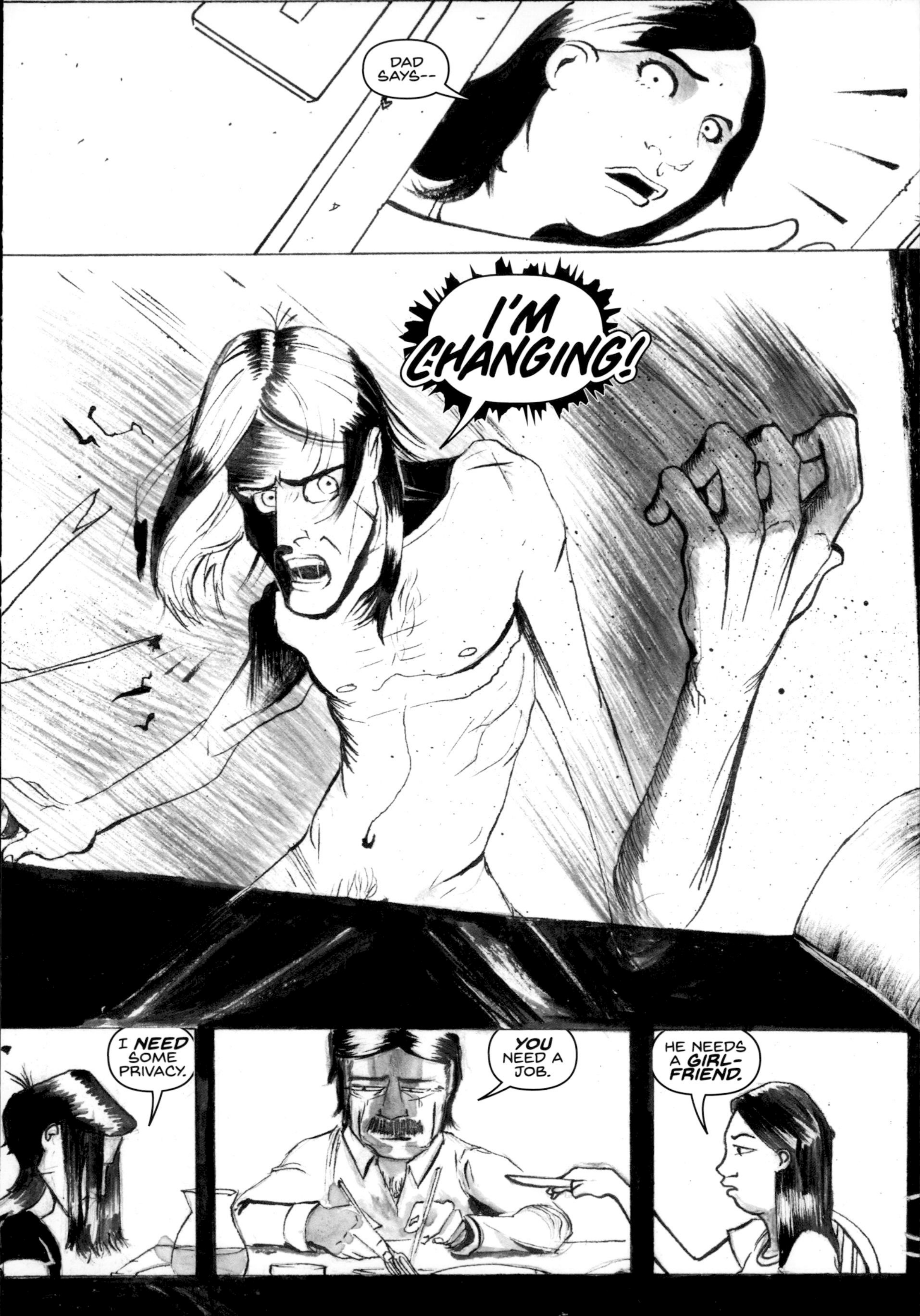
DAD SAYS--
I'M CHANGING!
I NEED SOME PRIVACY.
YOU NEED A JOB.
HE NEEDS A GIRL-FRIEND.

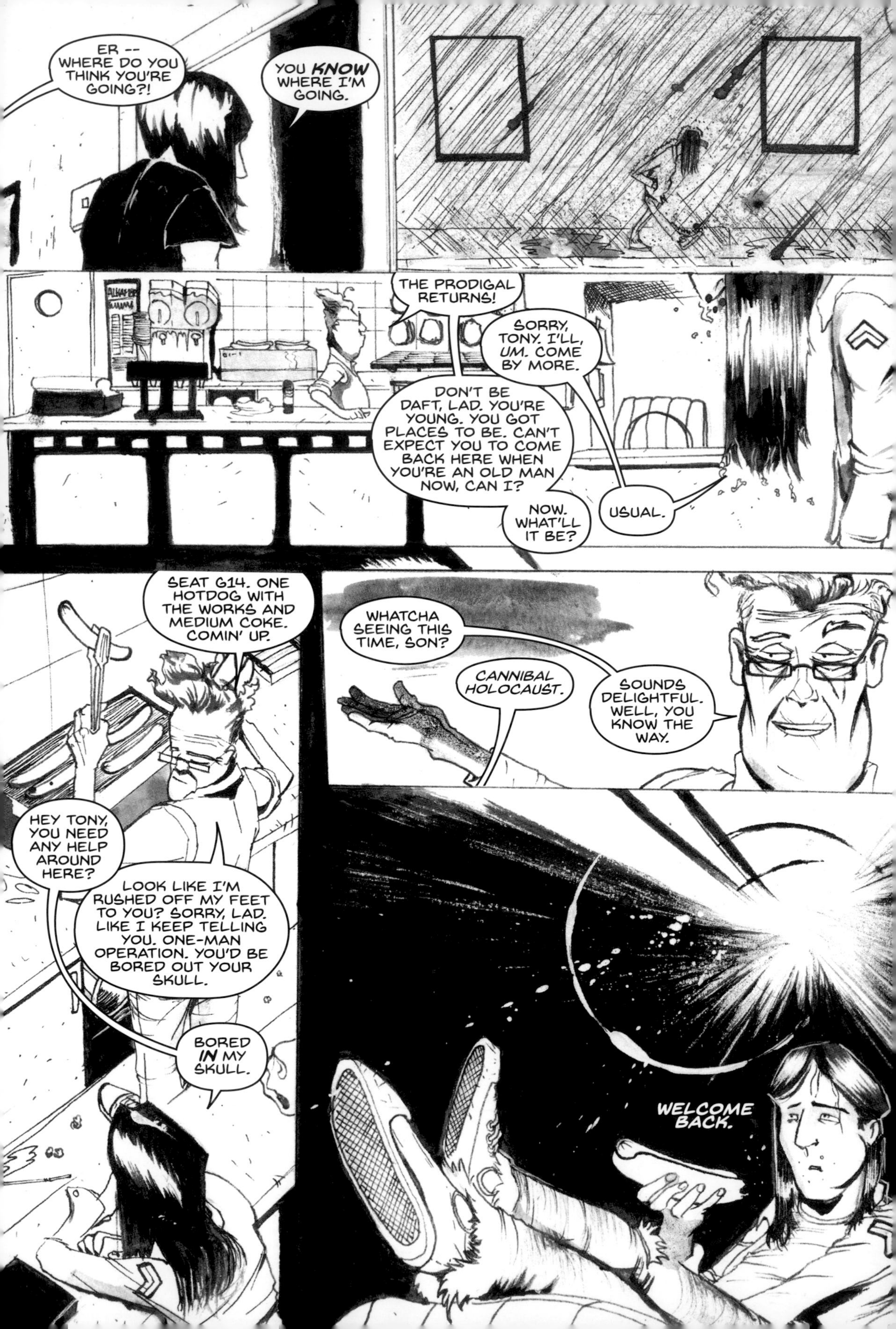
ER -- WHERE DO YOU THINK YOU'RE GOING?!
YOU KNOW WHERE I'M GOING.
THE PRODIGAL RETURNS!
SORRY, TONY. I'LL, UM. COME BY MORE.
DON'T BE DAFT, LAD. YOU'RE YOUNG. YOU GOT PLACES TO BE. CAN'T EXPECT YOU TO COME BACK HERE WHEN YOU'RE AN OLD MAN NOW, CAN I?
NOW. WHAT'LL IT BE?
USUAL.
SEAT G14. ONE HOTDOG WITH THE WORKS AND MEDIUM COKE. COMIN' UP.
HEY TONY, YOU NEED ANY HELP AROUND HERE?
LOOK LIKE I'M RUSHED OFF MY FEET TO YOU? SORRY, LAD. LIKE I KEEP TELLING YOU. ONE-MAN OPERATION. YOU'D BE BORED OUT YOUR SKULL.
BORED IN MY SKULL.
WHATCHA SEEING THIS TIME, SON?
CANNIBAL HOLOCAUST.
SOUNDS DELIGHTFUL. WELL, YOU KNOW THE WAY.
WELCOME BACK.

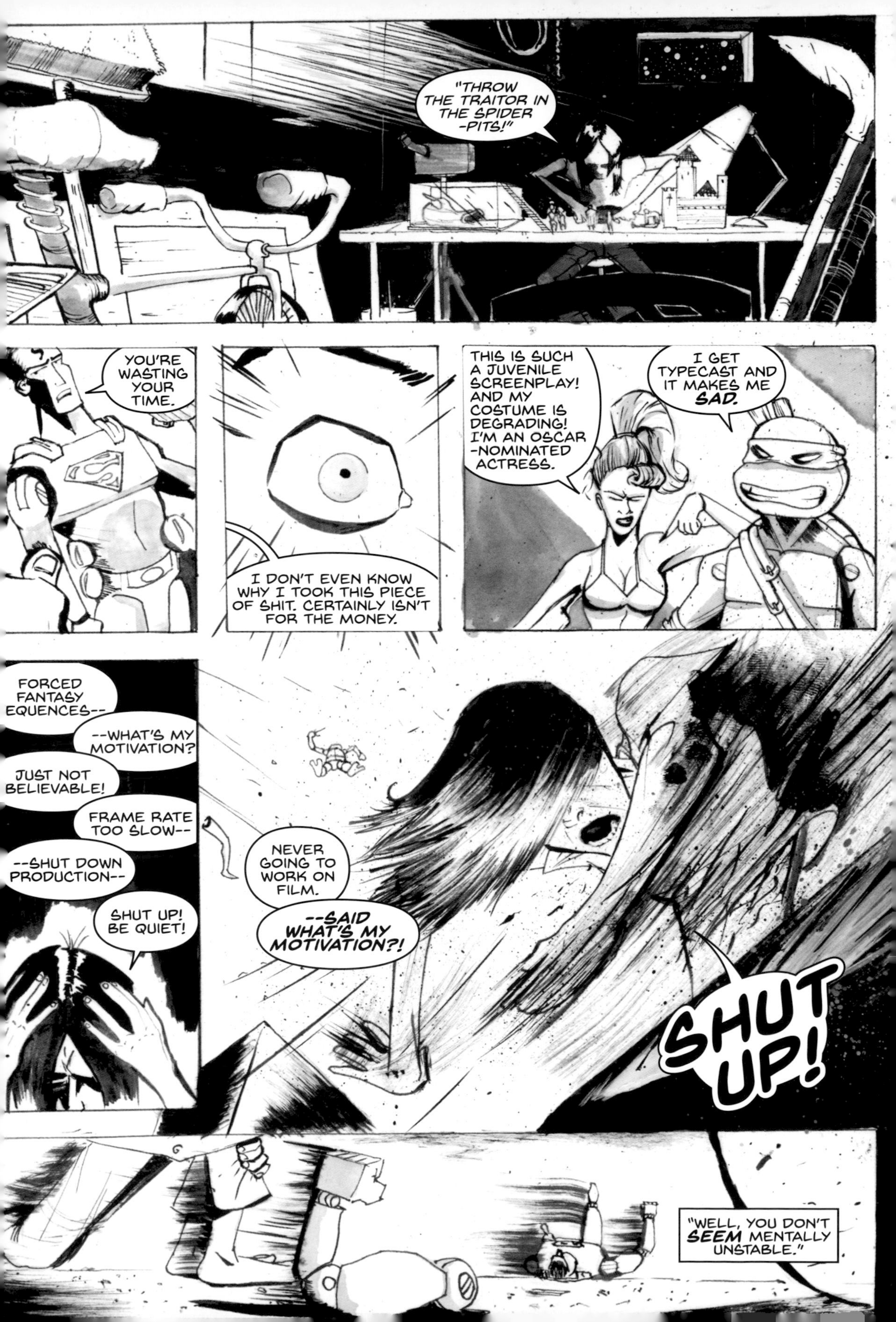
"THROW THE TRAITOR IN THE SPIDER -PITS!"
YOU'RE WASTING YOUR TIME.
I DON'T EVEN KNOW WHY I TOOK THIS PIECE OF SHIT. CERTAINLY ISN'T FOR THE MONEY.
THIS IS SUCH A JUVENILE SCREENPLAY! AND MY COSTUME IS DEGRADING! I'M AN OSCAR -NOMINATED ACTRESS.
I GET TYPECAST AND IT MAKES ME *SAD.*
FORCED FANTASY EQUENCES--
--WHAT'S MY MOTIVATION?
JUST NOT BELIEVABLE!
FRAME RATE TOO SLOW--
--SHUT DOWN PRODUCTION--
SHUT UP! BE QUIET!
NEVER GOING TO WORK ON FILM.
--SAID WHAT'S MY MOTIVATION?!
SHUT UP!
"WELL, YOU DON'T *SEEM* MENTALLY UNSTABLE."

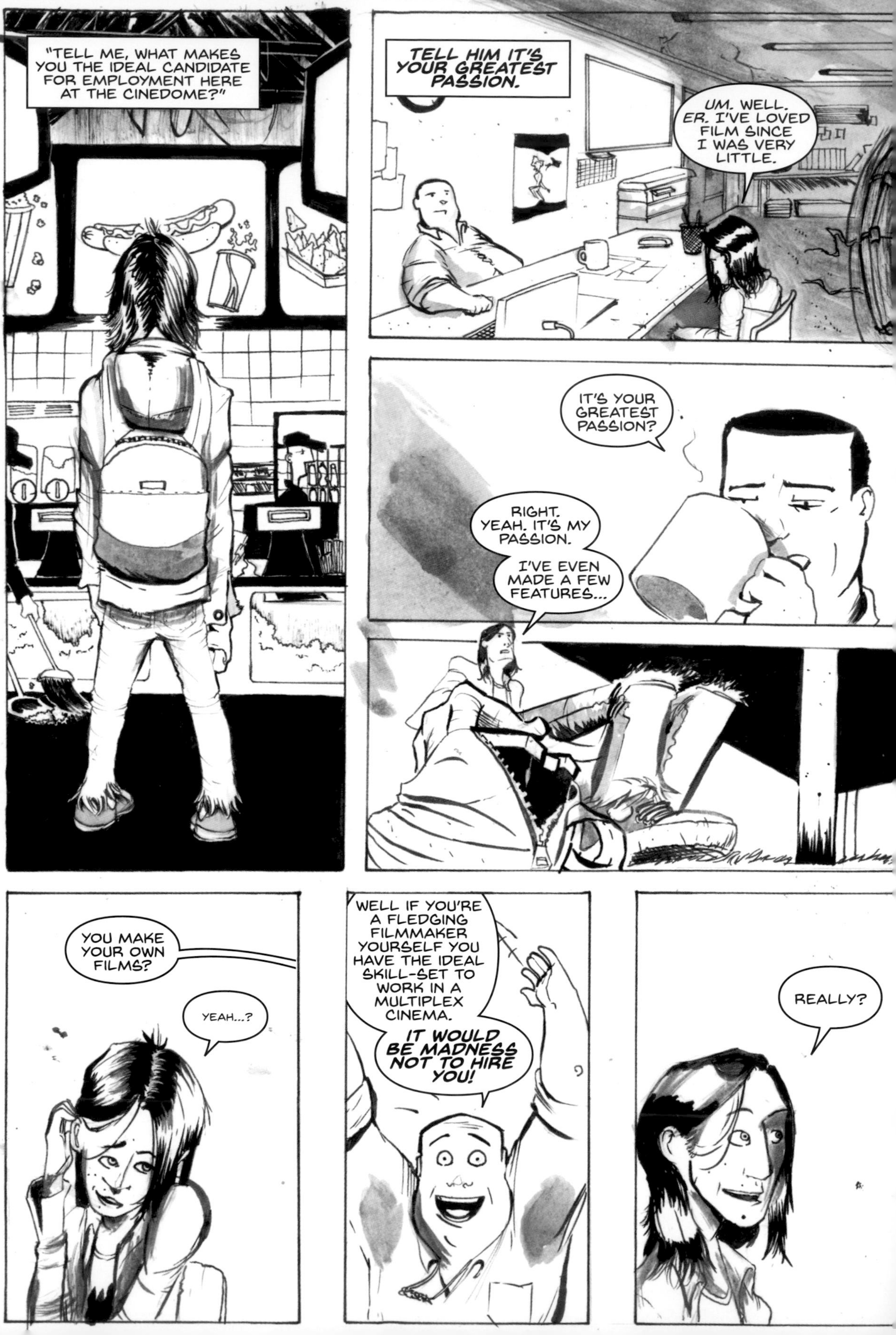

"TELL ME, WHAT MAKES YOU THE IDEAL CANDIDATE FOR EMPLOYMENT HERE AT THE CINEDOME?"
TELL HIM IT'S YOUR GREATEST PASSION.
UM. WELL. ER. I'VE LOVED FILM SINCE I WAS VERY LITTLE.
IT'S YOUR GREATEST PASSION?
RIGHT. YEAH. IT'S MY PASSION.
I'VE EVEN MADE A FEW FEATURES...
YOU MAKE YOUR OWN FILMS?
YEAH...?
WELL IF YOU'RE A FLEDGING FILMMAKER YOURSELF YOU HAVE THE IDEAL SKILL-SET TO WORK IN A MULTIPLEX CINEMA.
IT WOULD BE MADNESS NOT TO HIRE YOU!
REALLY?

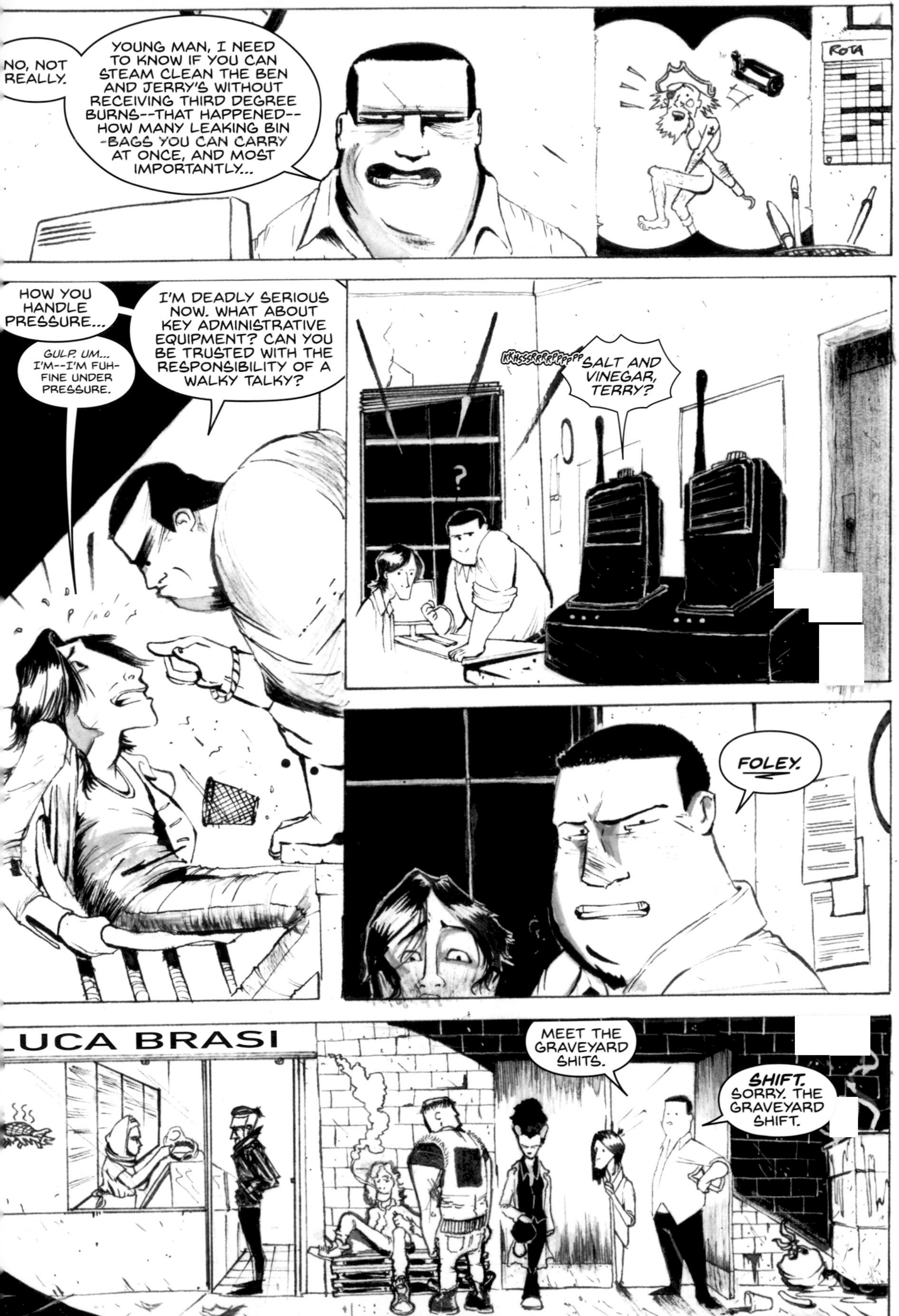
NO, NOT REALLY.
YOUNG MAN, I NEED TO KNOW IF YOU CAN STEAM CLEAN THE BEN AND JERRY'S WITHOUT RECEIVING THIRD DEGREE BURNS--THAT HAPPENED--HOW MANY LEAKING BIN-BAGS YOU CAN CARRY AT ONCE, AND MOST IMPORTANTLY...
ROTA
HOW YOU HANDLE PRESSURE...
GULP. UM... I'M--I'M FUH-FINE UNDER PRESSURE.
I'M DEADLY SERIOUS NOW. WHAT ABOUT KEY ADMINISTRATIVE EQUIPMENT? CAN YOU BE TRUSTED WITH THE RESPONSIBILITY OF A WALKY TALKY?
KKHSSSRRRRPPPPPP
SALT AND VINEGAR, TERRY?
?
FOLEY.
LUCA BRASI
MEET THE GRAVEYARD SHITS.
SHIFT. SORRY. THE GRAVEYARD SHIFT.

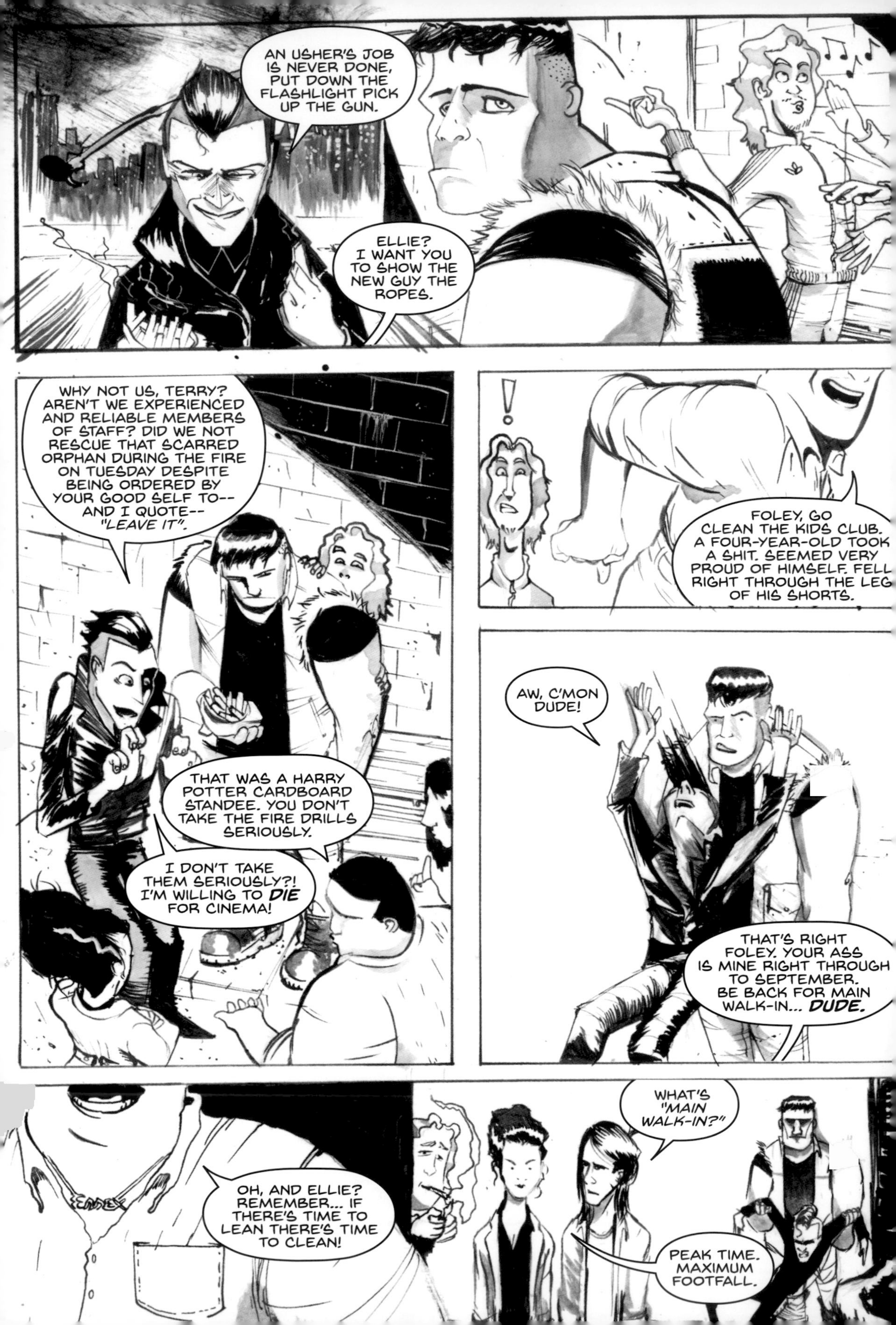
AN USHER'S JOB IS NEVER DONE, PUT DOWN THE FLASHLIGHT PICK UP THE GUN.
ELLIE? I WANT YOU TO SHOW THE NEW GUY THE ROPES.
WHY NOT US, TERRY? AREN'T WE EXPERIENCED AND RELIABLE MEMBERS OF STAFF? DID WE NOT RESCUE THAT SCARRED ORPHAN DURING THE FIRE ON TUESDAY DESPITE BEING ORDERED BY YOUR GOOD SELF TO-- AND I QUOTE-- "LEAVE IT".
THAT WAS A HARRY POTTER CARDBOARD STANDEE. YOU DON'T TAKE THE FIRE DRILLS SERIOUSLY.
I DON'T TAKE THEM SERIOUSLY?! I'M WILLING TO DIE FOR CINEMA!
!
FOLEY, GO CLEAN THE KIDS CLUB. A FOUR-YEAR-OLD TOOK A SHIT. SEEMED VERY PROUD OF HIMSELF. FELL RIGHT THROUGH THE LEG OF HIS SHORTS.
AW, C'MON DUDE!
THAT'S RIGHT FOLEY. YOUR ASS IS MINE RIGHT THROUGH TO SEPTEMBER. BE BACK FOR MAIN WALK-IN... DUDE.
OH, AND ELLIE? REMEMBER... IF THERE'S TIME TO LEAN THERE'S TIME TO CLEAN!
WHAT'S "MAIN WALK-IN?"
PEAK TIME. MAXIMUM FOOTFALL.

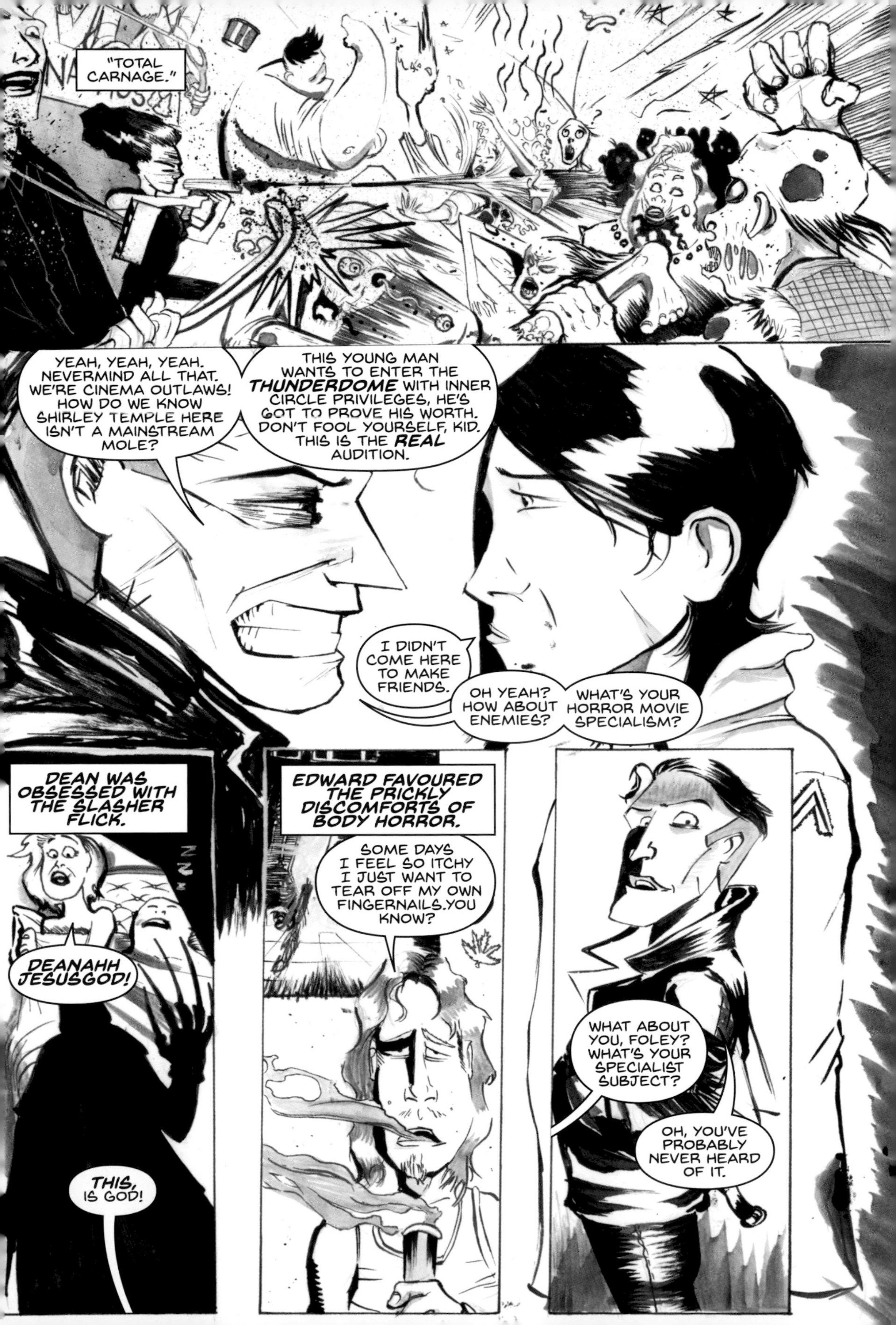
"TOTAL CARNAGE."
YEAH, YEAH, YEAH. NEVERMIND ALL THAT. WE'RE CINEMA OUTLAWS! HOW DO WE KNOW SHIRLEY TEMPLE HERE ISN'T A MAINSTREAM MOLE?
THIS YOUNG MAN WANTS TO ENTER THE THUNDERDOME WITH INNER CIRCLE PRIVILEGES, HE'S GOT TO PROVE HIS WORTH. DON'T FOOL YOURSELF, KID. THIS IS THE REAL AUDITION.
I DIDN'T COME HERE TO MAKE FRIENDS.
OH YEAH? HOW ABOUT ENEMIES?
WHAT'S YOUR HORROR MOVIE SPECIALISM?
DEAN WAS OBSESSED WITH THE SLASHER FLICK.
DEANAHH JESUSGOD!
THIS, IS GOD!
EDWARD FAVOURED THE PRICKLY DISCOMFORTS OF BODY HORROR.
SOME DAYS I FEEL SO ITCHY I JUST WANT TO TEAR OFF MY OWN FINGERNAILS.YOU KNOW?
WHAT ABOUT YOU, FOLEY? WHAT'S YOUR SPECIALIST SUBJECT?
OH, YOU'VE PROBABLY NEVER HEARD OF IT.

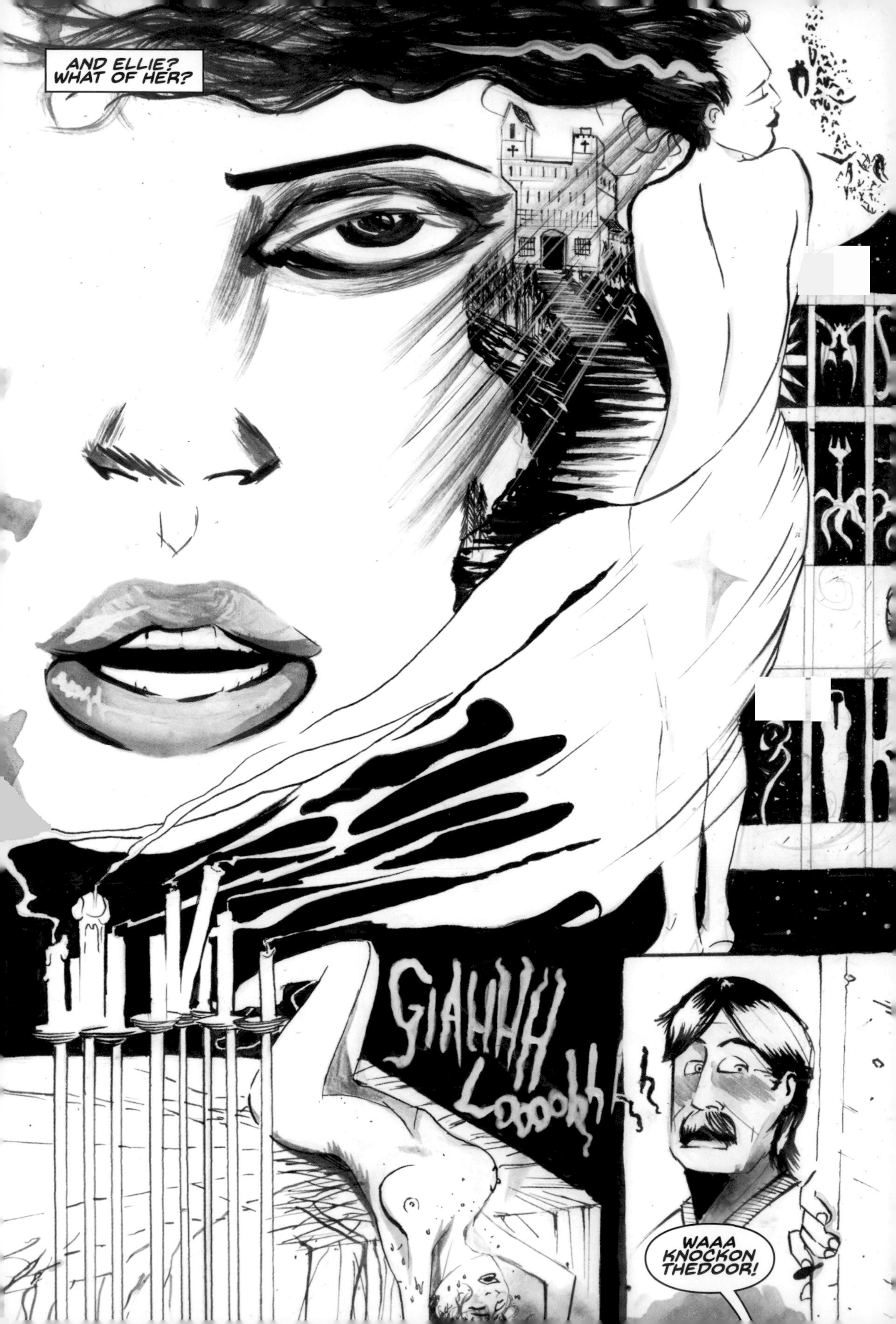
AND ELLIE? WHAT OF HER?
GIAHHH LOOOOHHHh
WAAA KNOCKON THEDOOR!

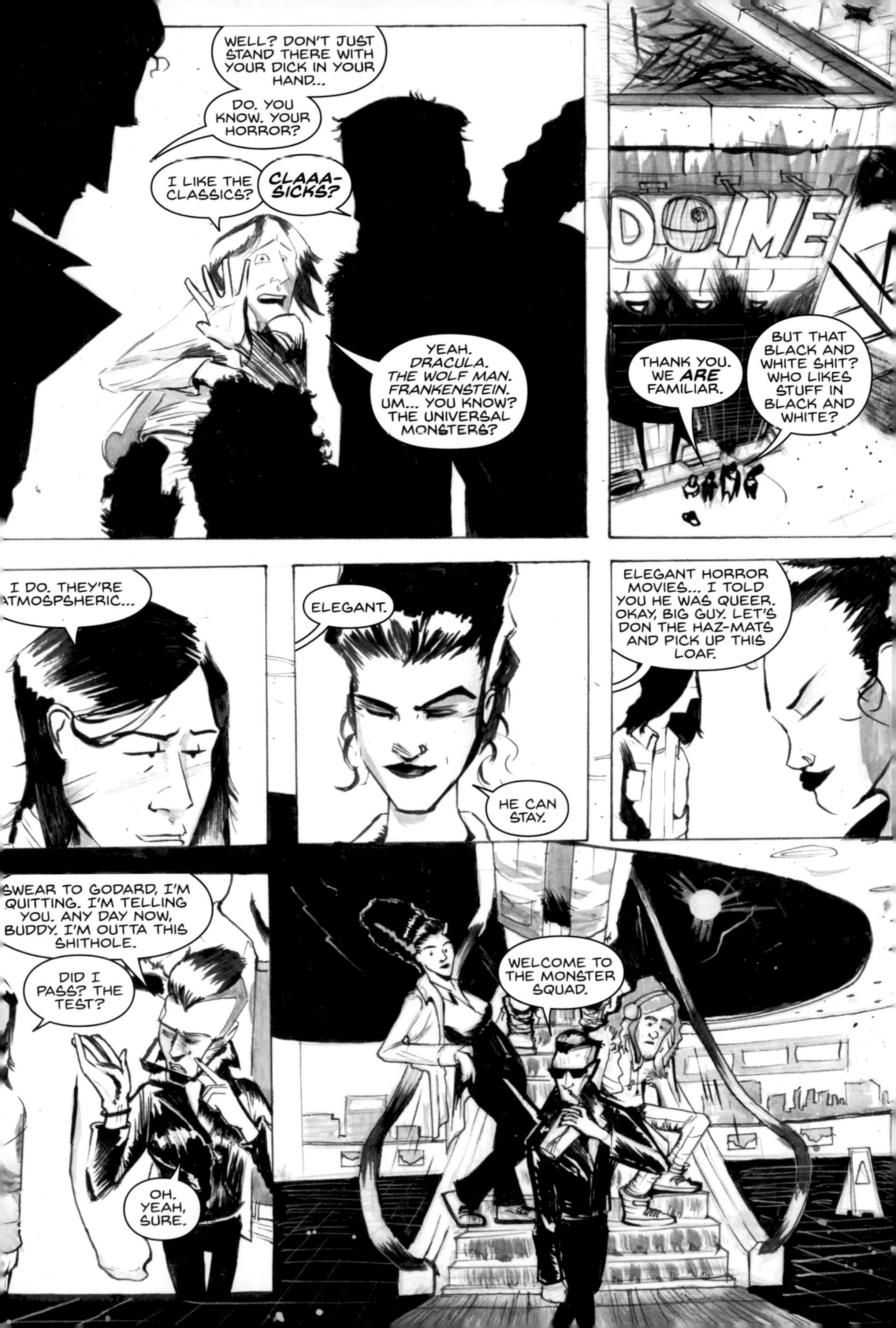
WELL? DON'T JUST STAND THERE WITH YOUR DICK IN YOUR HAND...
DO. YOU KNOW. YOUR HORROR?
I LIKE THE CLASSICS?
CLAAA-SICKS?
YEAH. DRACULA. THE WOLF MAN. FRANKENSTEIN. UM... YOU KNOW? THE UNIVERSAL MONSTERS?
DOME
THANK YOU. WE ARE FAMILIAR.
BUT THAT BLACK AND WHITE SHIT? WHO LIKES STUFF IN BLACK AND WHITE?
I DO. THEY'RE ATMOSPSHERIC...
ELEGANT.
HE CAN STAY.
ELEGANT HORROR MOVIES... I TOLD YOU HE WAS QUEER. OKAY, BIG GUY. LET'S DON THE HAZ-MATS AND PICK UP THIS LOAF.
SWEAR TO GODARD, I'M QUITTING. I'M TELLING YOU. ANY DAY NOW, BUDDY. I'M OUTTA THIS SHITHOLE.
DID I PASS? THE TEST?
OH. YEAH, SURE.
WELCOME TO THE MONSTER SQUAD.

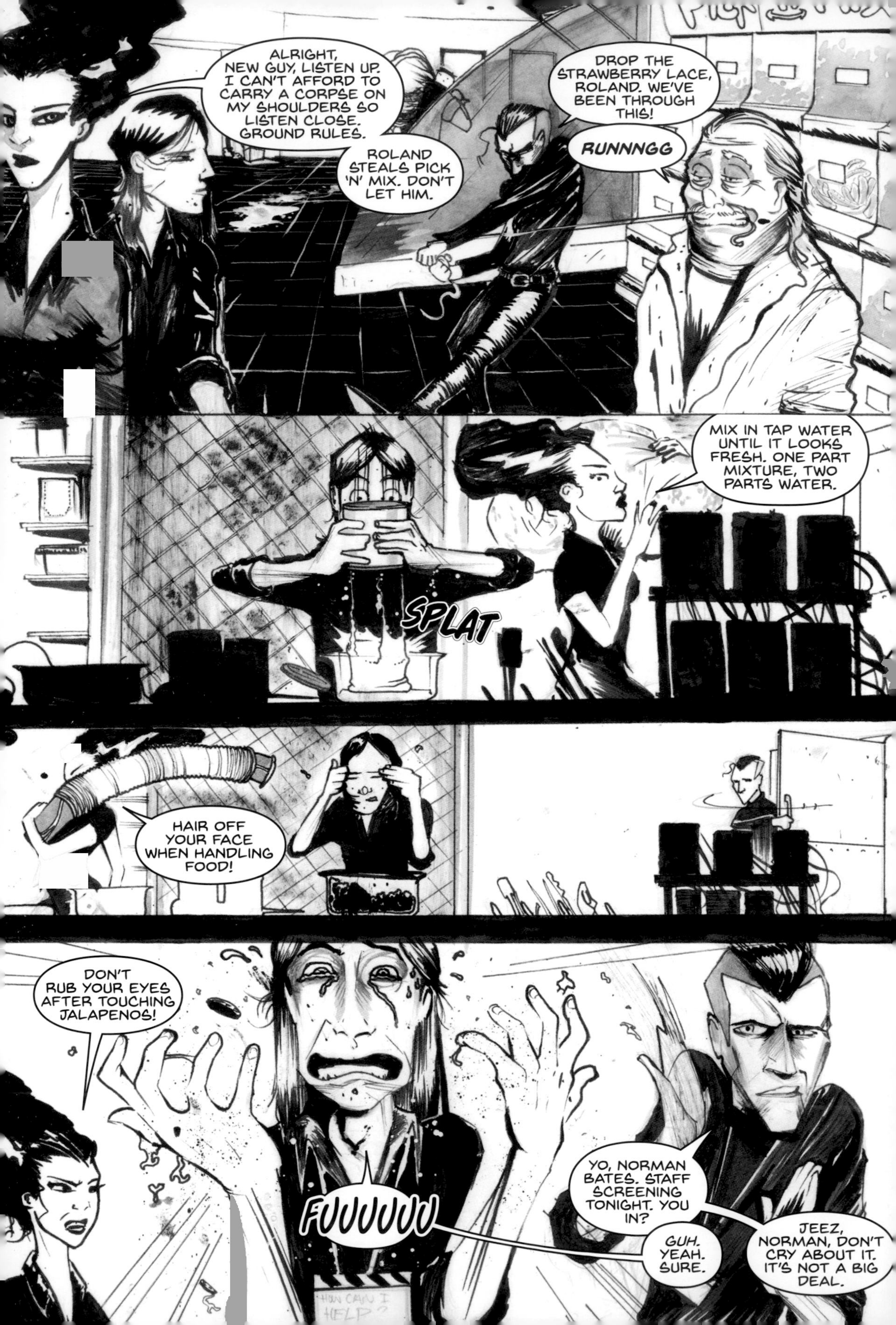
ALRIGHT, NEW GUY, LISTEN UP. I CAN'T AFFORD TO CARRY A CORPSE ON MY SHOULDERS SO LISTEN CLOSE. GROUND RULES.
ROLAND STEALS PICK 'N' MIX. DON'T LET HIM.
DROP THE STRAWBERRY LACE, ROLAND. WE'VE BEEN THROUGH THIS!
RUNNNGG
MIX IN TAP WATER UNTIL IT LOOKS FRESH. ONE PART MIXTURE, TWO PARTS WATER.
SPLAT
HAIR OFF YOUR FACE WHEN HANDLING FOOD!
DON'T RUB YOUR EYES AFTER TOUCHING JALAPENOS!
FUUUUUU
YO, NORMAN BATES. STAFF SCREENING TONIGHT. YOU IN?
GUH. YEAH. SURE.
JEEZ, NORMAN, DON'T CRY ABOUT IT. IT'S NOT A BIG DEAL.

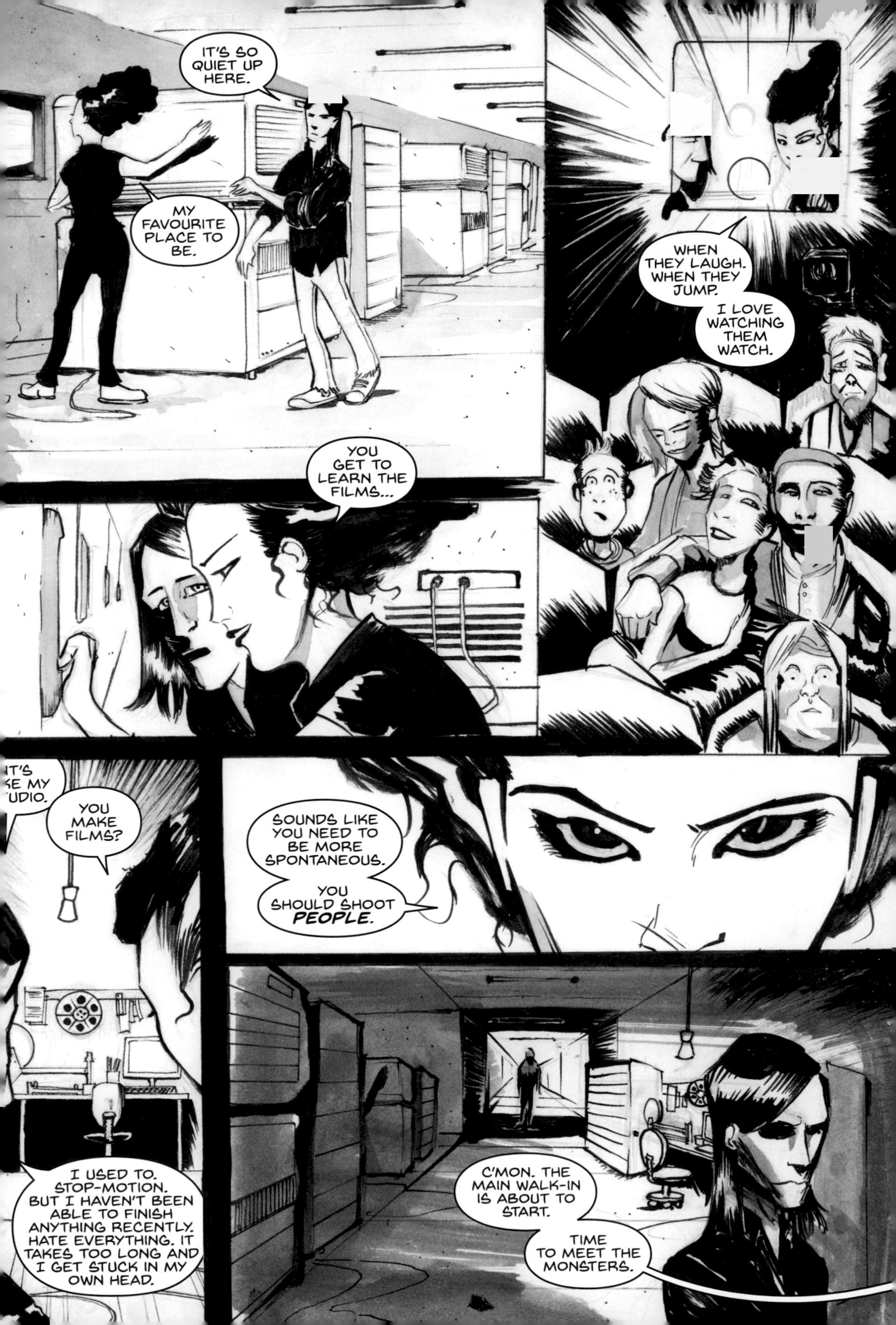
IT'S SO QUIET UP HERE.
MY FAVOURITE PLACE TO BE.
YOU GET TO LEARN THE FILMS...
WHEN THEY LAUGH. WHEN THEY JUMP.
I LOVE WATCHING THEM WATCH.
YOU MAKE FILMS?
I USED TO. STOP-MOTION. BUT I HAVEN'T BEEN ABLE TO FINISH ANYTHING RECENTLY. HATE EVERYTHING. IT TAKES TOO LONG AND I GET STUCK IN MY OWN HEAD.
SOUNDS LIKE YOU NEED TO BE MORE SPONTANEOUS.
YOU SHOULD SHOOT ***PEOPLE***.
C'MON. THE MAIN WALK-IN IS ABOUT TO START.
TIME TO MEET THE MONSTERS.

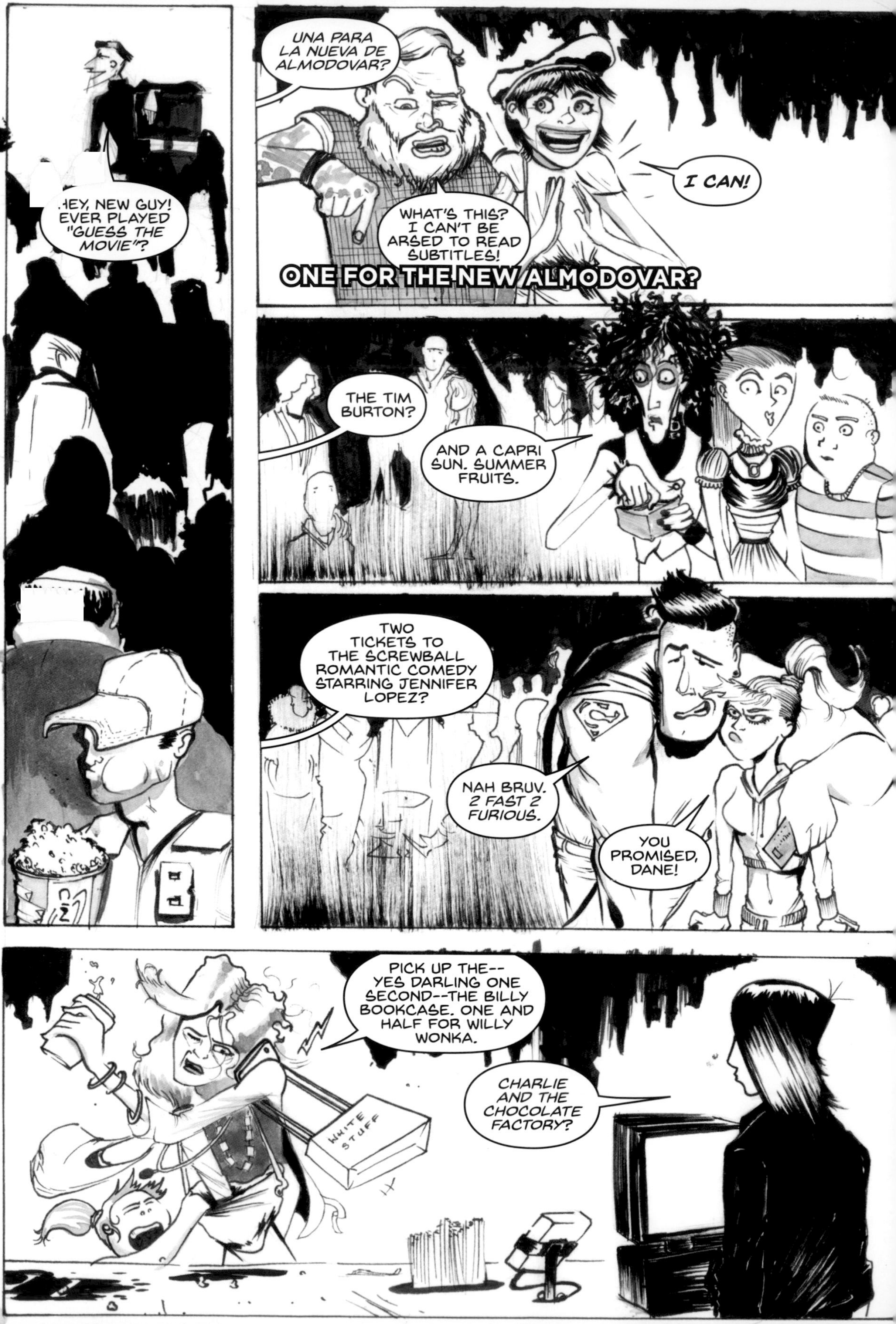
HEY, NEW GUY! EVER PLAYED "GUESS THE MOVIE"?
UNA PARA LA NUEVA DE ALMODOVAR?
WHAT'S THIS? I CAN'T BE ARSED TO READ SUBTITLES!
I CAN!
ONE FOR THE NEW ALMODOVAR?
THE TIM BURTON?
AND A CAPRI SUN. SUMMER FRUITS.
TWO TICKETS TO THE SCREWBALL ROMANTIC COMEDY STARRING JENNIFER LOPEZ?
NAH BRUV. 2 FAST 2 FURIOUS.
YOU PROMISED, DANE!
PICK UP THE-- YES DARLING ONE SECOND--THE BILLY BOOKCASE. ONE AND HALF FOR WILLY WONKA.
CHARLIE AND THE CHOCOLATE FACTORY?
WHITE STUFF

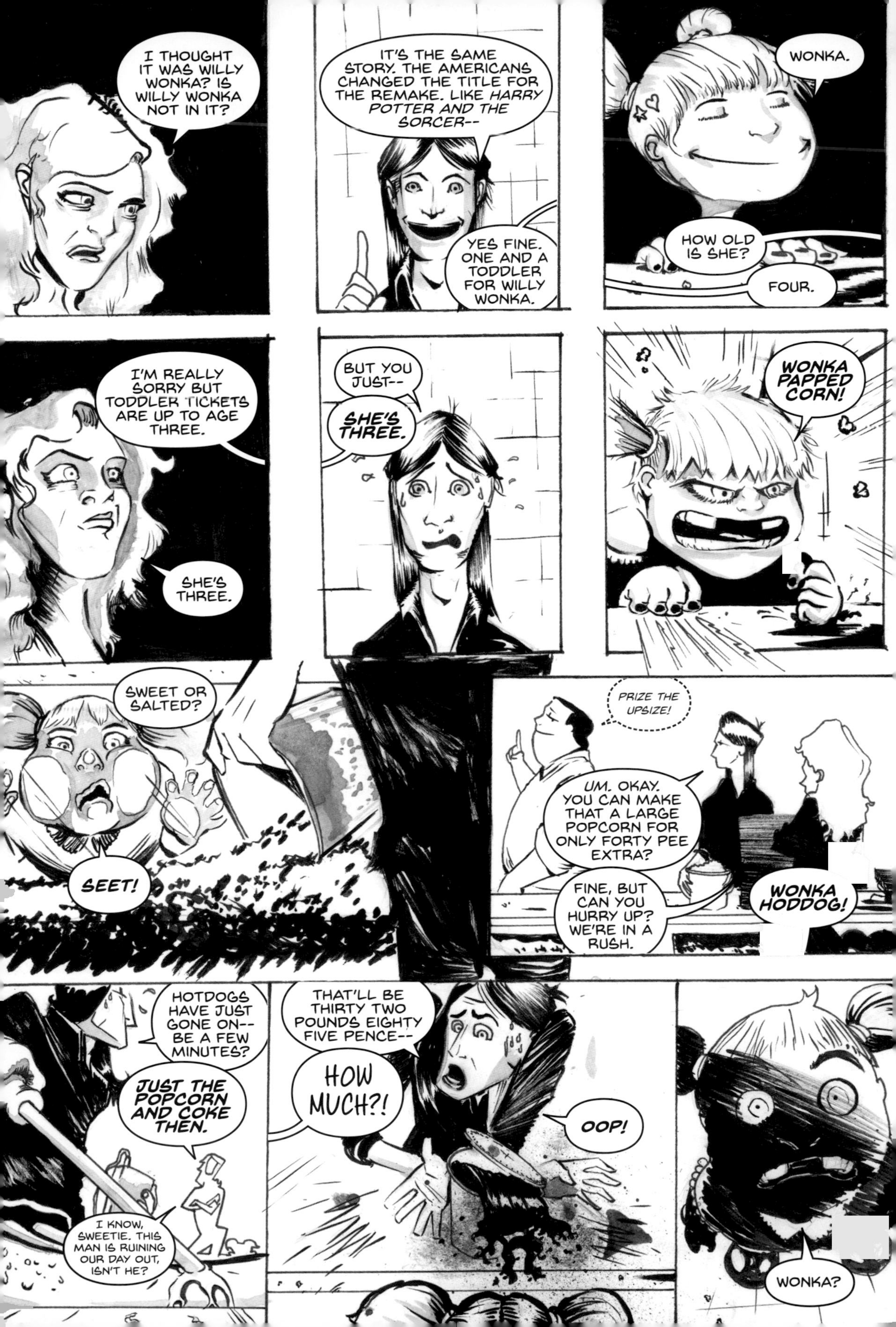
I THOUGHT IT WAS WILLY WONKA? IS WILLY WONKA NOT IN IT?
IT'S THE SAME STORY. THE AMERICANS CHANGED THE TITLE FOR THE REMAKE. LIKE *HARRY POTTER AND THE SORCER--*
YES FINE. ONE AND A TODDLER FOR WILLY WONKA.
WONKA.
HOW OLD IS SHE?
FOUR.
I'M REALLY SORRY BUT TODDLER TICKETS ARE UP TO AGE THREE.
SHE'S THREE.
BUT YOU JUST--
SHE'S THREE.
WONKA PAPPED CORN!
SWEET OR SALTED?
SEET!
PRIZE THE UPSIZE!
UM. OKAY. YOU CAN MAKE THAT A LARGE POPCORN FOR ONLY FORTY PEE EXTRA?
FINE, BUT CAN YOU HURRY UP? WE'RE IN A RUSH.
WONKA HODDOG!
HOTDOGS HAVE JUST GONE ON-- BE A FEW MINUTES?
JUST THE POPCORN AND COKE THEN.
I KNOW, SWEETIE. THIS MAN IS RUINING OUR DAY OUT, ISN'T HE?
THAT'LL BE THIRTY TWO POUNDS EIGHTY FIVE PENCE--
HOW MUCH?!
OOP!
WONKA?

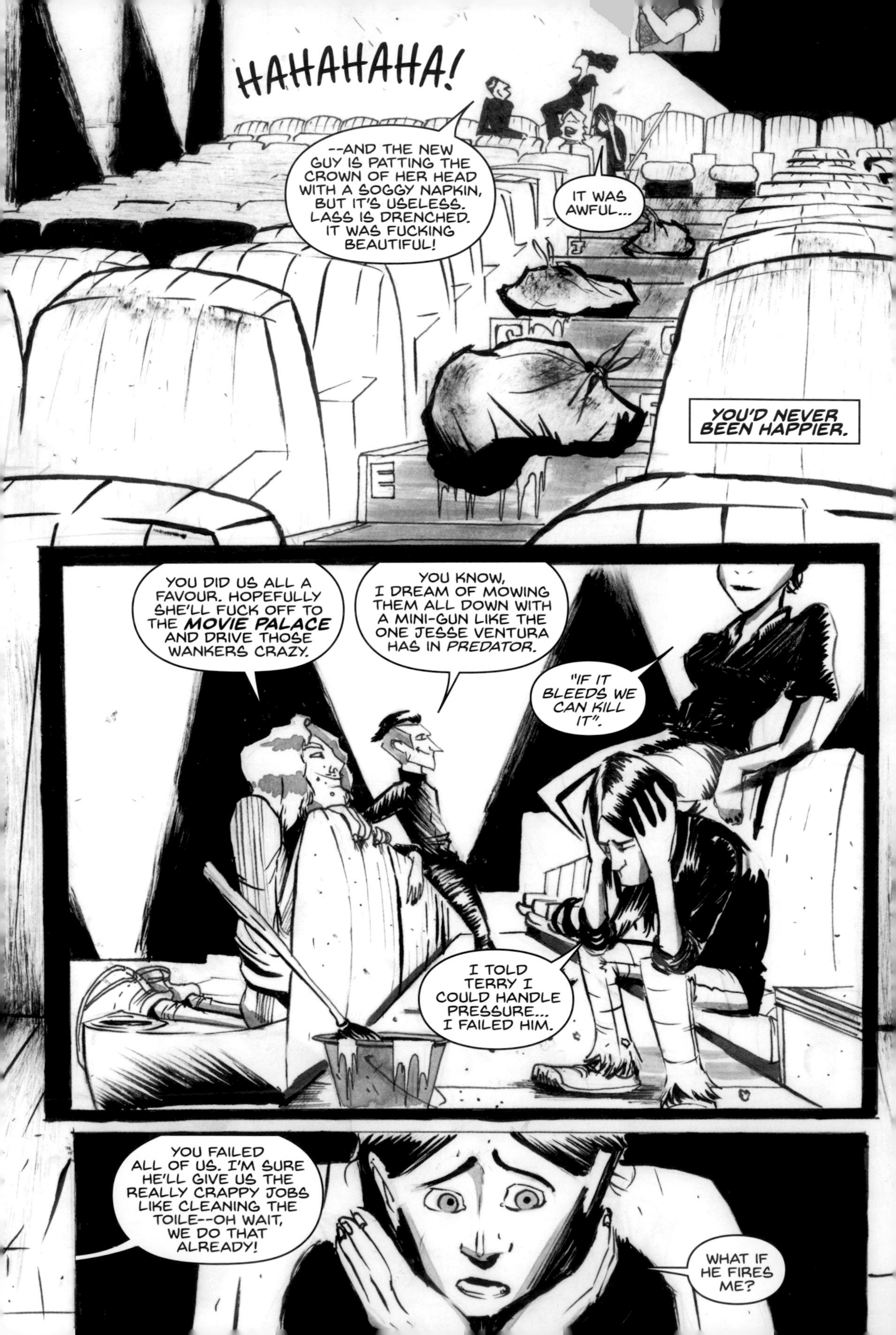
HAHAHAHA!
--AND THE NEW GUY IS PATTING THE CROWN OF HER HEAD WITH A SOGGY NAPKIN, BUT IT'S USELESS. LASS IS DRENCHED. IT WAS FUCKING BEAUTIFUL!
IT WAS AWFUL...
YOU'D NEVER BEEN HAPPIER.
YOU DID US ALL A FAVOUR. HOPEFULLY SHE'LL FUCK OFF TO THE MOVIE PALACE AND DRIVE THOSE WANKERS CRAZY.
YOU KNOW, I DREAM OF MOWING THEM ALL DOWN WITH A MINI-GUN LIKE THE ONE JESSE VENTURA HAS IN PREDATOR.
"IF IT BLEEDS WE CAN KILL IT".
I TOLD TERRY I COULD HANDLE PRESSURE... I FAILED HIM.
YOU FAILED ALL OF US. I'M SURE HE'LL GIVE US THE REALLY CRAPPY JOBS LIKE CLEANING THE TOILE--OH WAIT, WE DO THAT ALREADY!
WHAT IF HE FIRES ME?

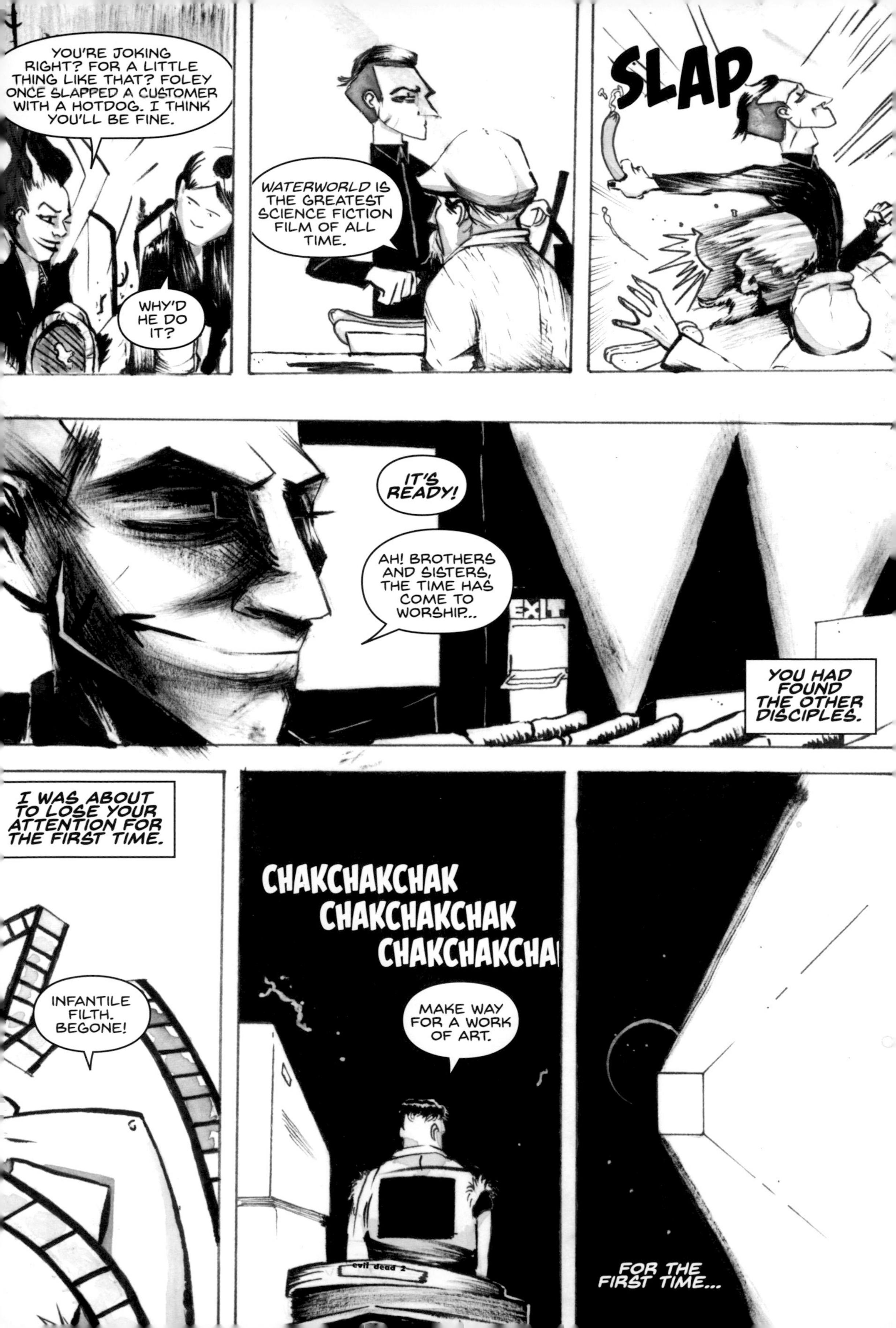
YOU'RE JOKING RIGHT? FOR A LITTLE THING LIKE THAT? FOLEY ONCE SLAPPED A CUSTOMER WITH A HOTDOG. I THINK YOU'LL BE FINE.
WHY'D HE DO IT?
WATERWORLD IS THE GREATEST SCIENCE FICTION FILM OF ALL TIME.
SLAP
IT'S READY!
AH! BROTHERS AND SISTERS, THE TIME HAS COME TO WORSHIP...
EXIT
YOU HAD FOUND THE OTHER DISCIPLES.
I WAS ABOUT TO LOSE YOUR ATTENTION FOR THE FIRST TIME.
INFANTILE FILTH. BEGONE!
CHAKCHAKCHAK
CHAKCHAKCHAK
CHAKCHAKCHA
MAKE WAY FOR A WORK OF ART.
evil dead 2
FOR THE FIRST TIME...

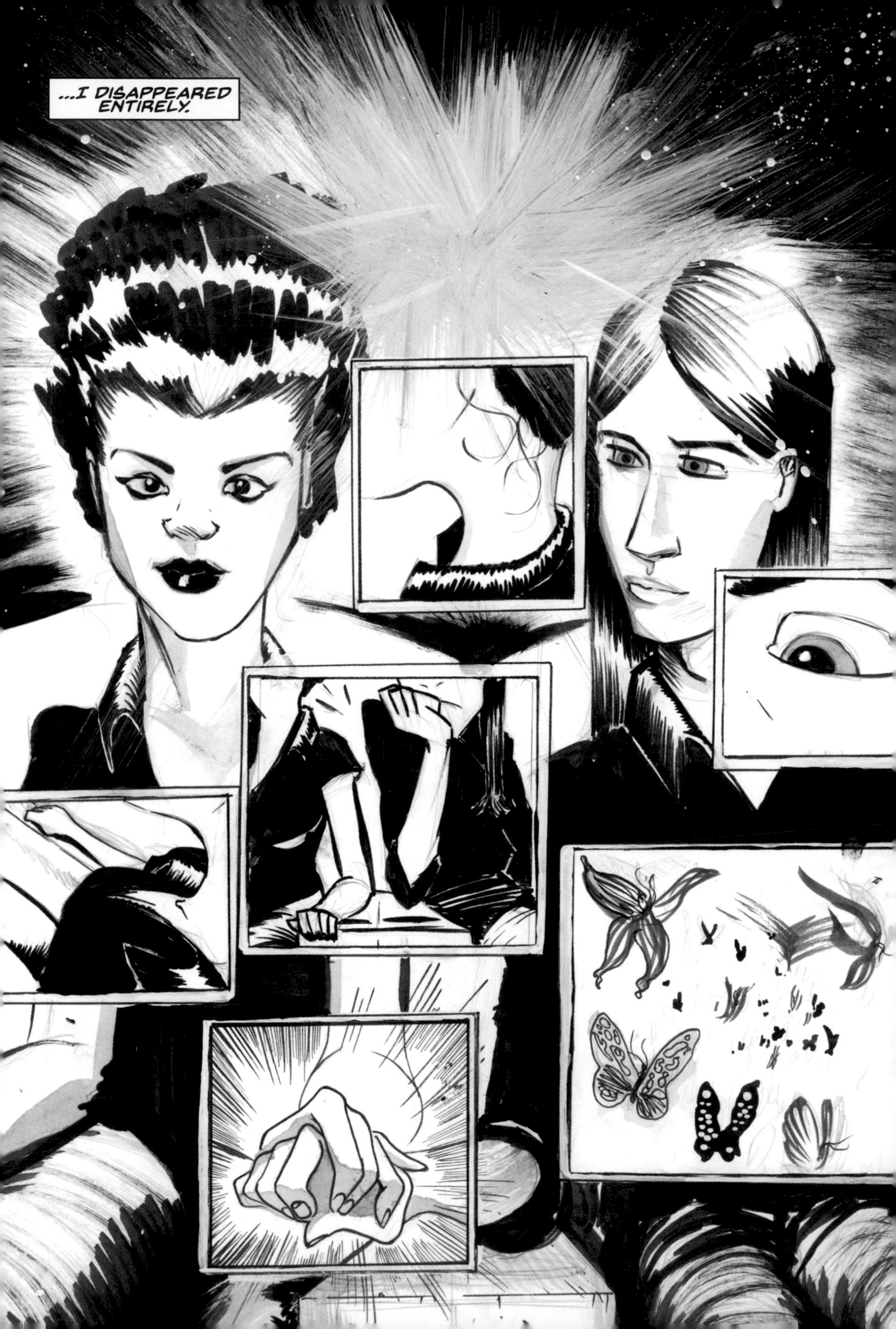
...I DISAPPEARED ENTIRELY.

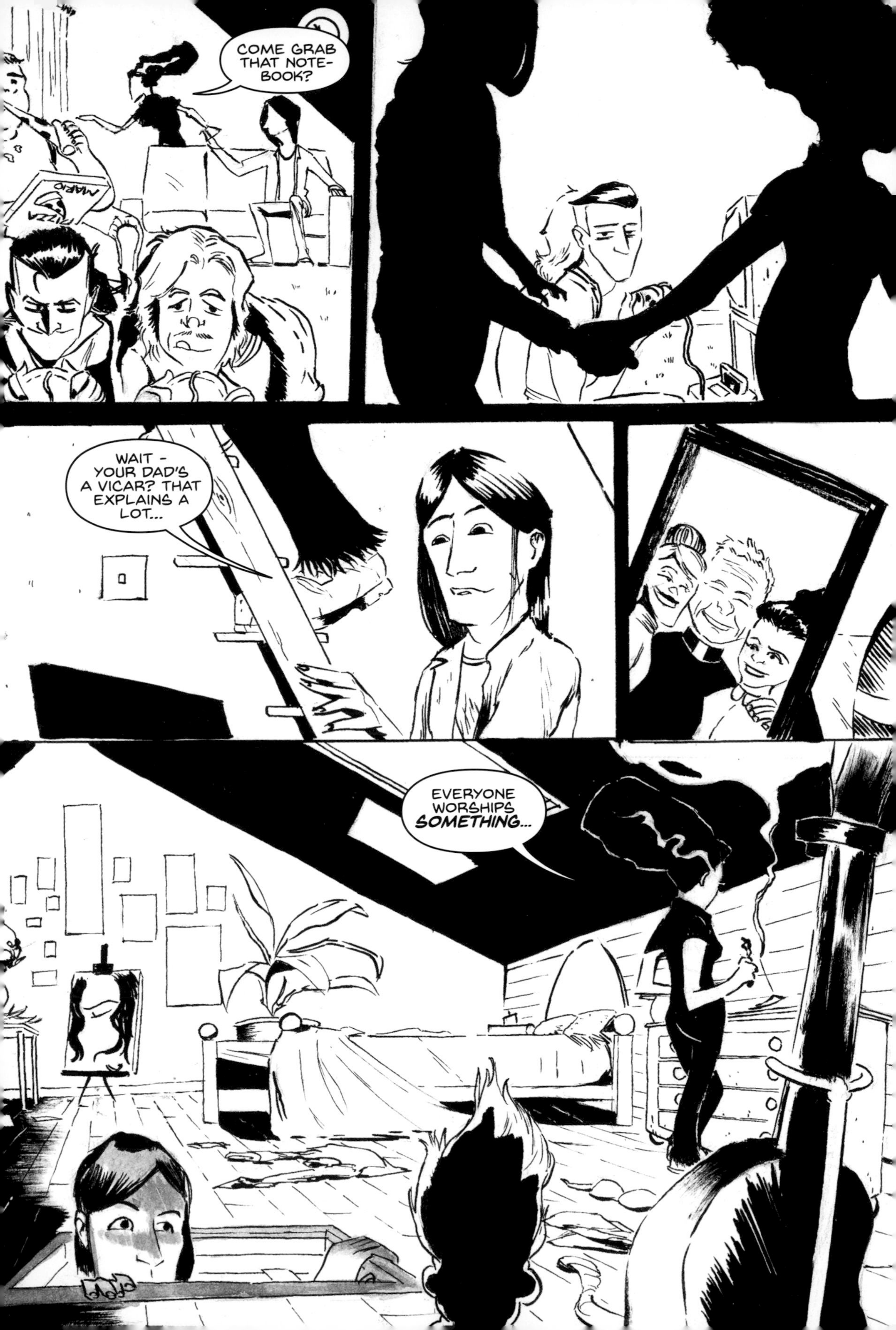
COME GRAB THAT NOTE-BOOK?
MARIO PIZZA
WAIT - YOUR DAD'S A VICAR? THAT EXPLAINS A LOT...
EVERYONE WORSHIPS *SOMETHING*...

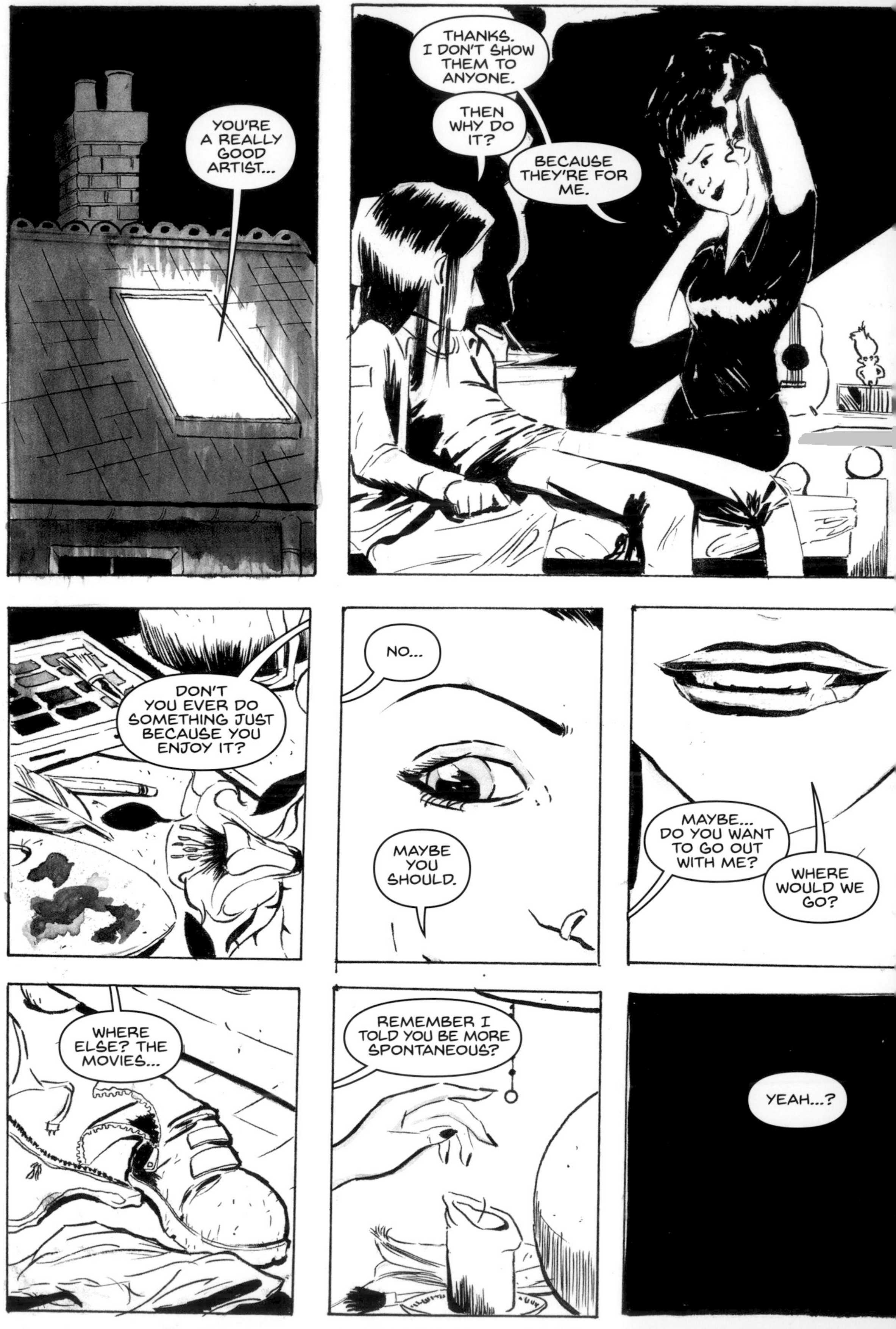
YOU'RE A REALLY GOOD ARTIST...
THANKS. I DON'T SHOW THEM TO ANYONE.
THEN WHY DO IT?
BECAUSE THEY'RE FOR ME.
DON'T YOU EVER DO SOMETHING JUST BECAUSE YOU ENJOY IT?
NO...
MAYBE YOU SHOULD.
MAYBE... DO YOU WANT TO GO OUT WITH ME?
WHERE WOULD WE GO?
WHERE ELSE? THE MOVIES...
REMEMBER I TOLD YOU BE MORE SPONTANEOUS?
YEAH...?

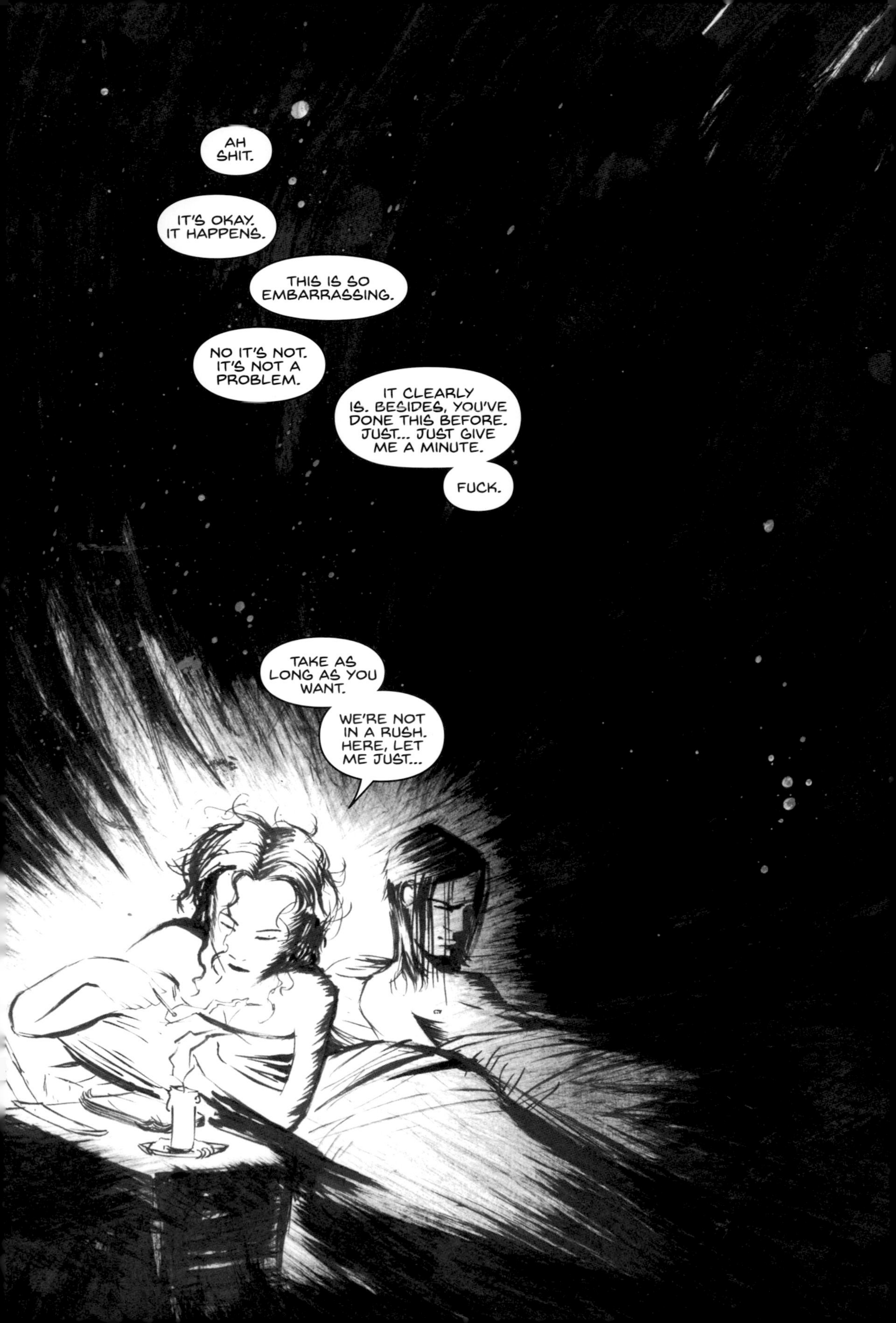
AH SHIT.
IT'S OKAY. IT HAPPENS.
THIS IS SO EMBARRASSING.
NO IT'S NOT. IT'S NOT A PROBLEM.
IT CLEARLY IS. BESIDES, YOU'VE DONE THIS BEFORE. JUST... JUST GIVE ME A MINUTE.
FUCK.
TAKE AS LONG AS YOU WANT.
WE'RE NOT IN A RUSH. HERE, LET ME JUST...

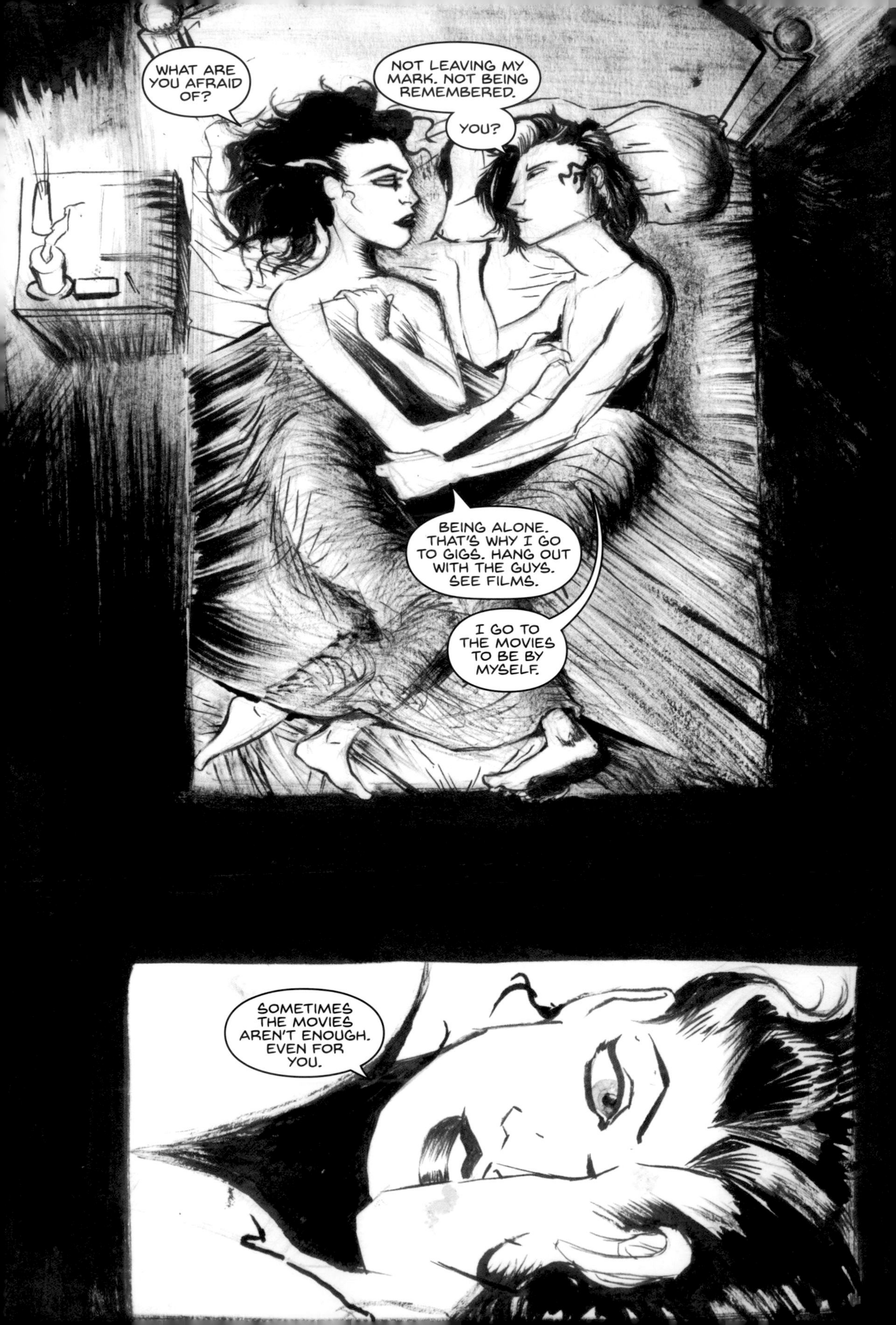
WHAT ARE YOU AFRAID OF?
NOT LEAVING MY MARK. NOT BEING REMEMBERED.
YOU?
BEING ALONE. THAT'S WHY I GO TO GIGS. HANG OUT WITH THE GUYS. SEE FILMS.
I GO TO THE MOVIES TO BE BY MYSELF.
SOMETIMES THE MOVIES AREN'T ENOUGH. EVEN FOR YOU.

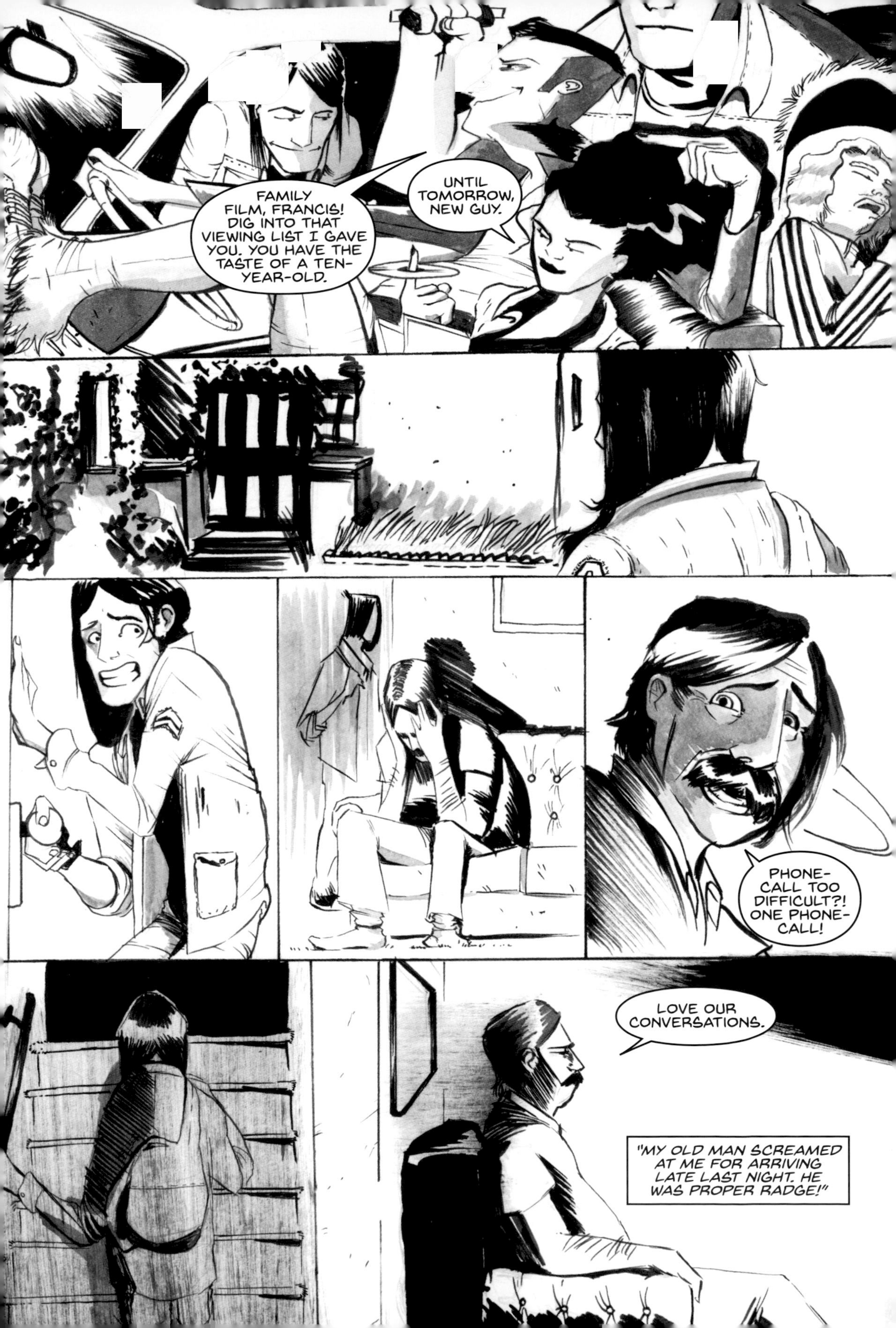
FAMILY FILM, FRANCIS! DIG INTO THAT VIEWING LIST I GAVE YOU. YOU HAVE THE TASTE OF A TEN-YEAR-OLD.
UNTIL TOMORROW, NEW GUY.
PHONE-CALL TOO DIFFICULT?! ONE PHONE-CALL!
LOVE OUR CONVERSATIONS.
"MY OLD MAN SCREAMED AT ME FOR ARRIVING LATE LAST NIGHT. HE WAS PROPER RADGE!"

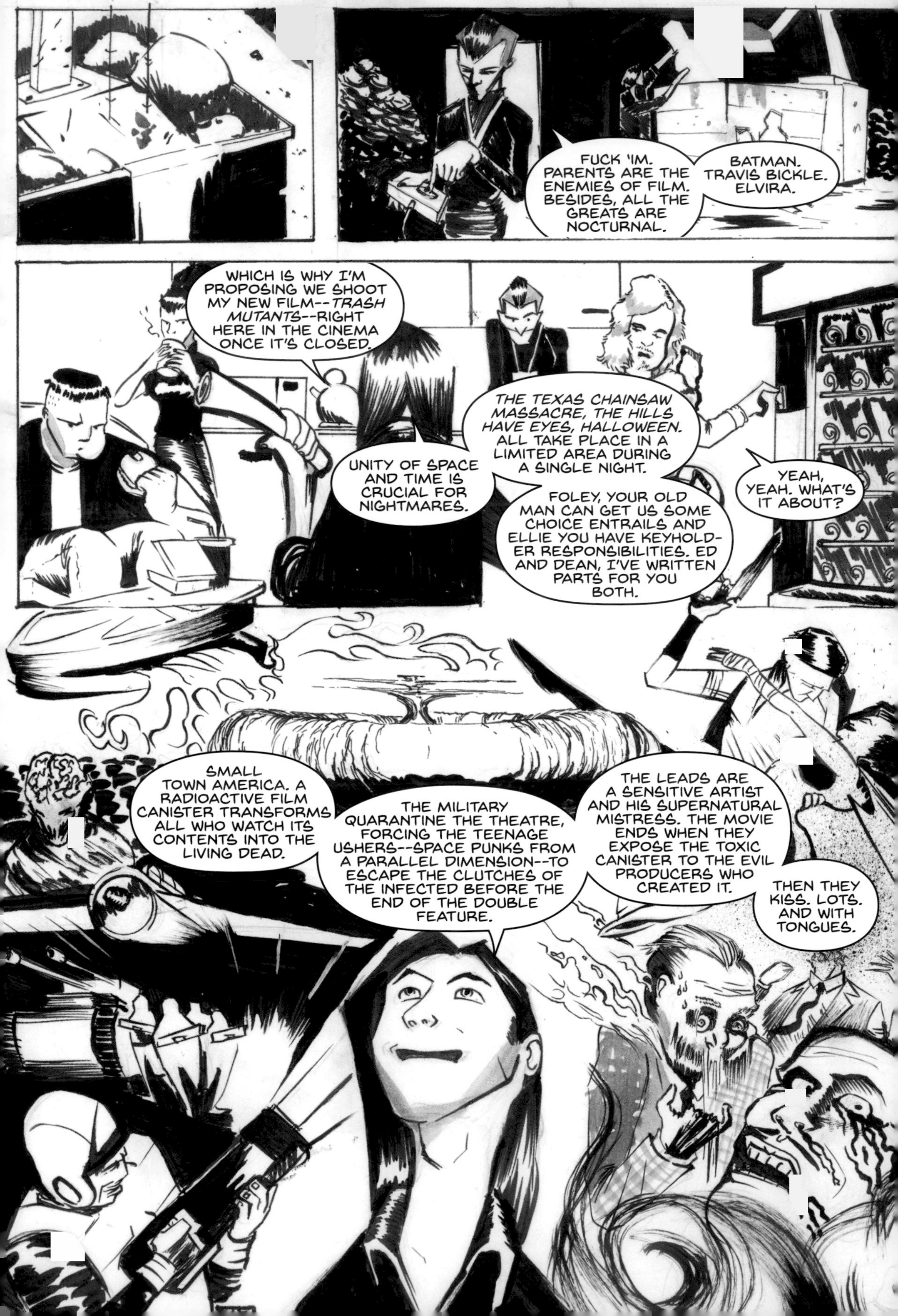
FUCK 'IM. PARENTS ARE THE ENEMIES OF FILM. BESIDES, ALL THE GREATS ARE NOCTURNAL.
BATMAN. TRAVIS BICKLE. ELVIRA.
WHICH IS WHY I'M PROPOSING WE SHOOT MY NEW FILM--*TRASH MUTANTS*--RIGHT HERE IN THE CINEMA ONCE IT'S CLOSED.
UNITY OF SPACE AND TIME IS CRUCIAL FOR NIGHTMARES.
THE TEXAS CHAINSAW MASSACRE, THE HILLS HAVE EYES, HALLOWEEN. ALL TAKE PLACE IN A LIMITED AREA DURING A SINGLE NIGHT.
FOLEY, YOUR OLD MAN CAN GET US SOME CHOICE ENTRAILS AND ELLIE YOU HAVE KEYHOLDER RESPONSIBILITIES. ED AND DEAN, I'VE WRITTEN PARTS FOR YOU BOTH.
YEAH, YEAH. WHAT'S IT ABOUT?
SMALL TOWN AMERICA. A RADIOACTIVE FILM CANISTER TRANSFORMS ALL WHO WATCH ITS CONTENTS INTO THE LIVING DEAD.
THE MILITARY QUARANTINE THE THEATRE, FORCING THE TEENAGE USHERS--SPACE PUNKS FROM A PARALLEL DIMENSION--TO ESCAPE THE CLUTCHES OF THE INFECTED BEFORE THE END OF THE DOUBLE FEATURE.
THE LEADS ARE A SENSITIVE ARTIST AND HIS SUPERNATURAL MISTRESS. THE MOVIE ENDS WHEN THEY EXPOSE THE TOXIC CANISTER TO THE EVIL PRODUCERS WHO CREATED IT.
THEN THEY KISS. LOTS. AND WITH TONGUES.

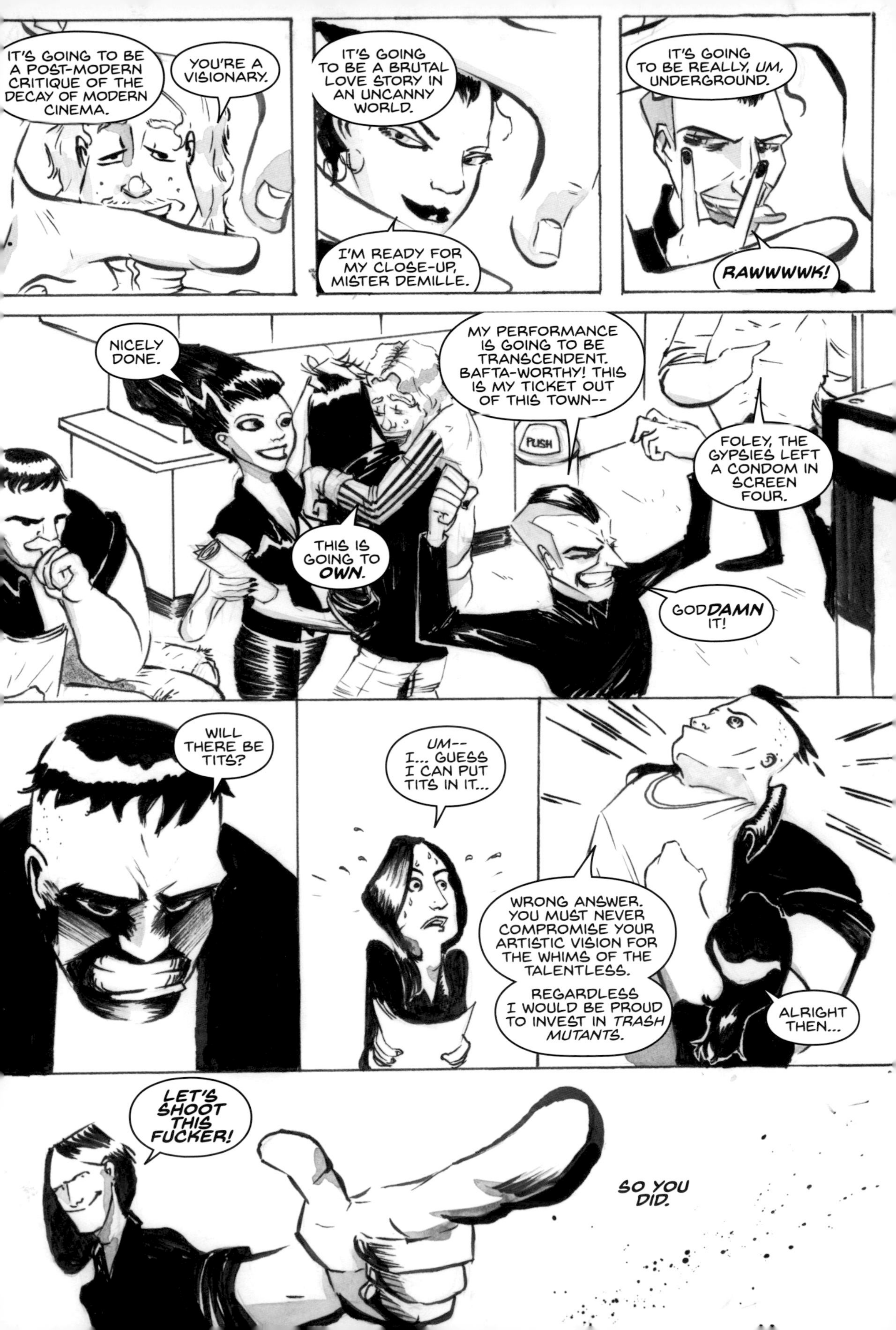

IT'S GOING TO BE A POST-MODERN CRITIQUE OF THE DECAY OF MODERN CINEMA.
YOU'RE A VISIONARY.
IT'S GOING TO BE A BRUTAL LOVE STORY IN AN UNCANNY WORLD.
I'M READY FOR MY CLOSE-UP, MISTER DEMILLE.
IT'S GOING TO BE REALLY, UM, UNDERGROUND.
RAWWWWK!
NICELY DONE.
MY PERFORMANCE IS GOING TO BE TRANSCENDENT. BAFTA-WORTHY! THIS IS MY TICKET OUT OF THIS TOWN--
PUSH
THIS IS GOING TO OWN.
FOLEY, THE GYPSIES LEFT A CONDOM IN SCREEN FOUR.
GODDAMN IT!
WILL THERE BE TITS?
UM-- I... GUESS I CAN PUT TITS IN IT...
WRONG ANSWER. YOU MUST NEVER COMPROMISE YOUR ARTISTIC VISION FOR THE WHIMS OF THE TALENTLESS.
REGARDLESS I WOULD BE PROUD TO INVEST IN TRASH MUTANTS.
ALRIGHT THEN...
LET'S SHOOT THIS FUCKER!
SO YOU DID.

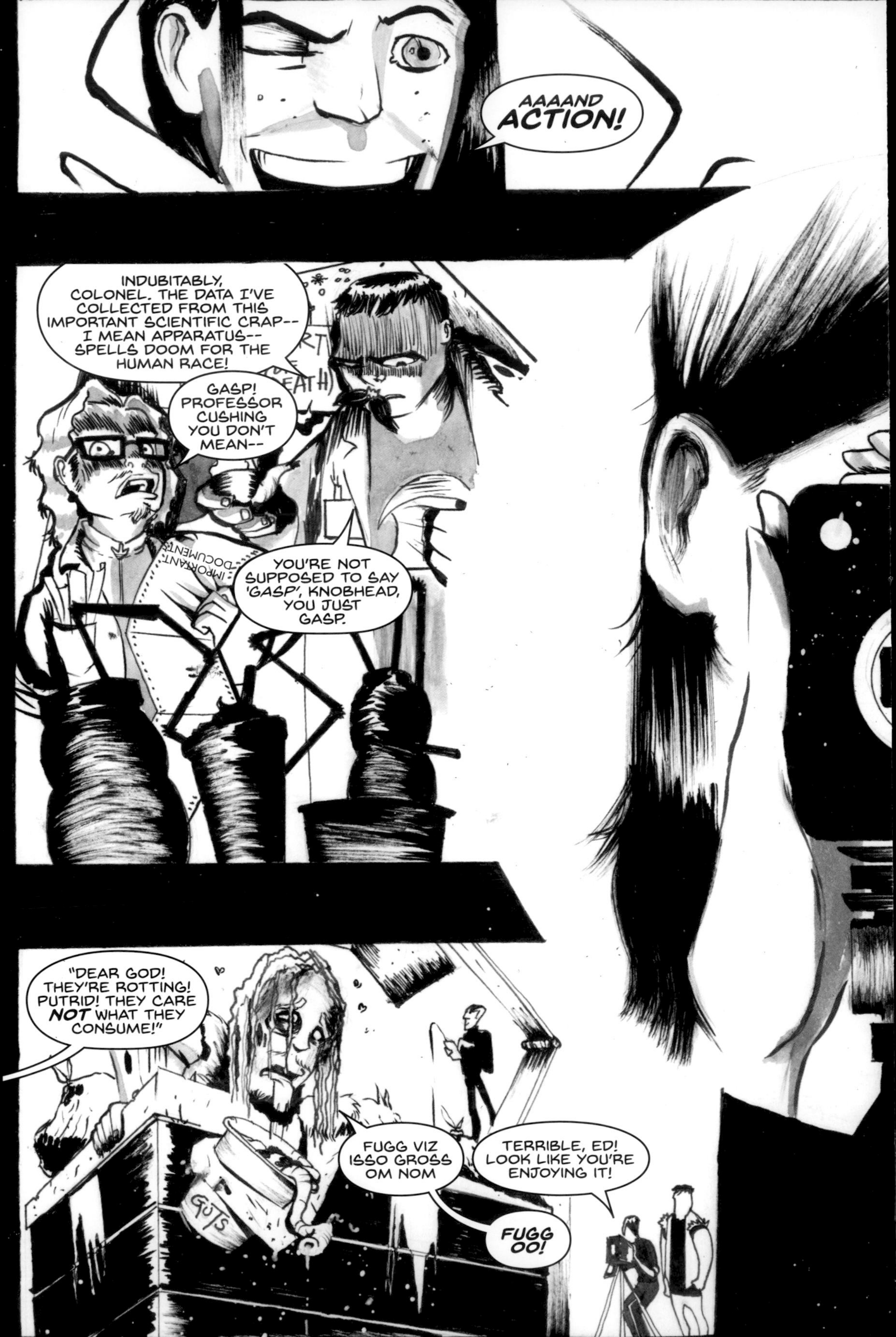
AAAAND ACTION!
INDUBITABLY, COLONEL. THE DATA I'VE COLLECTED FROM THIS IMPORTANT SCIENTIFIC CRAP-- I MEAN APPARATUS-- SPELLS DOOM FOR THE HUMAN RACE!
GASP! PROFESSOR CUSHING YOU DON'T MEAN--
IMPORTANT DOCUMENTS
YOU'RE NOT SUPPOSED TO SAY 'GASP', KNOBHEAD, YOU JUST GASP.
"DEAR GOD! THEY'RE ROTTING! PUTRID! THEY CARE NOT WHAT THEY CONSUME!"
GUTS
FUGG VIZ ISSO GROSS OM NOM
TERRIBLE, ED! LOOK LIKE YOU'RE ENJOYING IT!
FUGG OO!

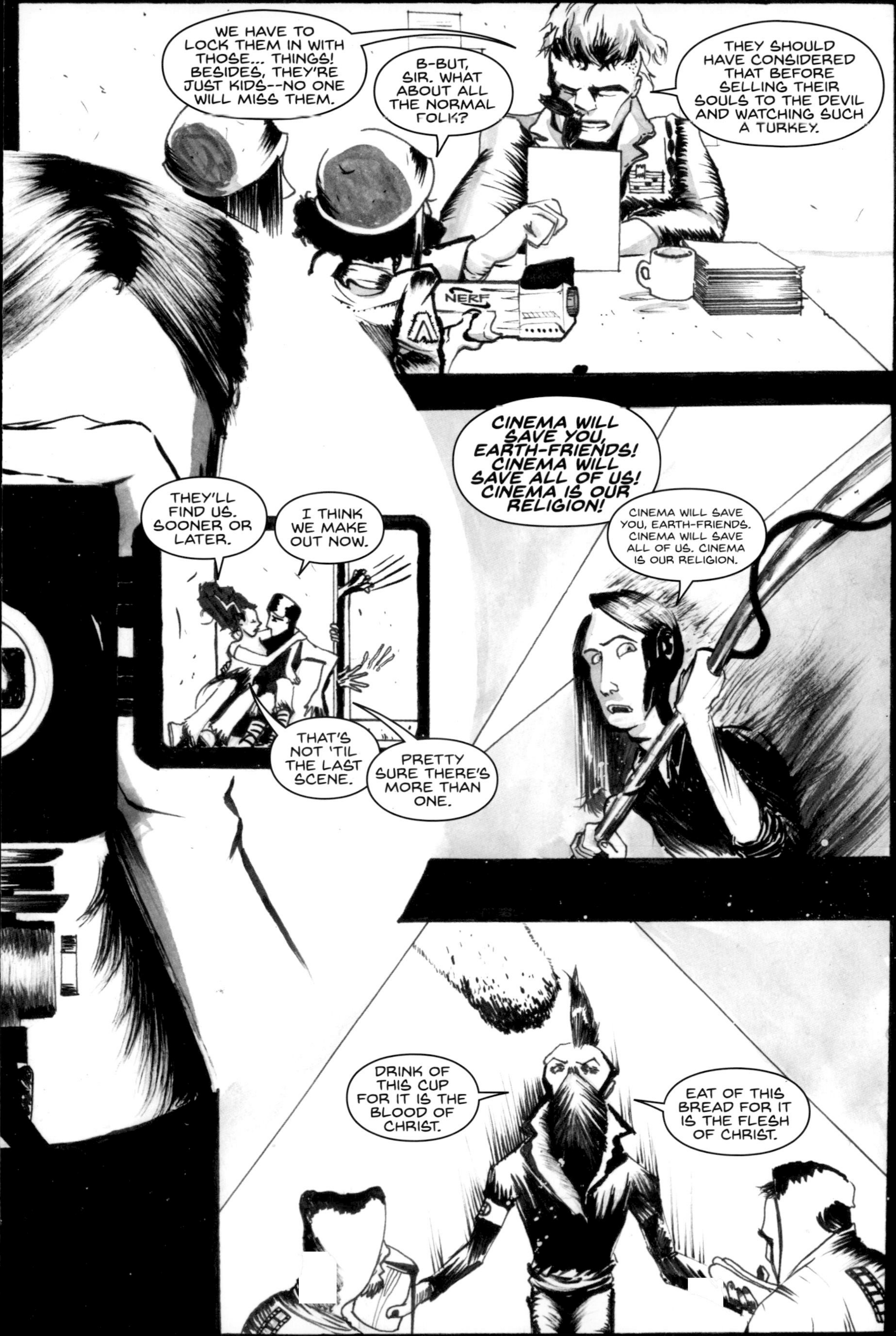
WE HAVE TO LOCK THEM IN WITH THOSE... THINGS! BESIDES, THEY'RE JUST KIDS--NO ONE WILL MISS THEM.
B-BUT, SIR. WHAT ABOUT ALL THE NORMAL FOLK?
THEY SHOULD HAVE CONSIDERED THAT BEFORE SELLING THEIR SOULS TO THE DEVIL AND WATCHING SUCH A TURKEY.
NERF
CINEMA WILL SAVE YOU, EARTH-FRIENDS! CINEMA WILL SAVE ALL OF US! CINEMA IS OUR RELIGION!
CINEMA WILL SAVE YOU, EARTH-FRIENDS. CINEMA WILL SAVE ALL OF US. CINEMA IS OUR RELIGION.
THEY'LL FIND US. SOONER OR LATER.
I THINK WE MAKE OUT NOW.
THAT'S NOT 'TIL THE LAST SCENE.
PRETTY SURE THERE'S MORE THAN ONE.
DRINK OF THIS CUP FOR IT IS THE BLOOD OF CHRIST.
EAT OF THIS BREAD FOR IT IS THE FLESH OF CHRIST.

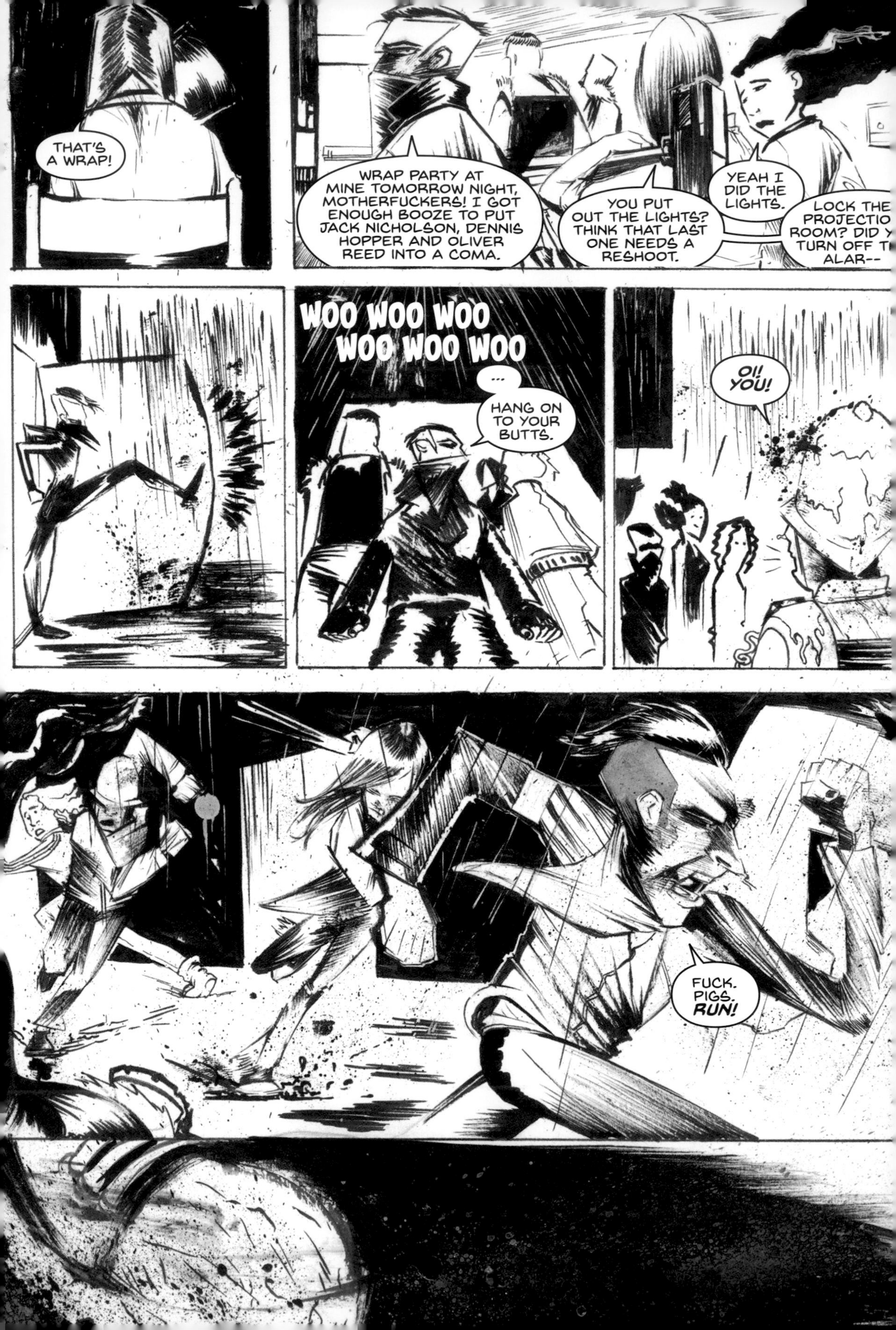
THAT'S A WRAP!
WRAP PARTY AT MINE TOMORROW NIGHT, MOTHERFUCKERS! I GOT ENOUGH BOOZE TO PUT JACK NICHOLSON, DENNIS HOPPER AND OLIVER REED INTO A COMA.
YOU PUT OUT THE LIGHTS? THINK THAT LAST ONE NEEDS A RESHOOT.
YEAH I DID THE LIGHTS.
LOCK THE PROJECTIO ROOM? DID Y TURN OFF T ALAR--
WOO WOO WOO
WOO WOO WOO
...
HANG ON TO YOUR BUTTS.
OI! YOU!
FUCK. PIGS. RUN!

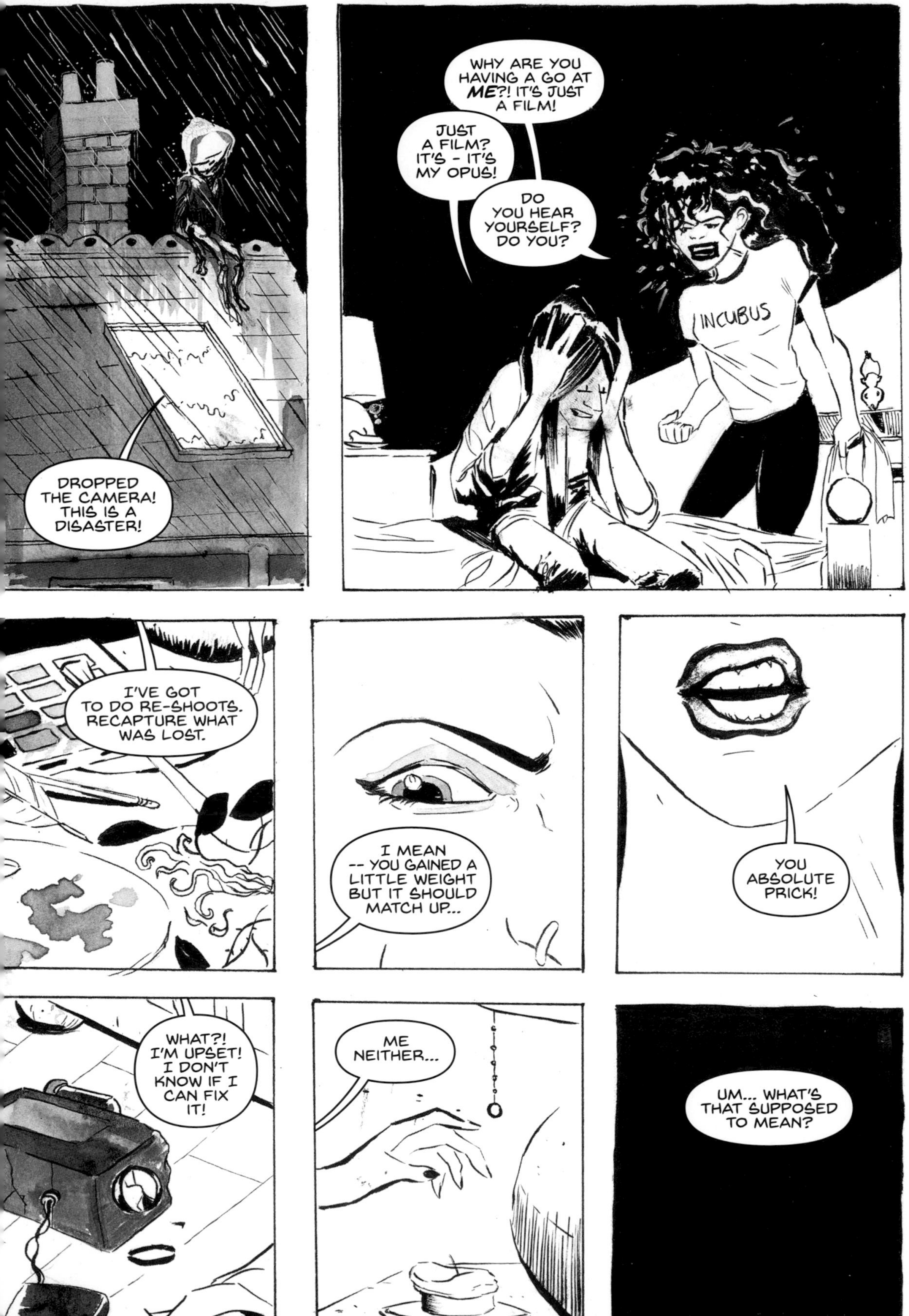
DROPPED THE CAMERA! THIS IS A DISASTER!
WHY ARE YOU HAVING A GO AT ME?! IT'S JUST A FILM!
JUST A FILM? IT'S - IT'S MY OPUS!
DO YOU HEAR YOURSELF? DO YOU?
INCUBUS
I'VE GOT TO DO RE-SHOOTS. RECAPTURE WHAT WAS LOST.
I MEAN -- YOU GAINED A LITTLE WEIGHT BUT IT SHOULD MATCH UP...
YOU ABSOLUTE PRICK!
WHAT?! I'M UPSET! I DON'T KNOW IF I CAN FIX IT!
ME NEITHER...
UM... WHAT'S THAT SUPPOSED TO MEAN?

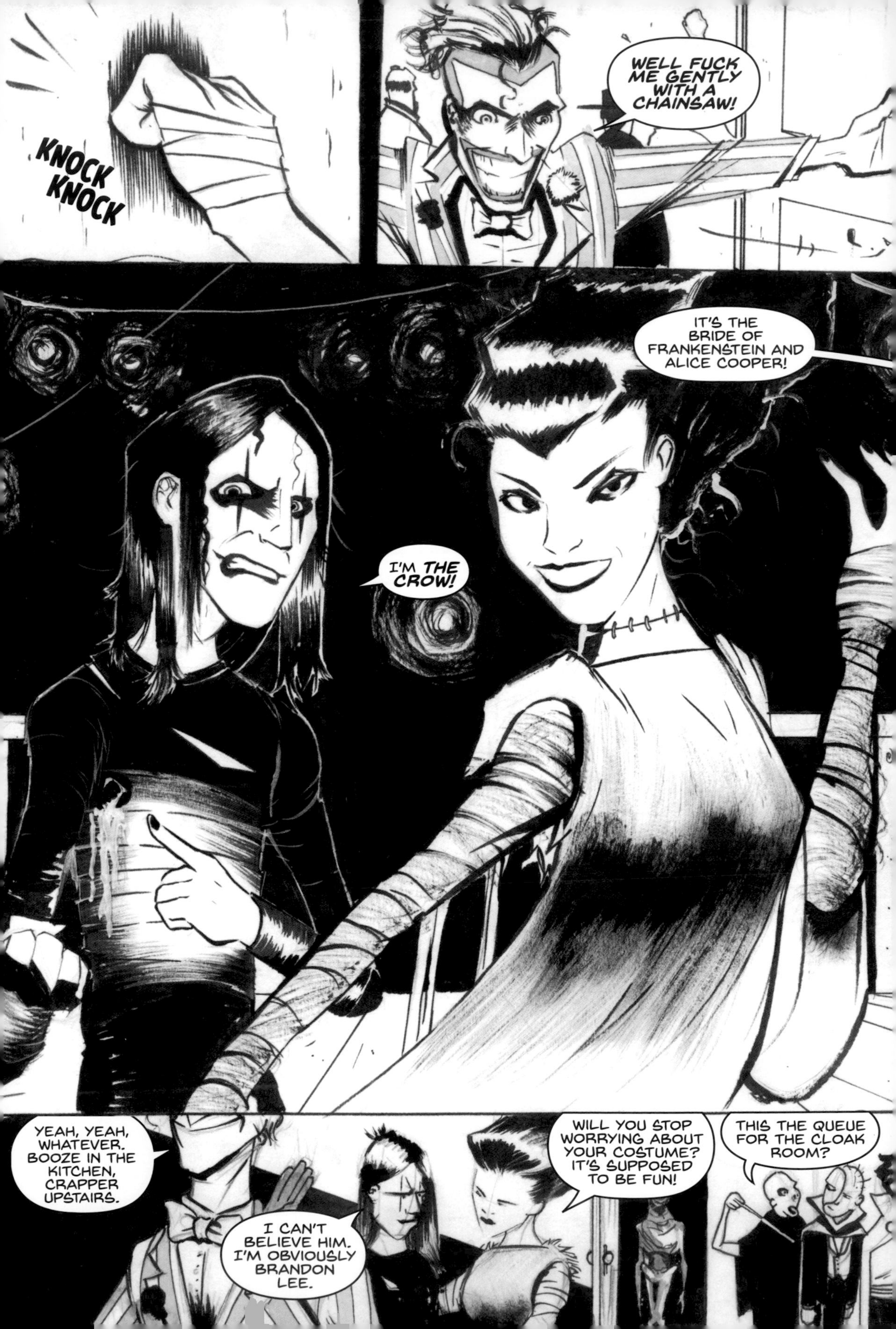
KNOCK KNOCK
WELL FUCK ME GENTLY WITH A CHAINSAW!
IT'S THE BRIDE OF FRANKENSTEIN AND ALICE COOPER!
I'M THE CROW!
YEAH, YEAH, WHATEVER. BOOZE IN THE KITCHEN, CRAPPER UPSTAIRS.
I CAN'T BELIEVE HIM. I'M OBVIOUSLY BRANDON LEE.
WILL YOU STOP WORRYING ABOUT YOUR COSTUME? IT'S SUPPOSED TO BE FUN!
THIS THE QUEUE FOR THE CLOAK ROOM?

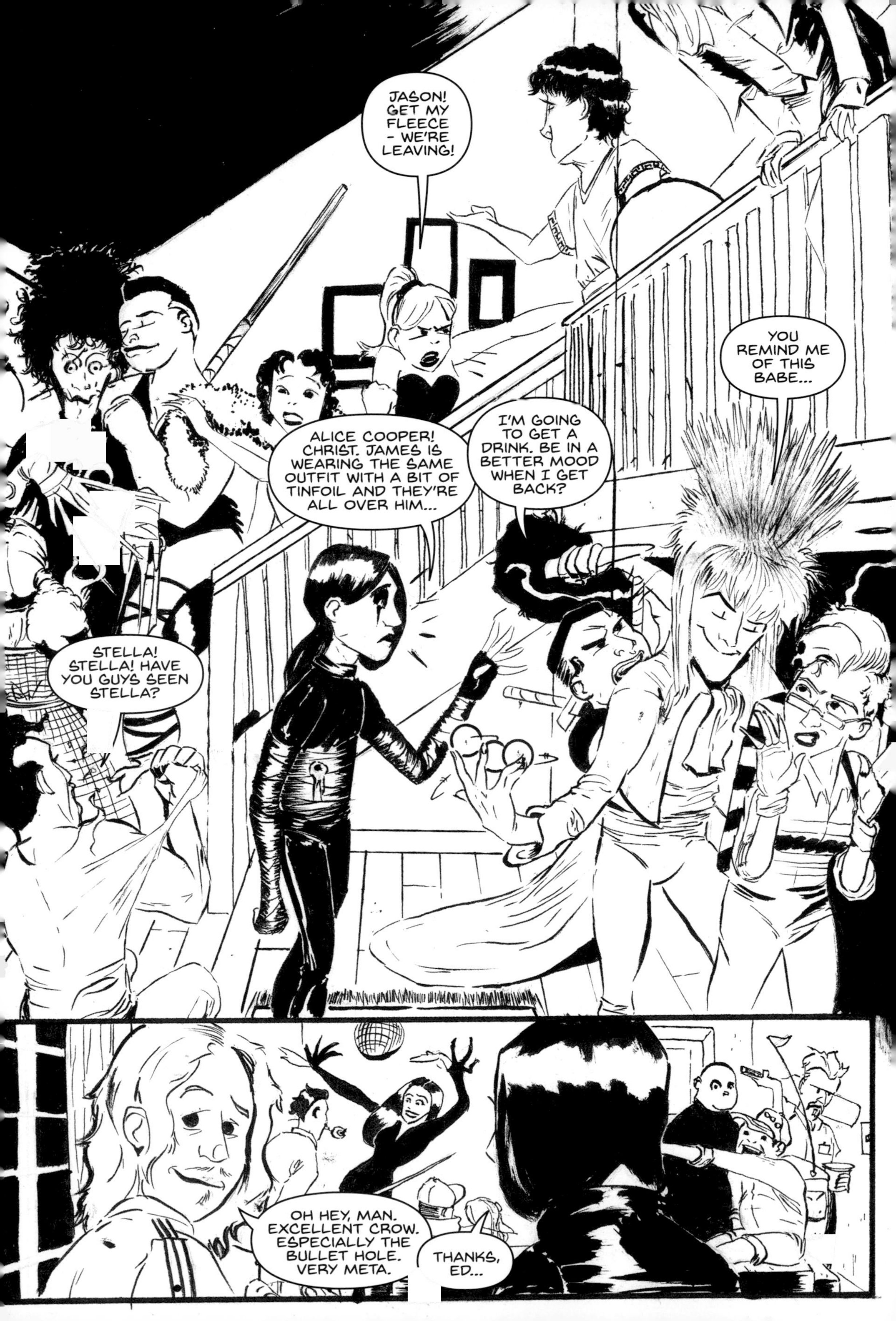
JASON! GET MY FLEECE - WE'RE LEAVING!
YOU REMIND ME OF THIS BABE...
I'M GOING TO GET A DRINK. BE IN A BETTER MOOD WHEN I GET BACK?
ALICE COOPER! CHRIST. JAMES IS WEARING THE SAME OUTFIT WITH A BIT OF TINFOIL AND THEY'RE ALL OVER HIM...
STELLA! STELLA! HAVE YOU GUYS SEEN STELLA?
OH HEY, MAN. EXCELLENT CROW. ESPECIALLY THE BULLET HOLE. VERY META.
THANKS, ED...

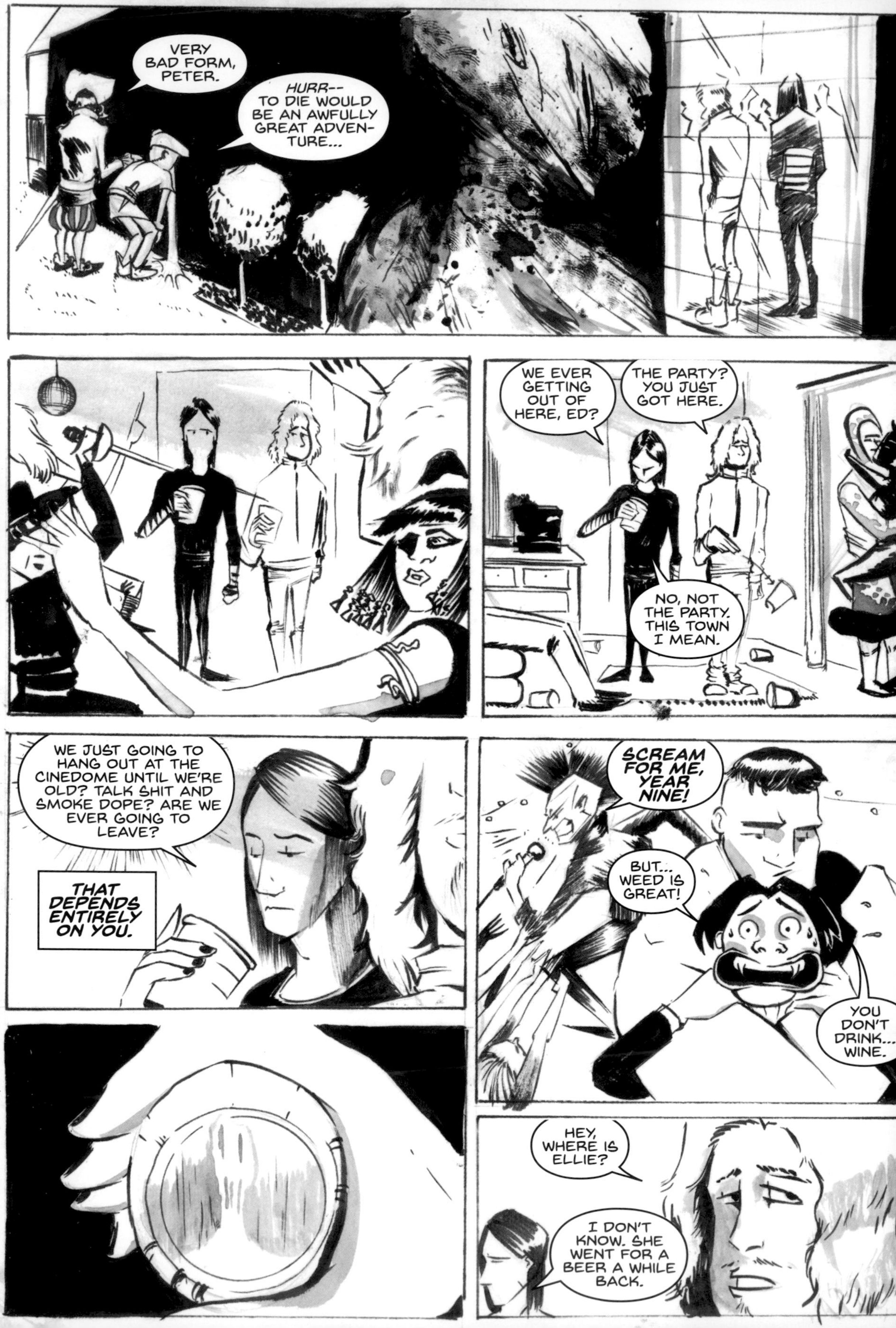
VERY BAD FORM, PETER.
HURR-- TO DIE WOULD BE AN AWFULLY GREAT ADVENTURE...
WE EVER GETTING OUT OF HERE, ED?
THE PARTY? YOU JUST GOT HERE.
NO, NOT THE PARTY. THIS TOWN I MEAN.
WE JUST GOING TO HANG OUT AT THE CINEDOME UNTIL WE'RE OLD? TALK SHIT AND SMOKE DOPE? ARE WE EVER GOING TO LEAVE?
THAT DEPENDS ENTIRELY ON YOU.
SCREAM FOR ME, YEAR NINE!
BUT... WEED IS GREAT!
YOU DON'T DRINK... WINE.
HEY, WHERE IS ELLIE?
I DON'T KNOW. SHE WENT FOR A BEER A WHILE BACK.

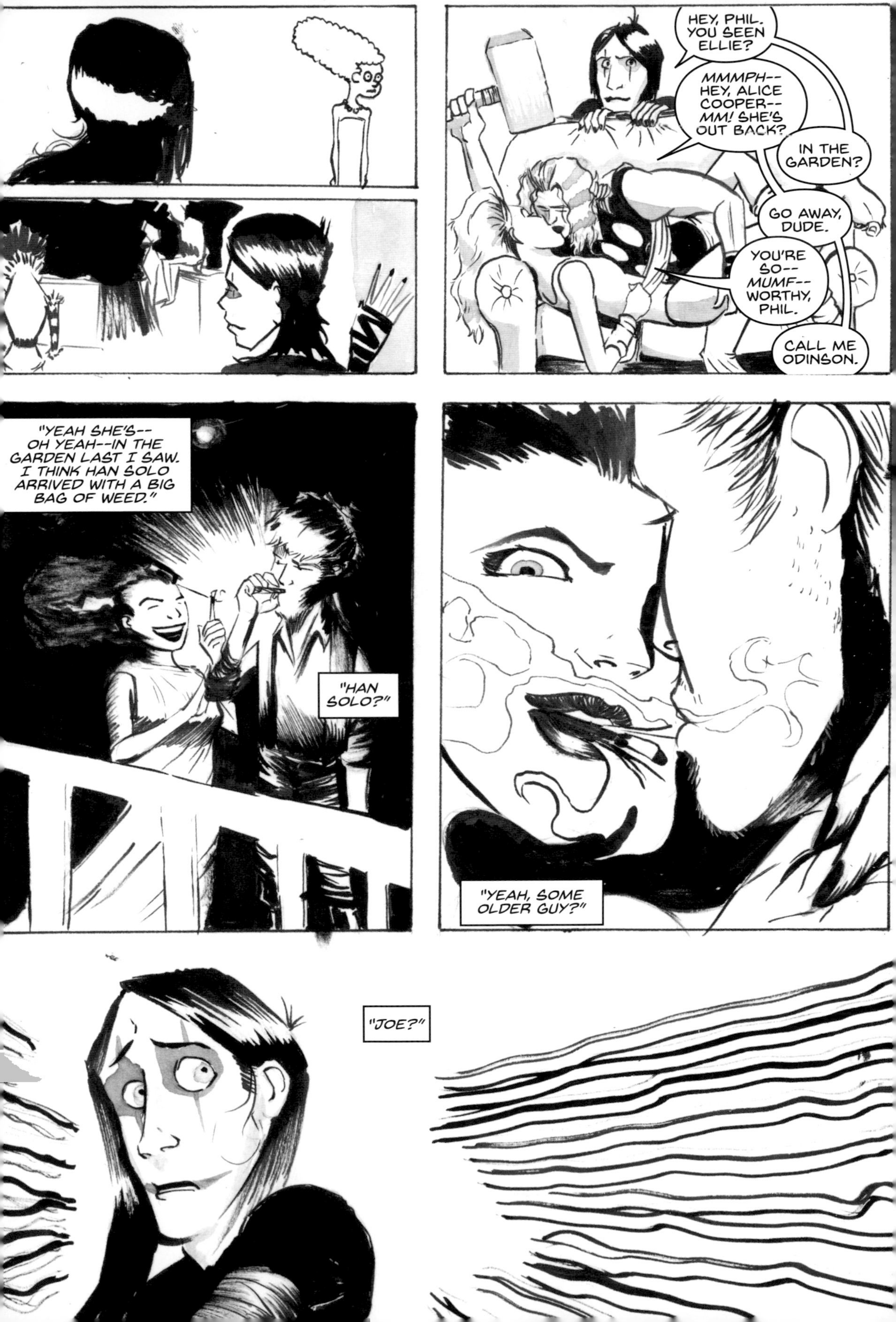

HEY, PHIL. YOU SEEN ELLIE?
MMMPH-- HEY, ALICE COOPER-- MM! SHE'S OUT BACK?
IN THE GARDEN?
GO AWAY, DUDE.
YOU'RE SO-- MUMF-- WORTHY, PHIL.
CALL ME ODINSON.
"YEAH SHE'S-- OH YEAH--IN THE GARDEN LAST I SAW. I THINK HAN SOLO ARRIVED WITH A BIG BAG OF WEED."
"HAN SOLO?"
"YEAH, SOME OLDER GUY?"
"JOE?"

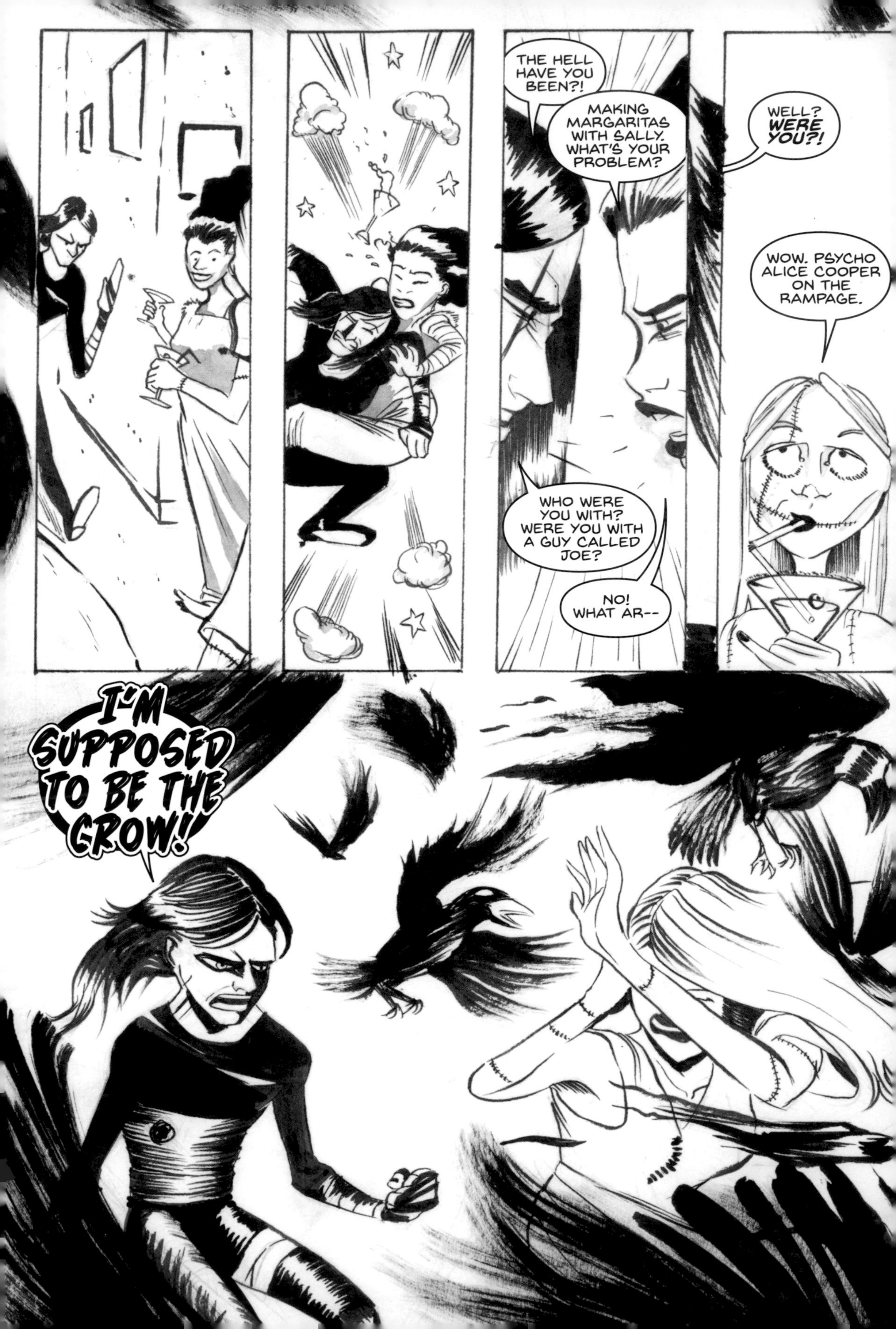
THE HELL HAVE YOU BEEN?!
MAKING MARGARITAS WITH SALLY. WHAT'S YOUR PROBLEM?
WHO WERE YOU WITH? WERE YOU WITH A GUY CALLED JOE?
NO! WHAT AR--
WELL? WERE YOU?!
WOW. PSYCHO ALICE COOPER ON THE RAMPAGE.
I'M SUPPOSED TO BE THE CROW!

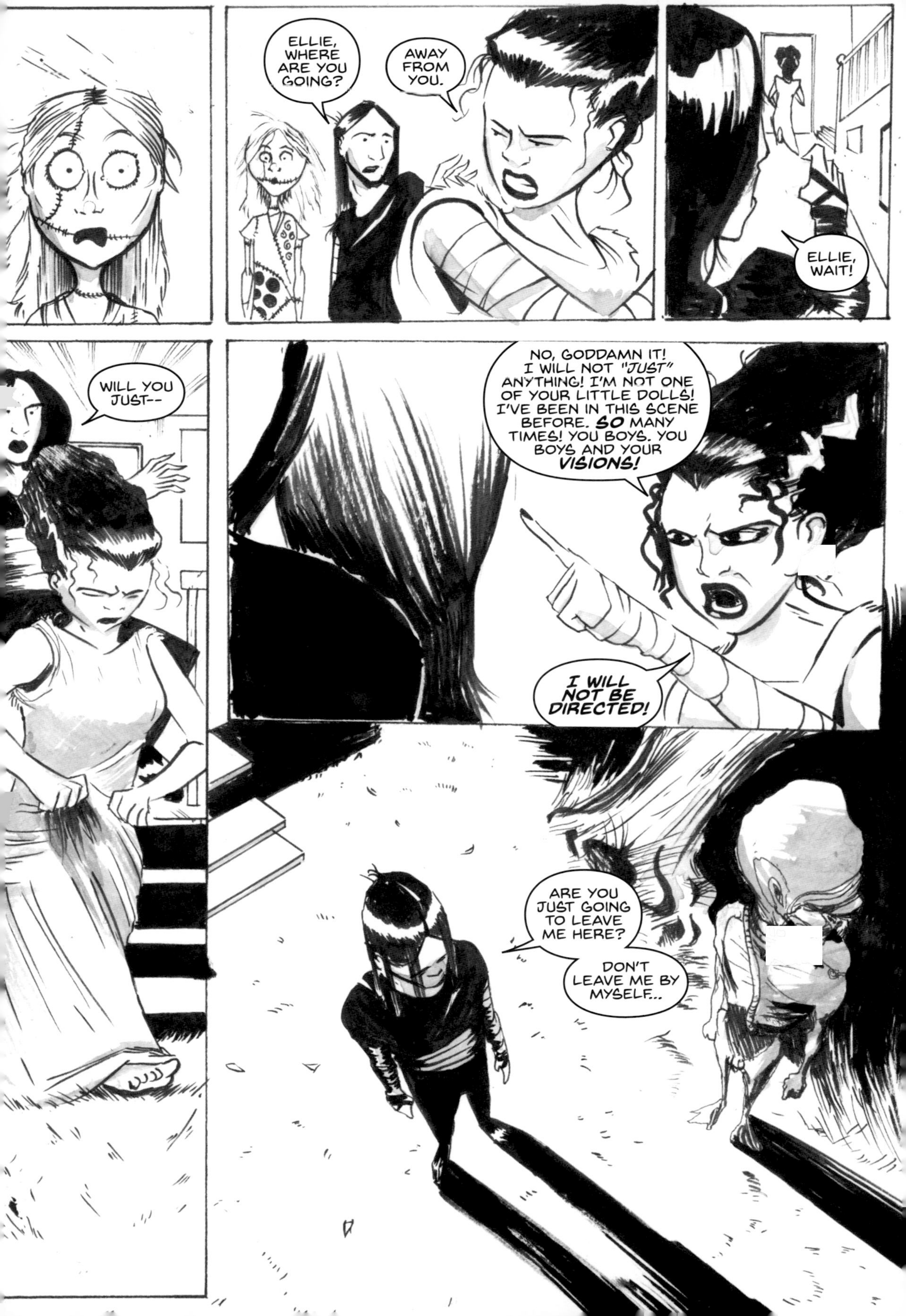

ELLIE, WHERE ARE YOU GOING?
AWAY FROM YOU.
ELLIE, WAIT!
WILL YOU JUST--
NO, GODDAMN IT! I WILL NOT "JUST" ANYTHING! I'M NOT ONE OF YOUR LITTLE DOLLS! I'VE BEEN IN THIS SCENE BEFORE. SO MANY TIMES! YOU BOYS. YOU BOYS AND YOUR VISIONS!
I WILL NOT BE DIRECTED!
ARE YOU JUST GOING TO LEAVE ME HERE?
DON'T LEAVE ME BY MYSELF...

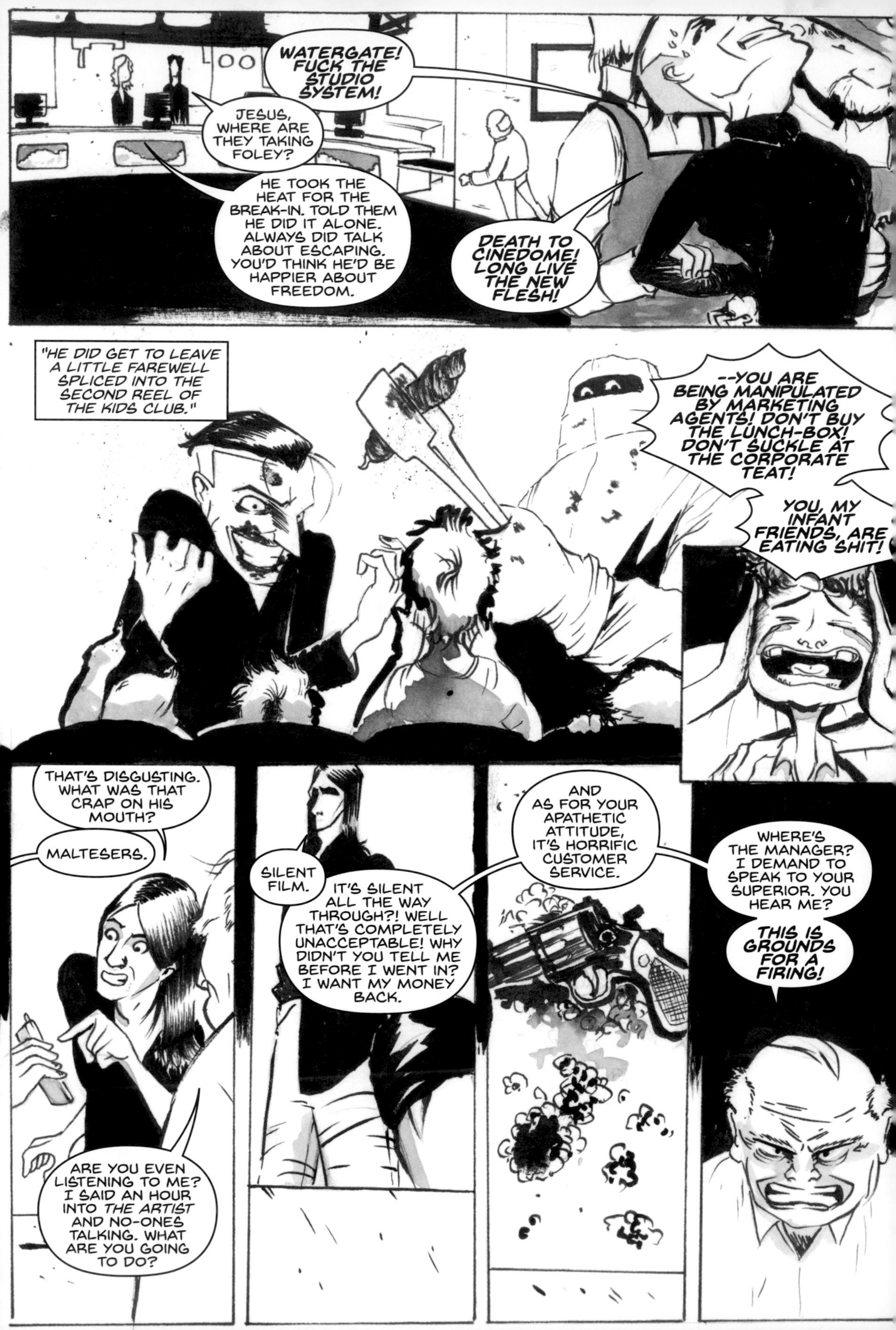
WATERGATE! FUCK THE STUDIO SYSTEM!
JESUS, WHERE ARE THEY TAKING FOLEY?
HE TOOK THE HEAT FOR THE BREAK-IN. TOLD THEM HE DID IT ALONE. ALWAYS DID TALK ABOUT ESCAPING. YOU'D THINK HE'D BE HAPPIER ABOUT FREEDOM.
DEATH TO CINEDOME! LONG LIVE THE NEW FLESH!
"HE DID GET TO LEAVE A LITTLE FAREWELL SPLICED INTO THE SECOND REEL OF THE KIDS CLUB."
--YOU ARE BEING MANIPULATED BY MARKETING AGENTS! DON'T BUY THE LUNCH-BOX! DON'T SUCKLE AT THE CORPORATE TEAT!
YOU, MY INFANT FRIENDS, ARE EATING SHIT!
THAT'S DISGUSTING. WHAT WAS THAT CRAP ON HIS MOUTH?
MALTESERS.
ARE YOU EVEN LISTENING TO ME? I SAID AN HOUR INTO *THE ARTIST* AND NO-ONES TALKING. WHAT ARE YOU GOING TO DO?
SILENT FILM.
IT'S SILENT ALL THE WAY THROUGH?! WELL THAT'S COMPLETELY UNACCEPTABLE! WHY DIDN'T YOU TELL ME BEFORE I WENT IN? I WANT MY MONEY BACK.
AND AS FOR YOUR APATHETIC ATTITUDE, IT'S HORRIFIC CUSTOMER SERVICE.
WHERE'S THE MANAGER? I DEMAND TO SPEAK TO YOUR SUPERIOR. YOU HEAR ME?
THIS IS GROUNDS FOR A FIRING!

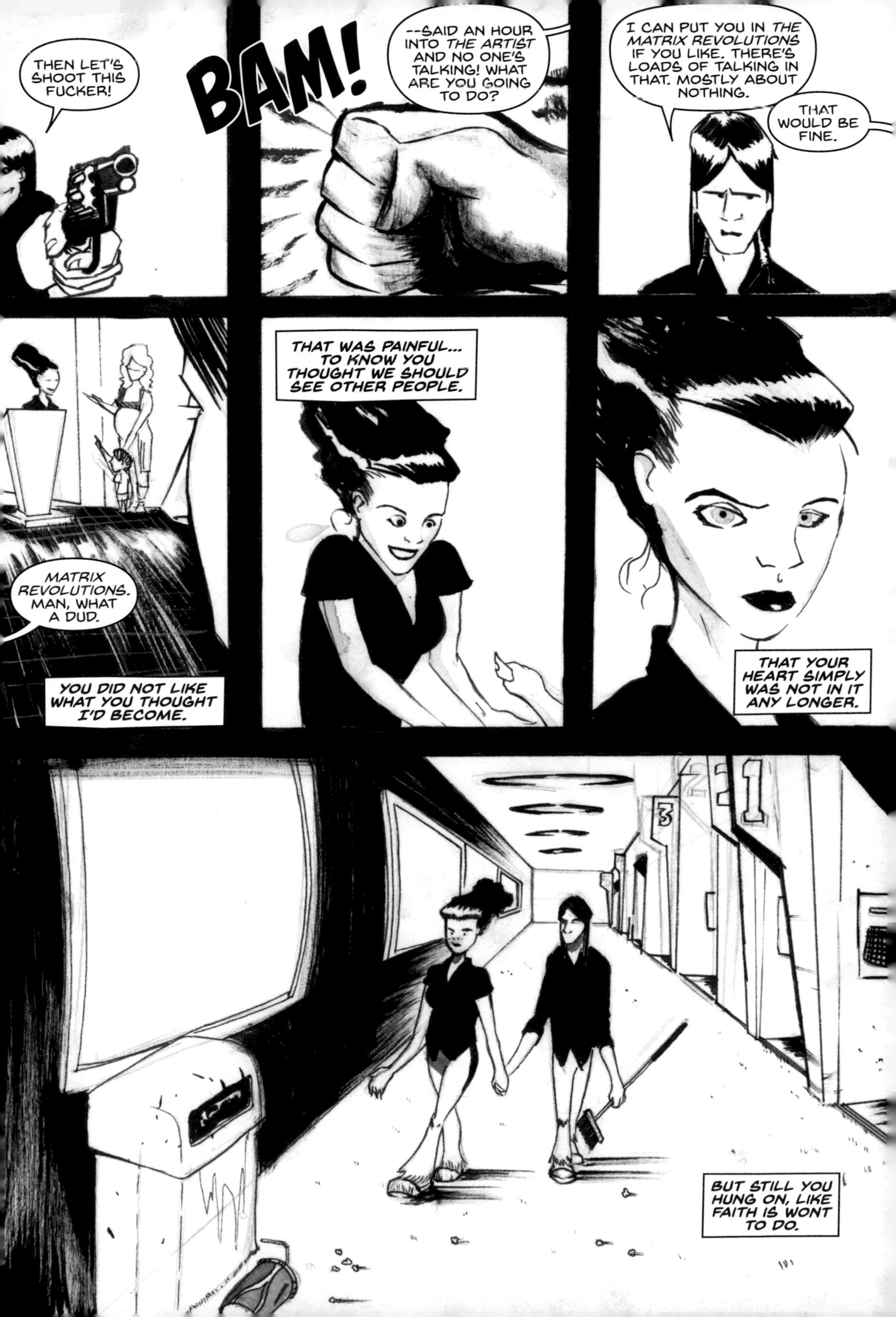
THEN LET'S SHOOT THIS FUCKER!
BAM!
--SAID AN HOUR INTO THE ARTIST AND NO ONE'S TALKING! WHAT ARE YOU GOING TO DO?
I CAN PUT YOU IN THE MATRIX REVOLUTIONS IF YOU LIKE. THERE'S LOADS OF TALKING IN THAT. MOSTLY ABOUT NOTHING.
THAT WOULD BE FINE.
MATRIX REVOLUTIONS. MAN, WHAT A DUD.
YOU DID NOT LIKE WHAT YOU THOUGHT I'D BECOME.
THAT WAS PAINFUL... TO KNOW YOU THOUGHT WE SHOULD SEE OTHER PEOPLE.
THAT YOUR HEART SIMPLY WAS NOT IN IT ANY LONGER.
BUT STILL YOU HUNG ON, LIKE FAITH IS WONT TO DO.

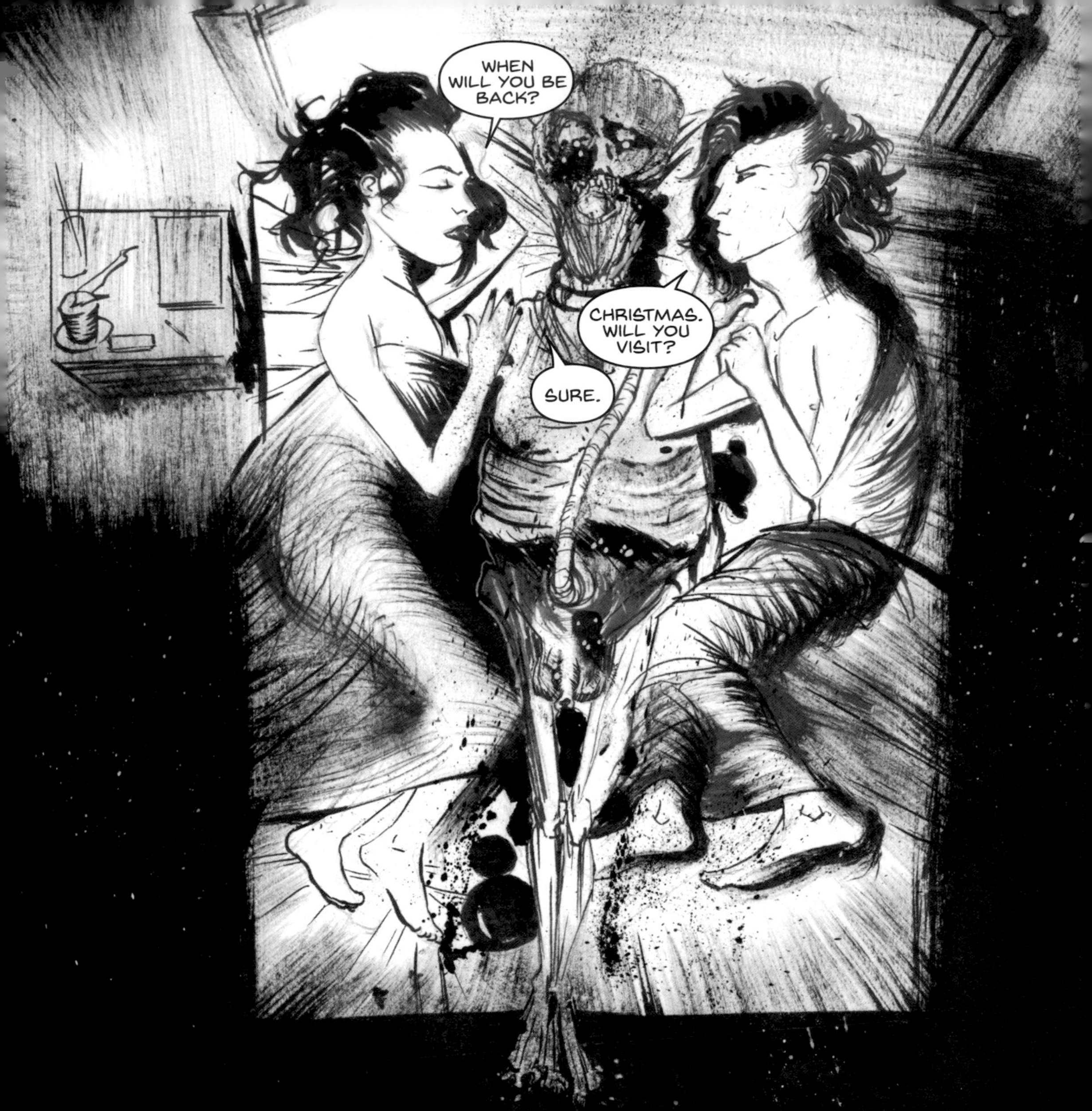
WHEN WILL YOU BE BACK?
CHRISTMAS. WILL YOU VISIT?
SURE.

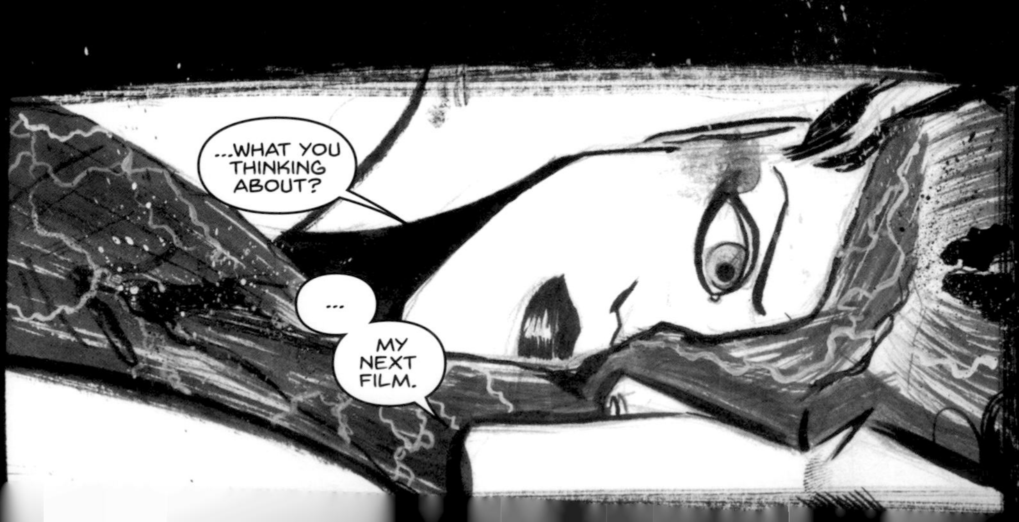
...WHAT YOU THINKING ABOUT?
...
MY NEXT FILM.

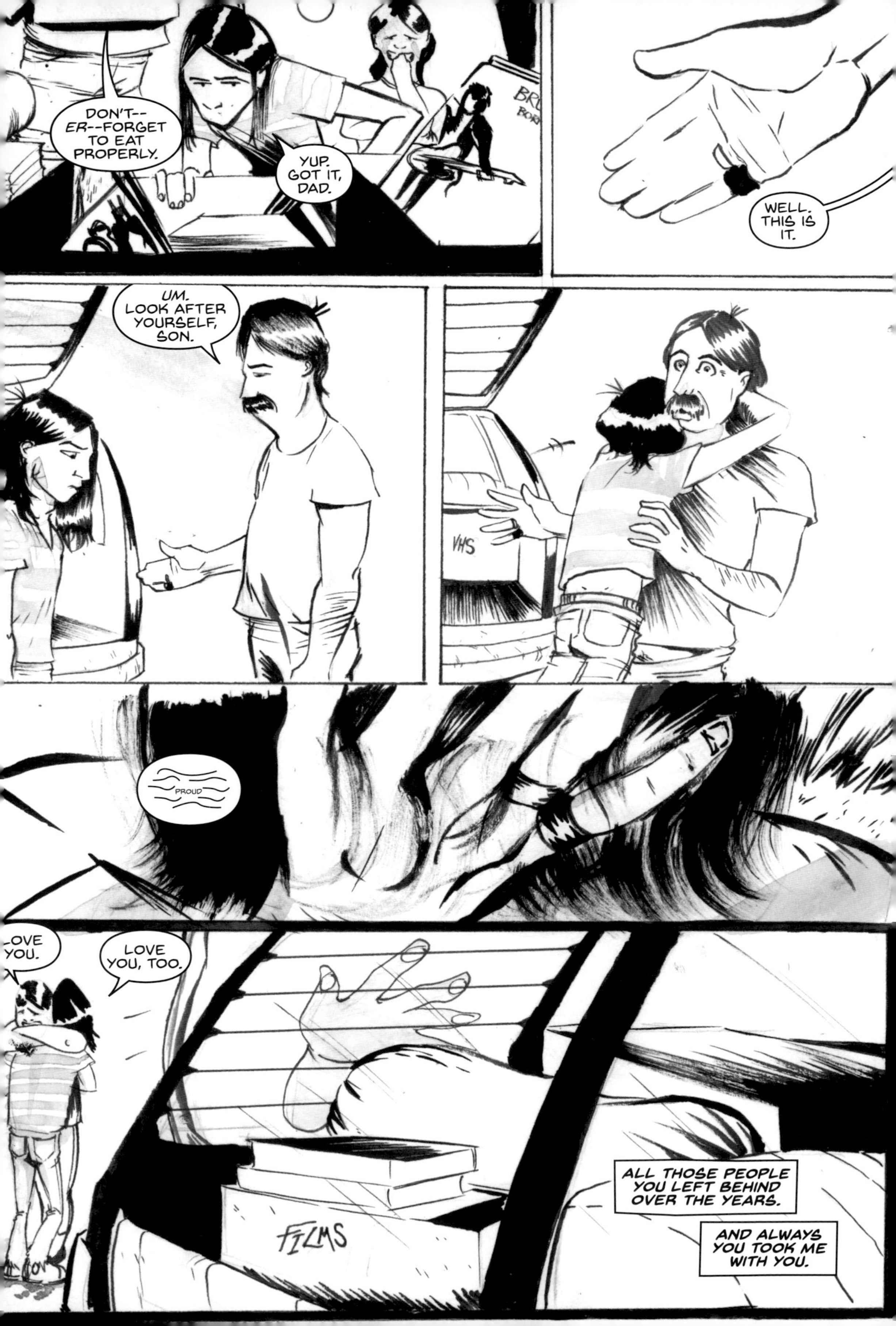
DON'T-- ER--FORGET TO EAT PROPERLY.
YUP. GOT IT, DAD.
WELL. THIS IS IT.
UM. LOOK AFTER YOURSELF, SON.
VHS
PROUD
LOVE YOU.
LOVE YOU, TOO.
FILMS
ALL THOSE PEOPLE YOU LEFT BEHIND OVER THE YEARS.
AND ALWAYS YOU TOOK ME WITH YOU.

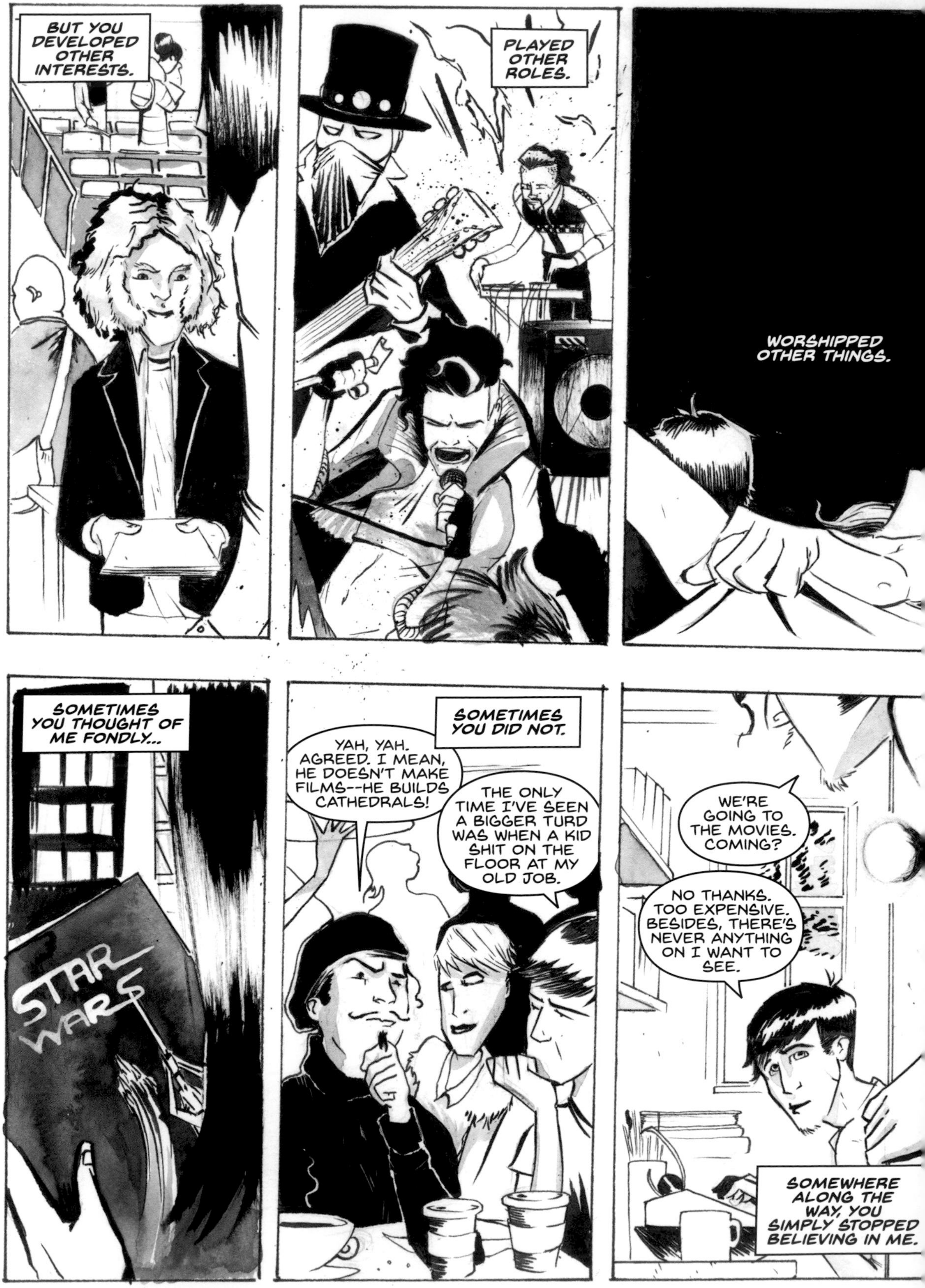
BUT YOU DEVELOPED OTHER INTERESTS.
PLAYED OTHER ROLES.
WORSHIPPED OTHER THINGS.
SOMETIMES YOU THOUGHT OF ME FONDLY...
STAR WARS
SOMETIMES YOU DID NOT.
YAH, YAH. AGREED. I MEAN, HE DOESN'T MAKE FILMS--HE BUILDS CATHEDRALS!
THE ONLY TIME I'VE SEEN A BIGGER TURD WAS WHEN A KID SHIT ON THE FLOOR AT MY OLD JOB.
WE'RE GOING TO THE MOVIES. COMING?
NO THANKS. TOO EXPENSIVE. BESIDES, THERE'S NEVER ANYTHING ON I WANT TO SEE.
SOMEWHERE ALONG THE WAY, YOU SIMPLY STOPPED BELIEVING IN ME.

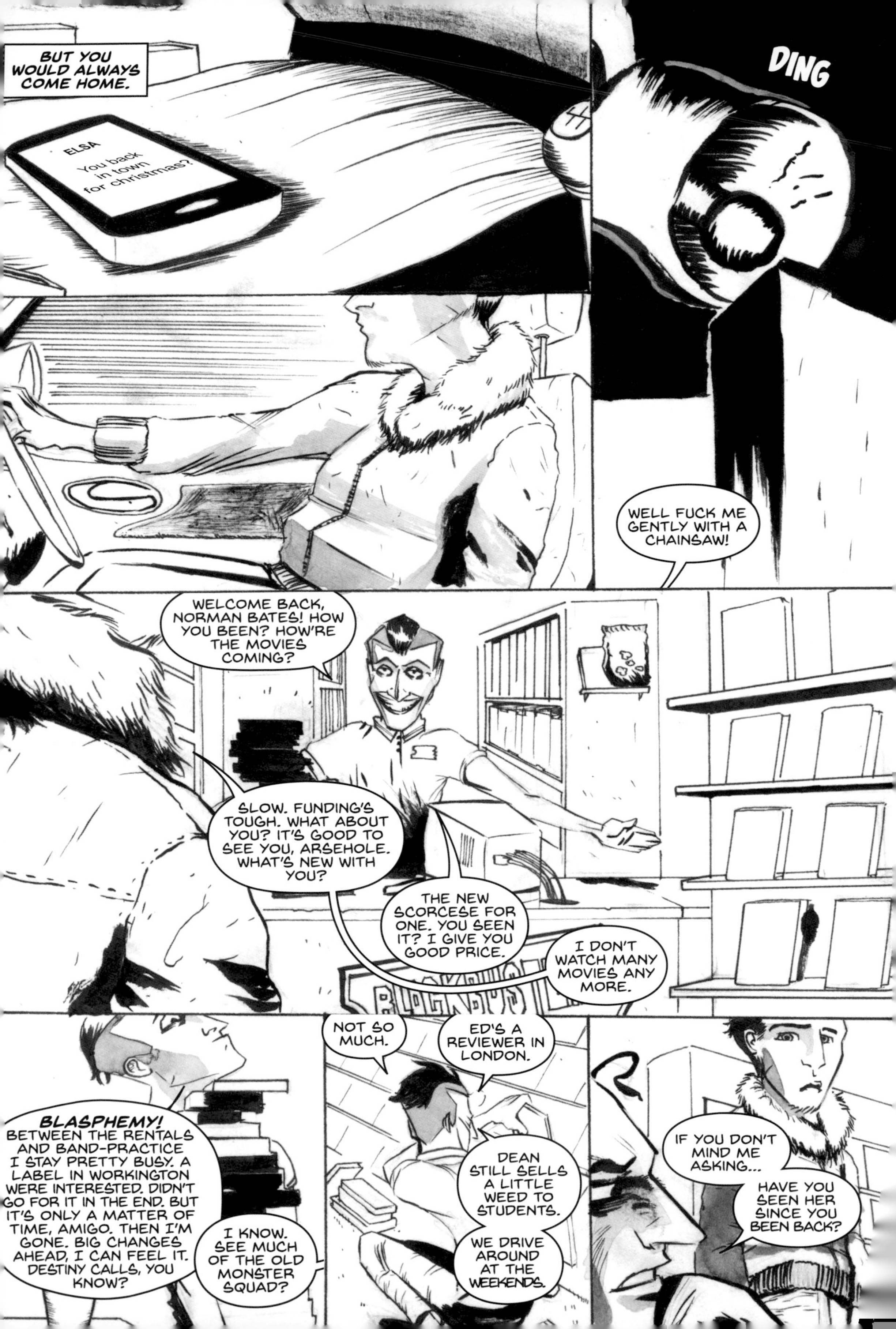
BUT YOU WOULD ALWAYS COME HOME.
ELSA
You back in town for christmas?
DING
WELL FUCK ME GENTLY WITH A CHAINSAW!
WELCOME BACK, NORMAN BATES! HOW YOU BEEN? HOW'RE THE MOVIES COMING?
SLOW. FUNDING'S TOUGH. WHAT ABOUT YOU? IT'S GOOD TO SEE YOU, ARSEHOLE. WHAT'S NEW WITH YOU?
THE NEW SCORCESE FOR ONE. YOU SEEN IT? I GIVE YOU GOOD PRICE.
I DON'T WATCH MANY MOVIES ANY MORE.
BLASPHEMY! BETWEEN THE RENTALS AND BAND-PRACTICE I STAY PRETTY BUSY. A LABEL IN WORKINGTON WERE INTERESTED. DIDN'T GO FOR IT IN THE END. BUT IT'S ONLY A MATTER OF TIME, AMIGO. THEN I'M GONE. BIG CHANGES AHEAD, I CAN FEEL IT. DESTINY CALLS, YOU KNOW?
I KNOW. SEE MUCH OF THE OLD MONSTER SQUAD?
NOT SO MUCH.
ED'S A REVIEWER IN LONDON.
DEAN STILL SELLS A LITTLE WEED TO STUDENTS.
WE DRIVE AROUND AT THE WEEKENDS.
IF YOU DON'T MIND ME ASKING...
HAVE YOU SEEN HER SINCE YOU BEEN BACK?

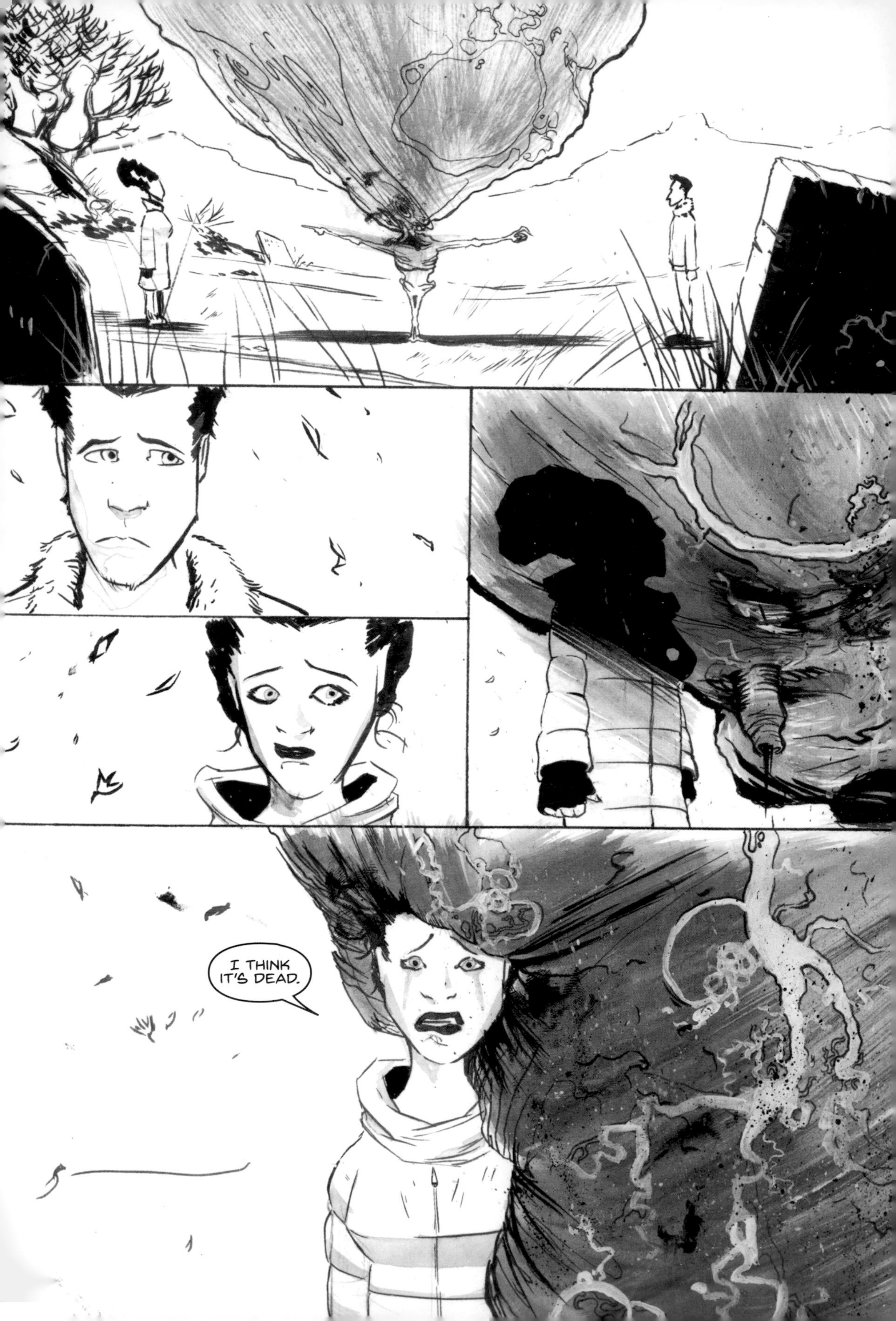
I THINK IT'S DEAD.

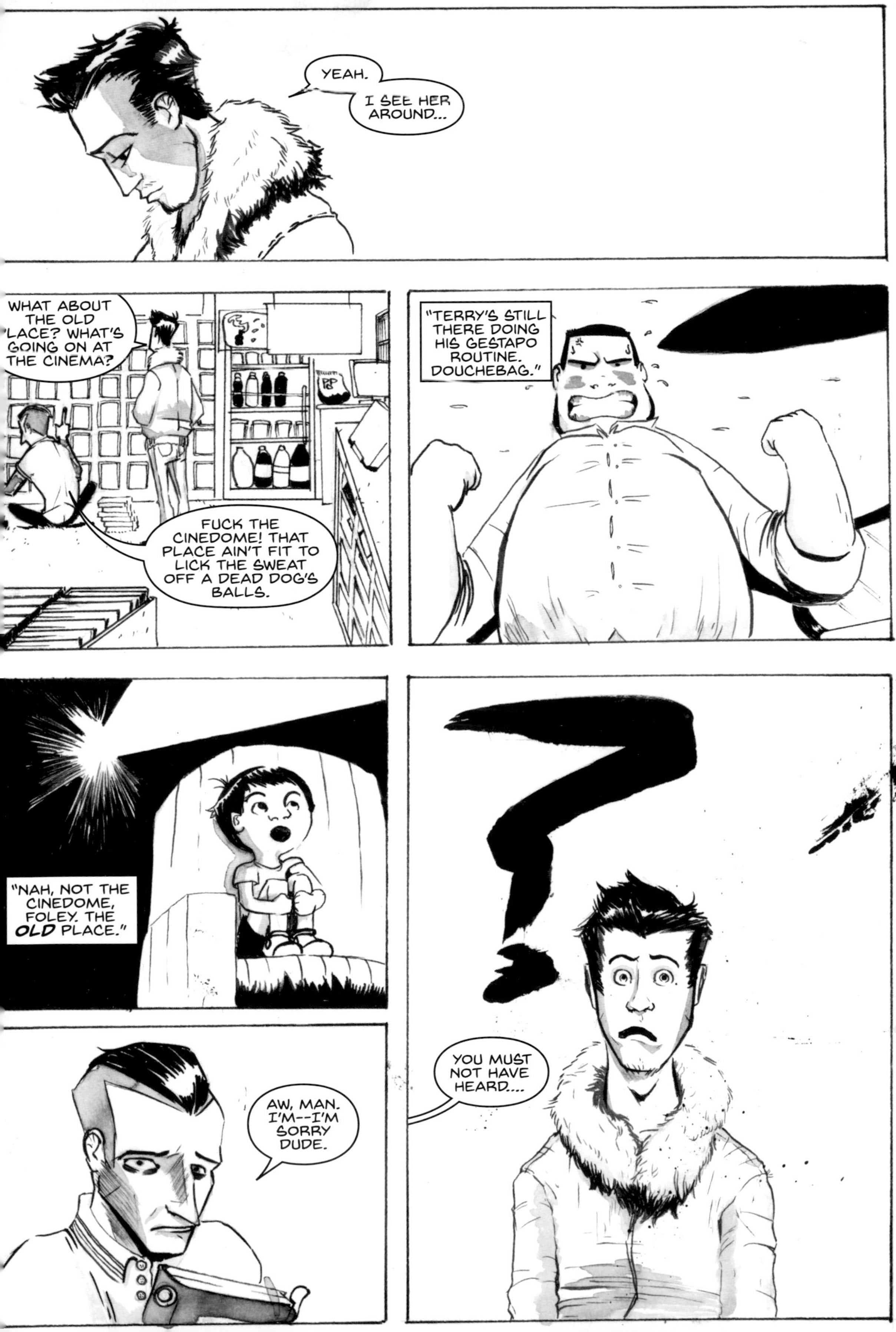
YEAH.
I SEE HER AROUND...
WHAT ABOUT THE OLD 'LACE? WHAT'S GOING ON AT THE CINEMA?
FUCK THE CINEDOME! THAT PLACE AIN'T FIT TO LICK THE SWEAT OFF A DEAD DOG'S BALLS.
"TERRY'S STILL THERE DOING HIS GESTAPO ROUTINE. DOUCHEBAG."
"NAH, NOT THE CINEDOME, FOLEY. THE OLD PLACE."
YOU MUST NOT HAVE HEARD....
AW, MAN. I'M--I'M SORRY DUDE.

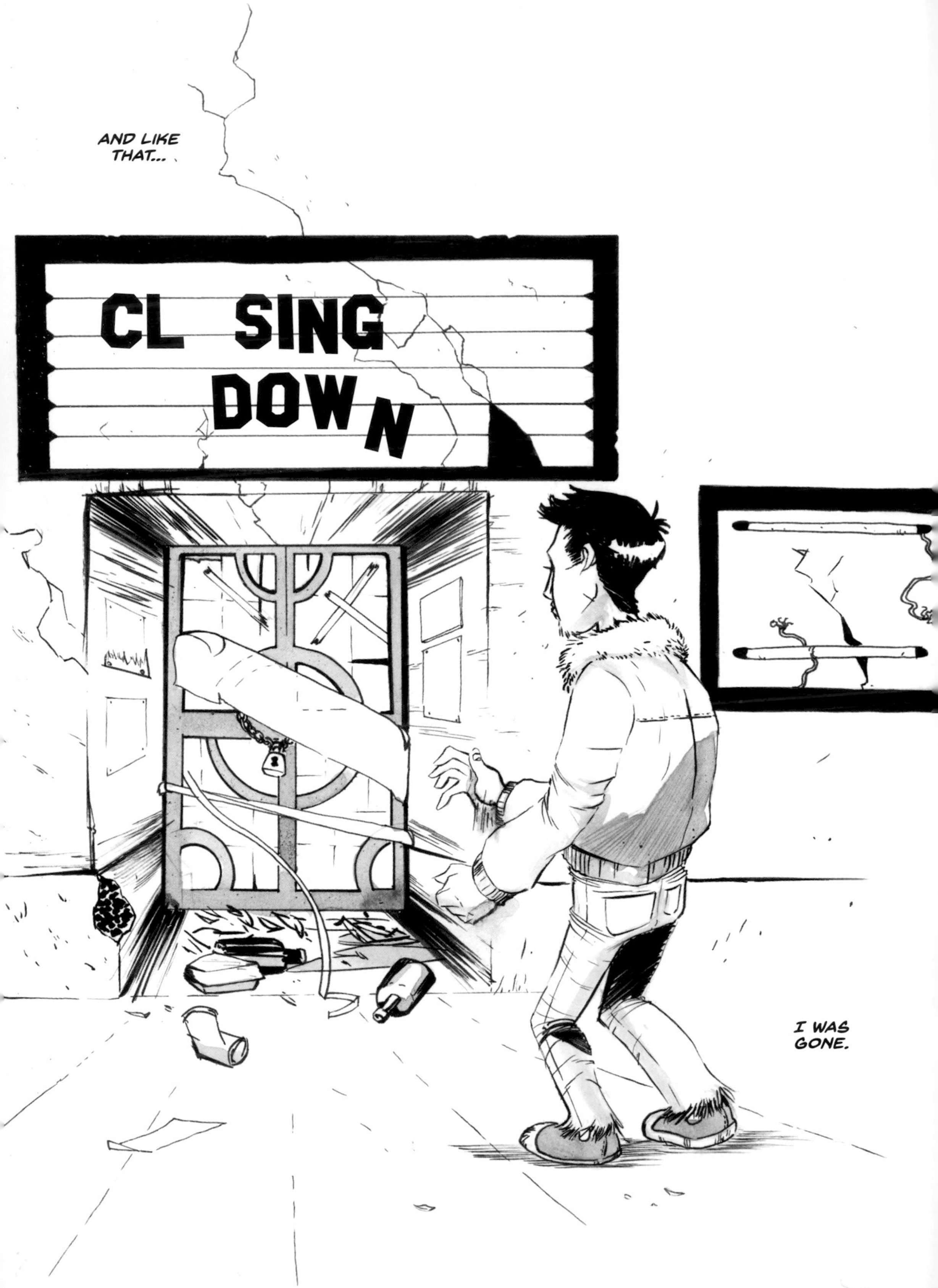
AND LIKE THAT...
CL SING DOWN
I WAS GONE.

ACT THREE
ADMISSIONS

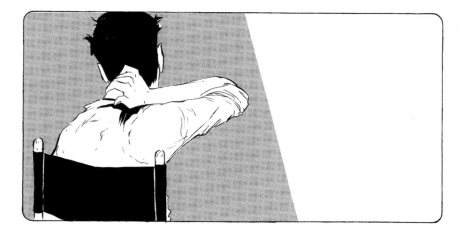

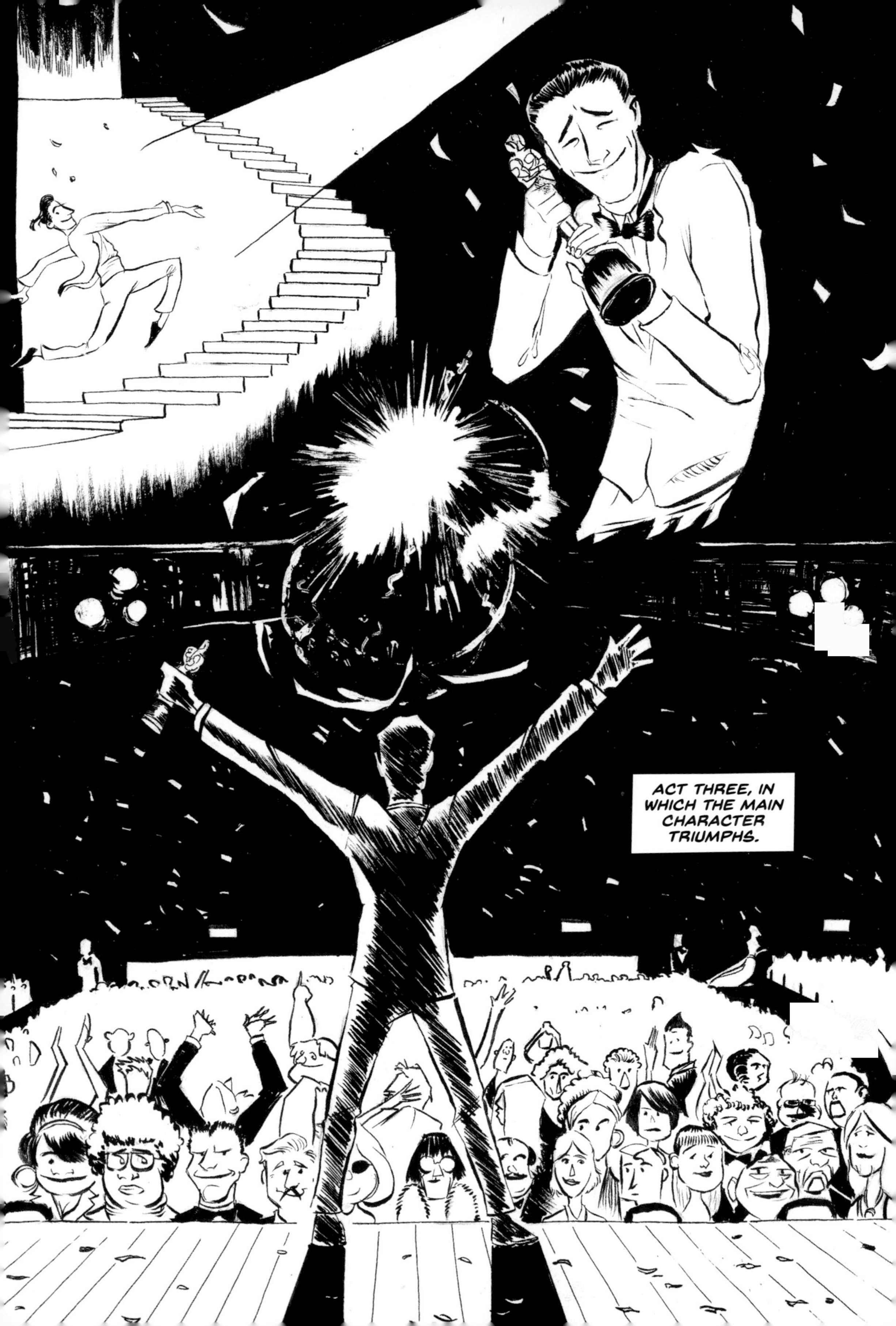
ACT THREE, IN WHICH THE MAIN CHARACTER TRIUMPHS.

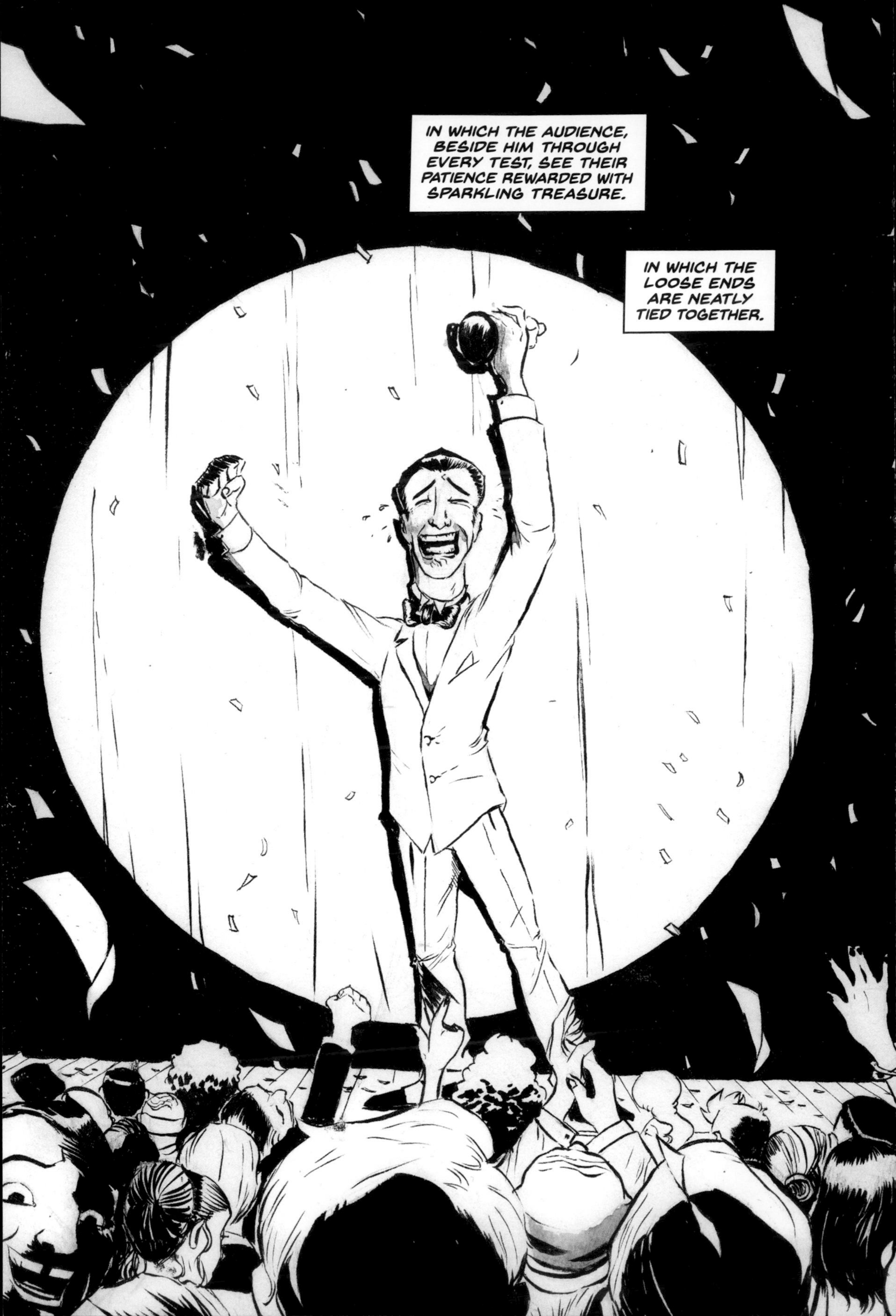
IN WHICH THE AUDIENCE, BESIDE HIM THROUGH EVERY TEST, SEE THEIR PATIENCE REWARDED WITH SPARKLING TREASURE.
IN WHICH THE LOOSE ENDS ARE NEATLY TIED TOGETHER.

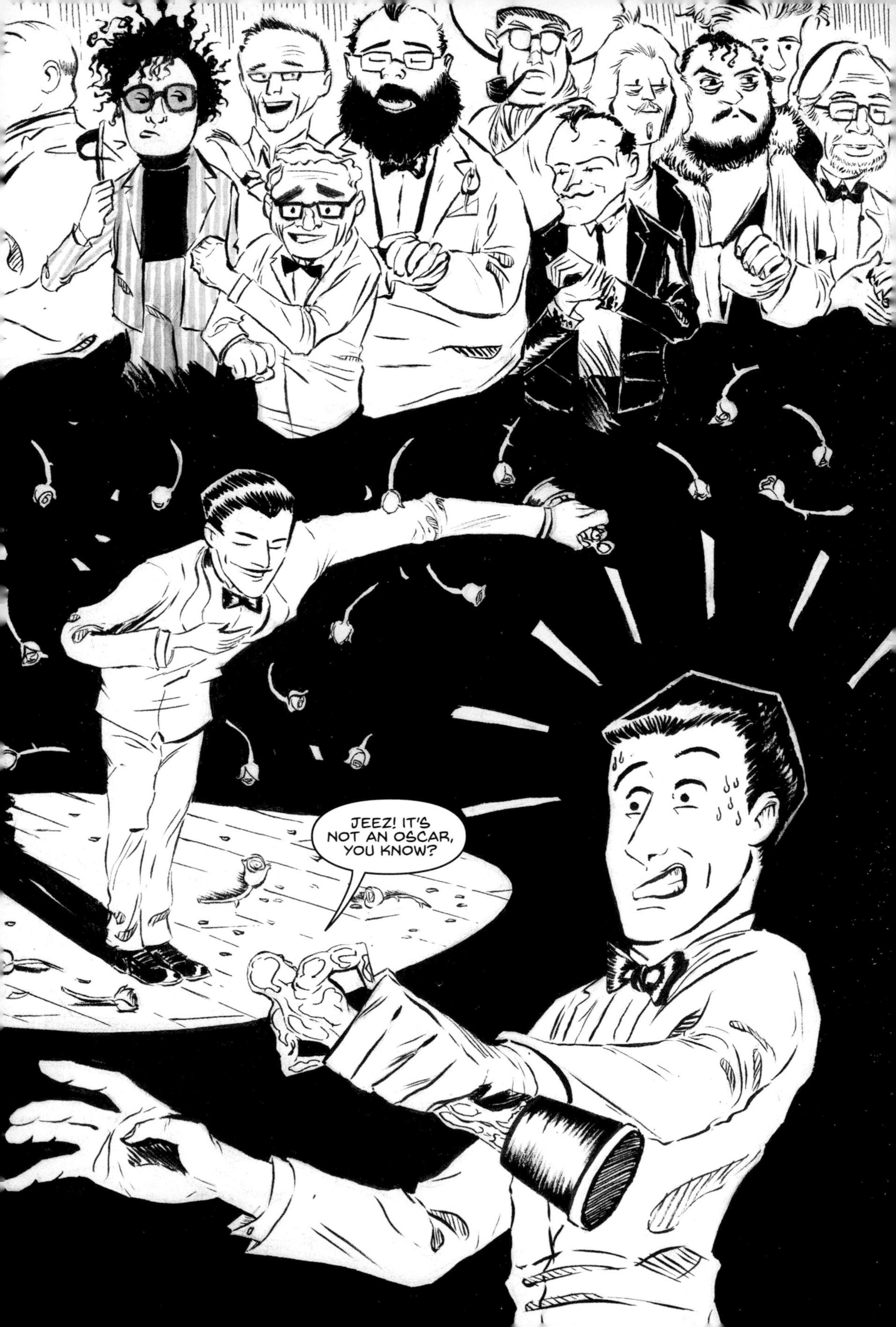
JEEZ! IT'S NOT AN OSCAR, YOU KNOW?

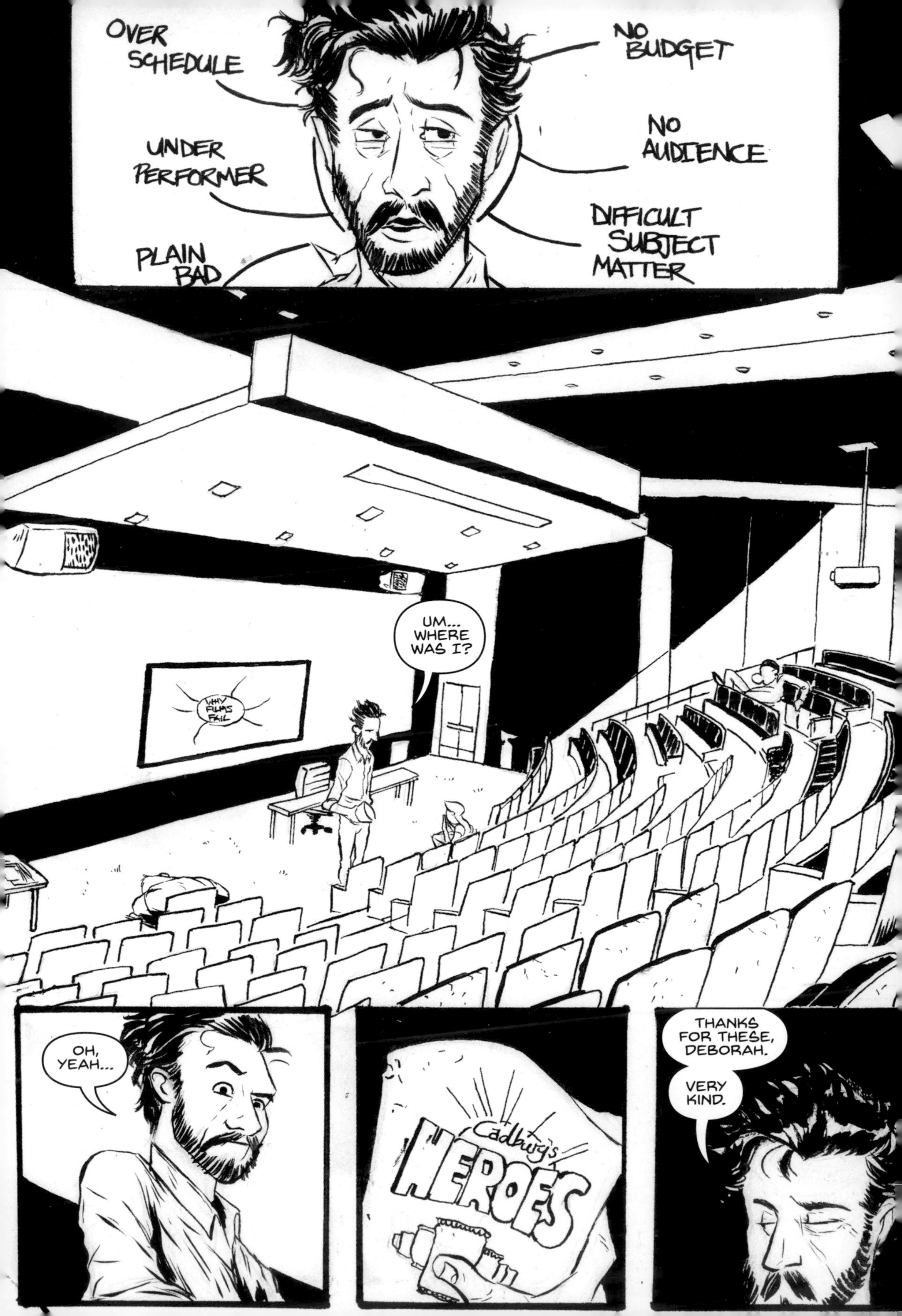
OVER SCHEDULE
NO BUDGET
UNDER PERFORMER
NO AUDIENCE
DIFFICULT SUBJECT MATTER
PLAIN BAD
WHY FILMS FAIL
UM... WHERE WAS I?
OH, YEAH...
Cadbury's HEROES
THANKS FOR THESE, DEBORAH.
VERY KIND.

YOUR RESPONSIBILITIES HAD BLOOMED. YOUR DREAMS, DIMINISHED.

YOU HAD FOLLOWERS. STUDENTS WHO WORSHIPPED ME LIKE YOU.

BUT YOU NO LONGER BELIEVED IN MY POWER, NO LONGER FOUND PLEASURE IN MY SIMPLE VOICE.

OVER SCHEDULE

UNDER PERFORMER

WHY FILMS FAIL

NO BUDGET

NO AUDIENCE

DIFFICULT SUBJECT MATTER

PLAIN BAD TALENT

IN TRUTH, YOU HAD NEVER FELT FURTHER AWAY.

RUH. HEADACHE. LET'S WATCH THE TRAILER ASSIGNMENTS FOR YOUR AUTUMN TERM FEATURES, SHALL WE?

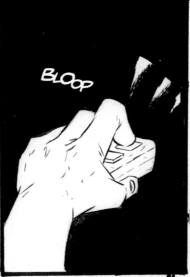

BLOOP

DEBORAH, YOU'RE FIRST UP!

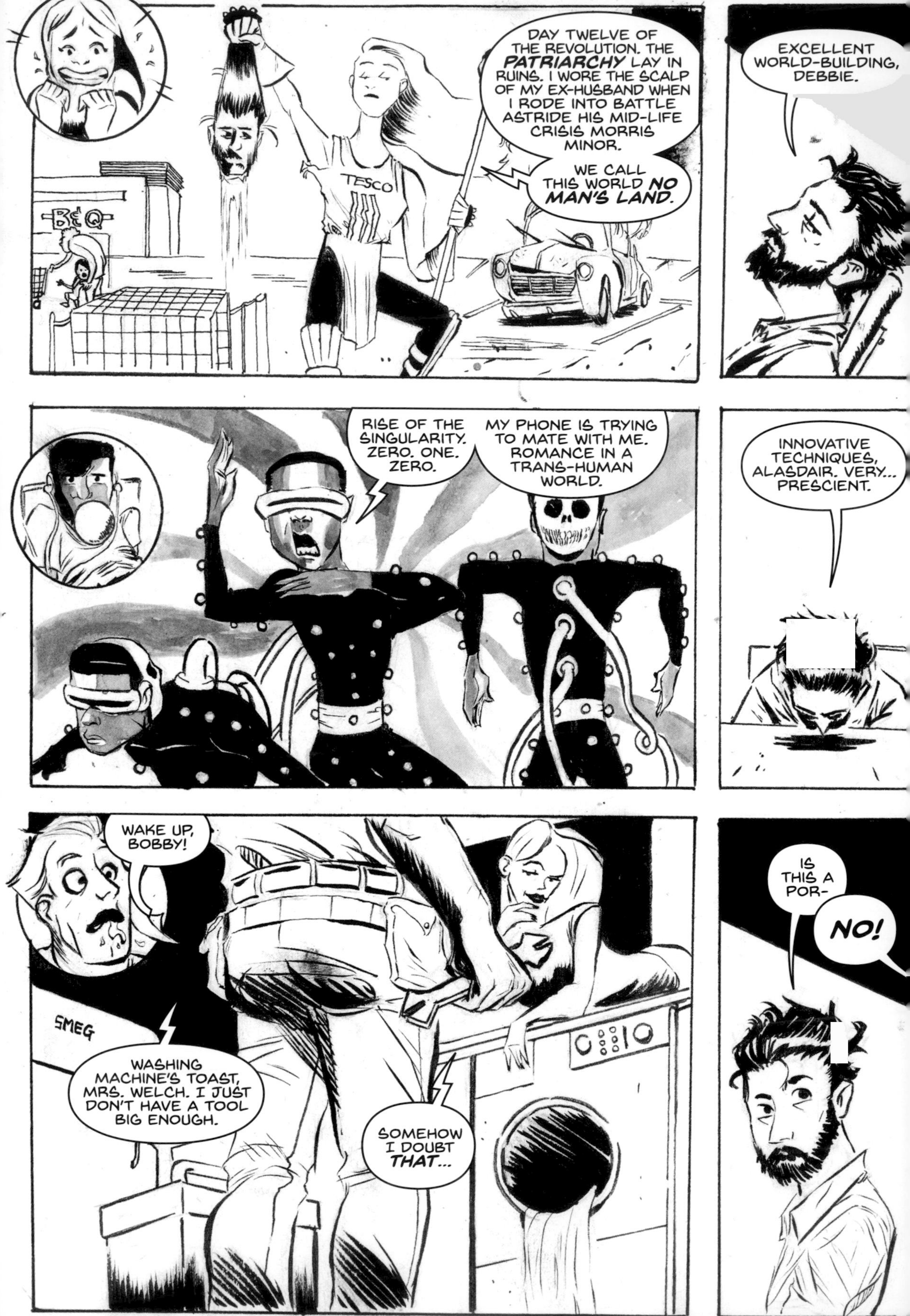
DAY TWELVE OF THE REVOLUTION. THE PATRIARCHY LAY IN RUINS. I WORE THE SCALP OF MY EX-HUSBAND WHEN I RODE INTO BATTLE ASTRIDE HIS MID-LIFE CRISIS MORRIS MINOR.
WE CALL THIS WORLD NO MAN'S LAND.
B&Q
TESCO
EXCELLENT WORLD-BUILDING, DEBBIE.
RISE OF THE SINGULARITY. ZERO. ONE. ZERO.
MY PHONE IS TRYING TO MATE WITH ME. ROMANCE IN A TRANS-HUMAN WORLD.
INNOVATIVE TECHNIQUES, ALASDAIR. VERY... PRESCIENT.
WAKE UP, BOBBY!
SMEG
WASHING MACHINE'S TOAST, MRS. WELCH. I JUST DON'T HAVE A TOOL BIG ENOUGH.
SOMEHOW I DOUBT THAT...
IS THIS A POR-
NO!

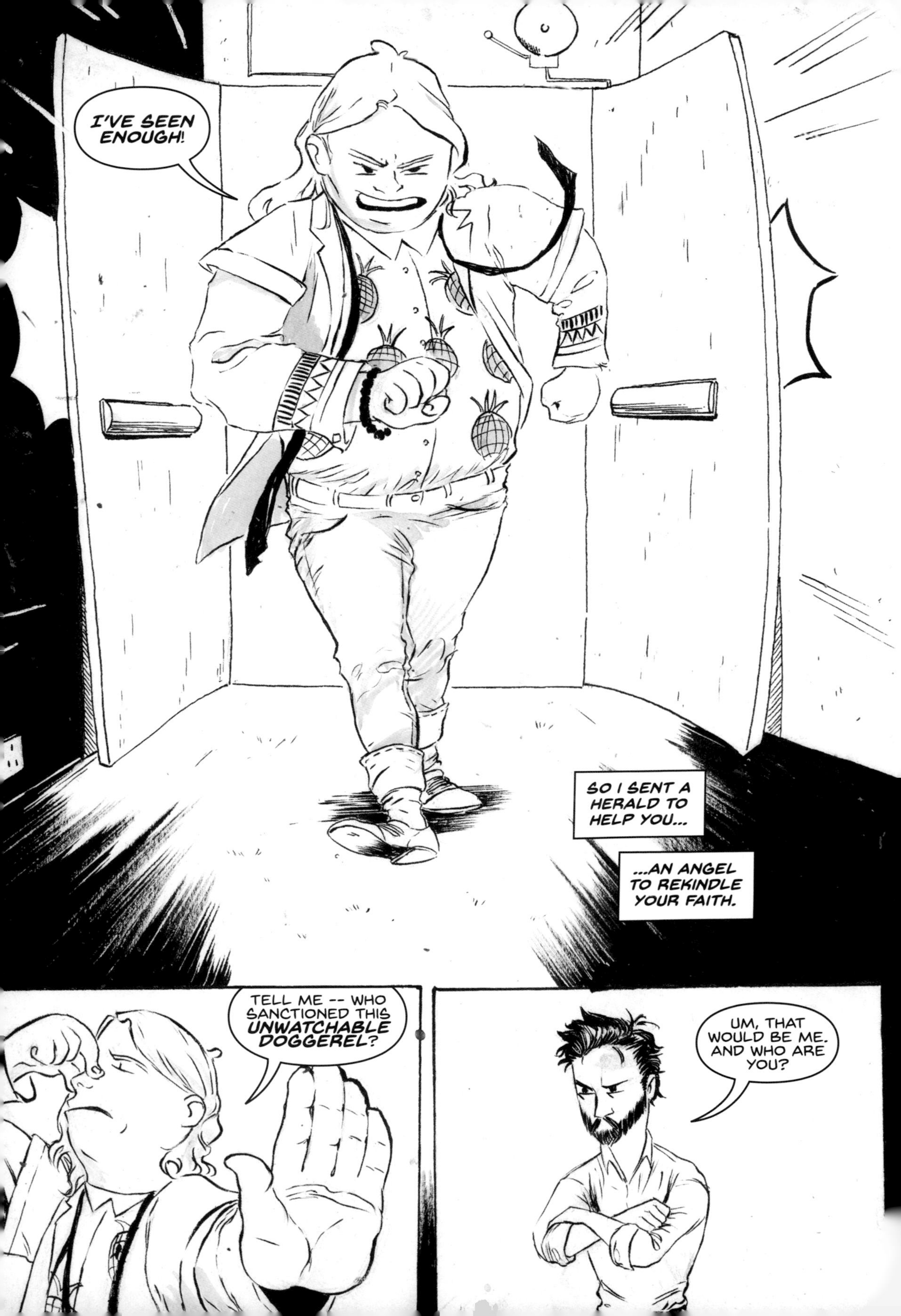
I'VE SEEN ENOUGH!
SO I SENT A HERALD TO HELP YOU...
...AN ANGEL TO REKINDLE YOUR FAITH.
TELL ME -- WHO SANCTIONED THIS UNWATCHABLE DOGGEREL?
UM, THAT WOULD BE ME. AND WHO ARE YOU?

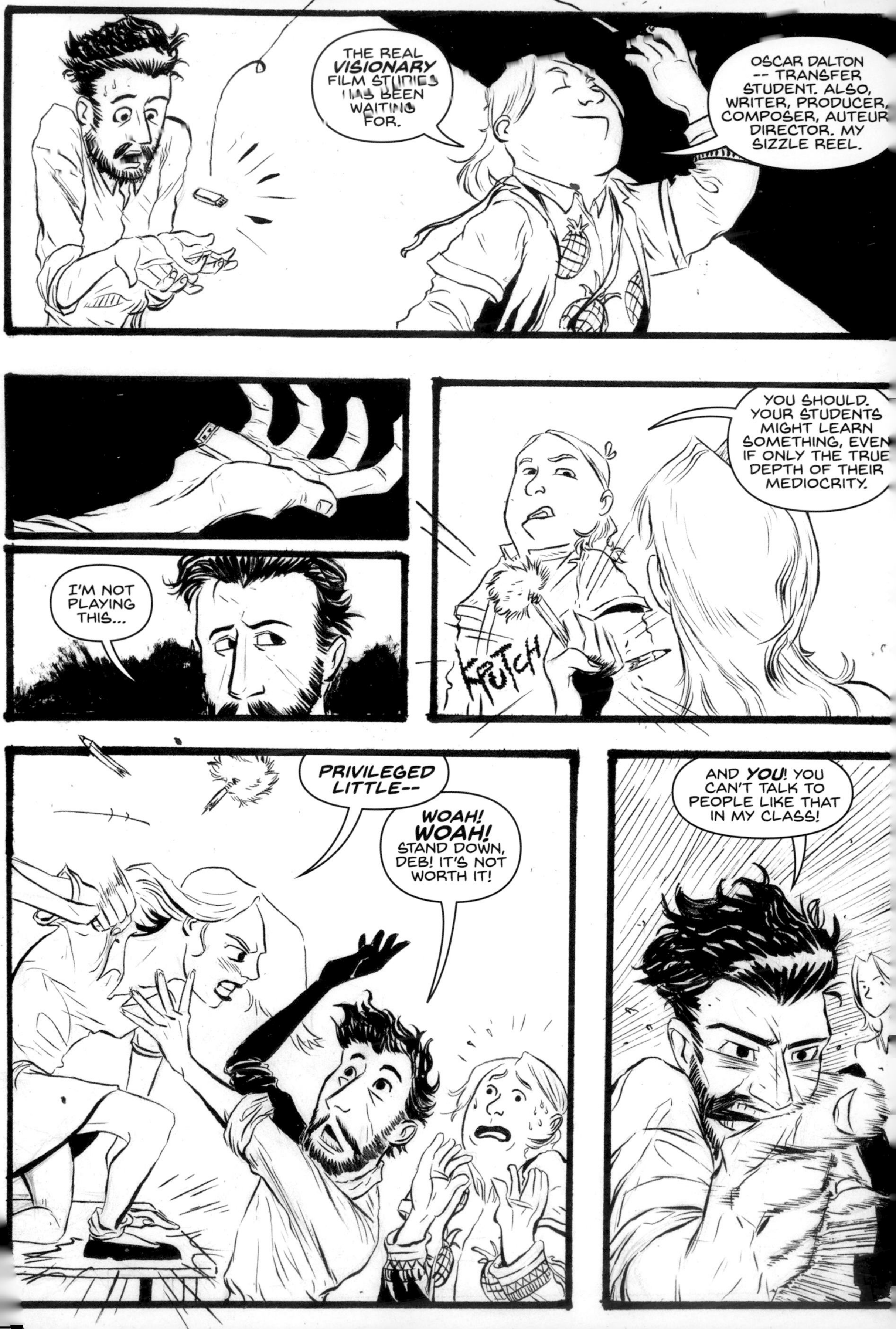
THE REAL VISIONARY FILM STUDIES HAS BEEN WAITING FOR.
OSCAR DALTON -- TRANSFER STUDENT. ALSO, WRITER, PRODUCER, COMPOSER, AUTEUR DIRECTOR. MY SIZZLE REEL.
I'M NOT PLAYING THIS...
YOU SHOULD. YOUR STUDENTS MIGHT LEARN SOMETHING, EVEN IF ONLY THE TRUE DEPTH OF THEIR MEDIOCRITY.
KRUTCH
PRIVILEGED LITTLE--
WOAH! WOAH! STAND DOWN, DEB! IT'S NOT WORTH IT!
AND YOU! YOU CAN'T TALK TO PEOPLE LIKE THAT IN MY CLASS!

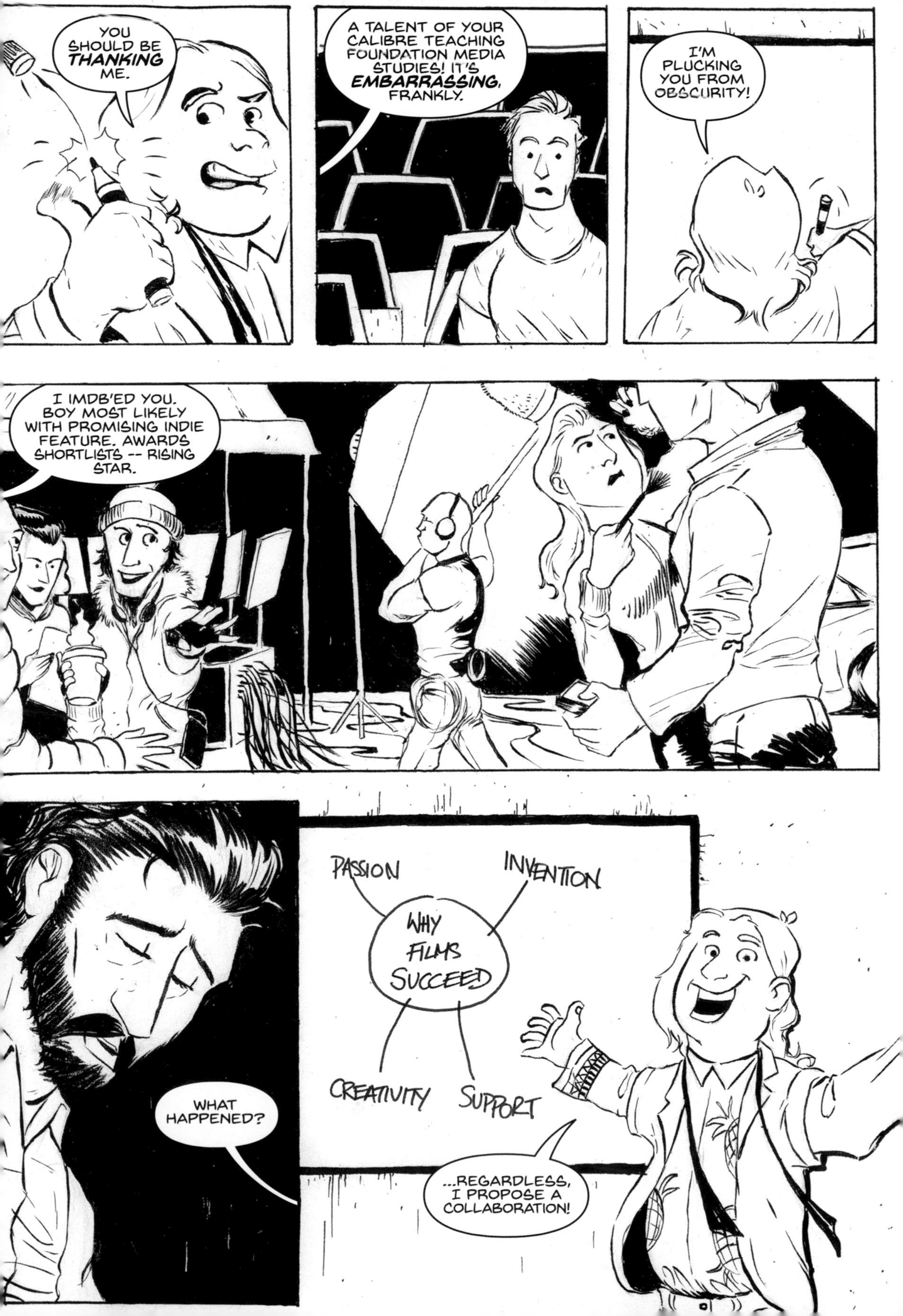
YOU SHOULD BE THANKING ME.
A TALENT OF YOUR CALIBRE TEACHING FOUNDATION MEDIA STUDIES! IT'S EMBARRASSING, FRANKLY.
I'M PLUCKING YOU FROM OBSCURITY!
I IMDB'ED YOU. BOY MOST LIKELY WITH PROMISING INDIE FEATURE. AWARDS SHORTLISTS -- RISING STAR.
PASSION
INVENTION
WHY FILMS SUCCEED
CREATIVITY
SUPPORT
WHAT HAPPENED?
...REGARDLESS, I PROPOSE A COLLABORATION!

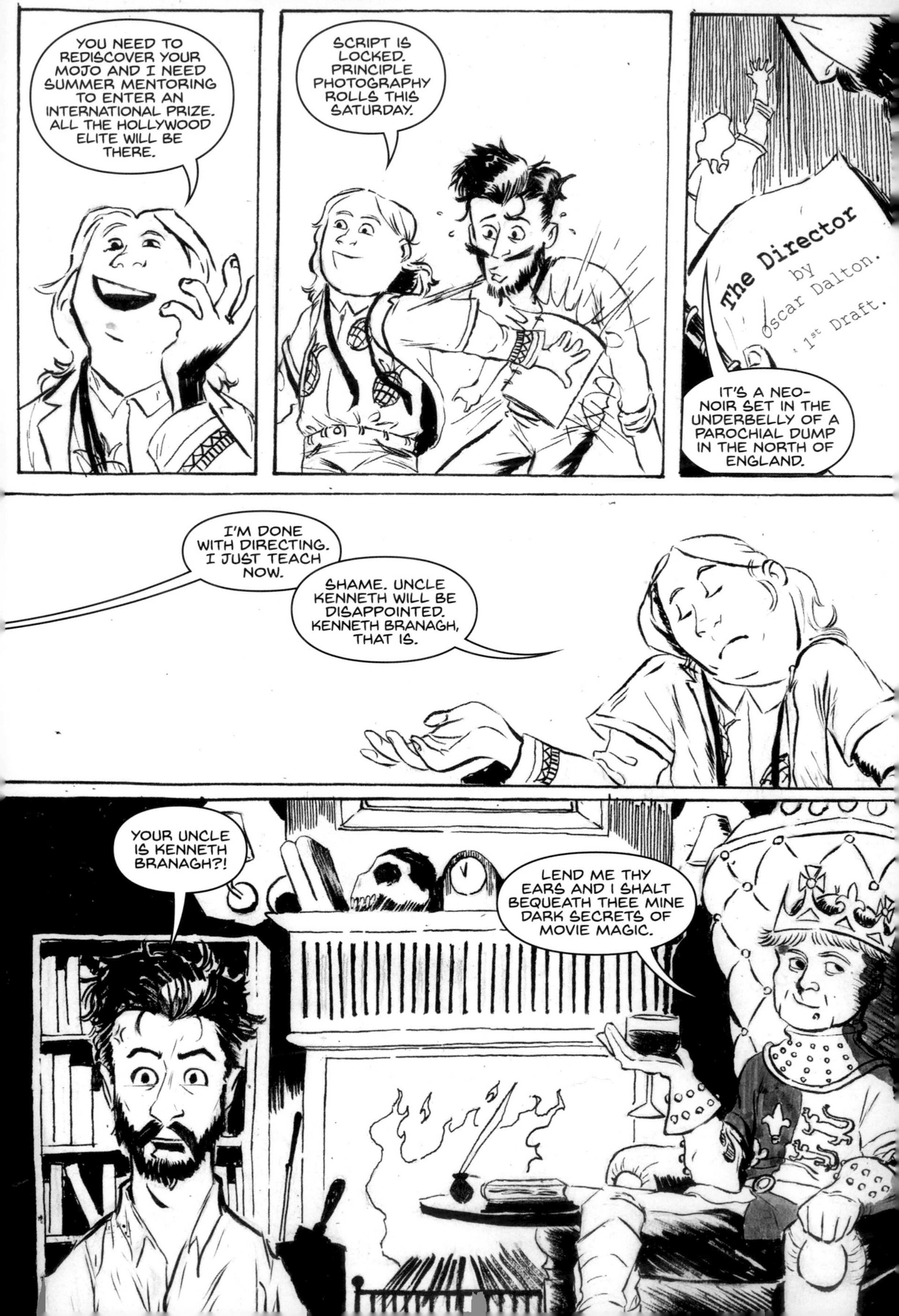
YOU NEED TO REDISCOVER YOUR MOJO AND I NEED SUMMER MENTORING TO ENTER AN INTERNATIONAL PRIZE. ALL THE HOLLYWOOD ELITE WILL BE THERE.
SCRIPT IS LOCKED. PRINCIPLE PHOTOGRAPHY ROLLS THIS SATURDAY.
The Director
by
Oscar Dalton.
1st Draft.
IT'S A NEO-NOIR SET IN THE UNDERBELLY OF A PAROCHIAL DUMP IN THE NORTH OF ENGLAND.
I'M DONE WITH DIRECTING. I JUST TEACH NOW.
SHAME. UNCLE KENNETH WILL BE DISAPPOINTED. KENNETH BRANAGH, THAT IS.
YOUR UNCLE IS KENNETH BRANAGH?!
LEND ME THY EARS AND I SHALT BEQUEATH THEE MINE DARK SECRETS OF MOVIE MAGIC.

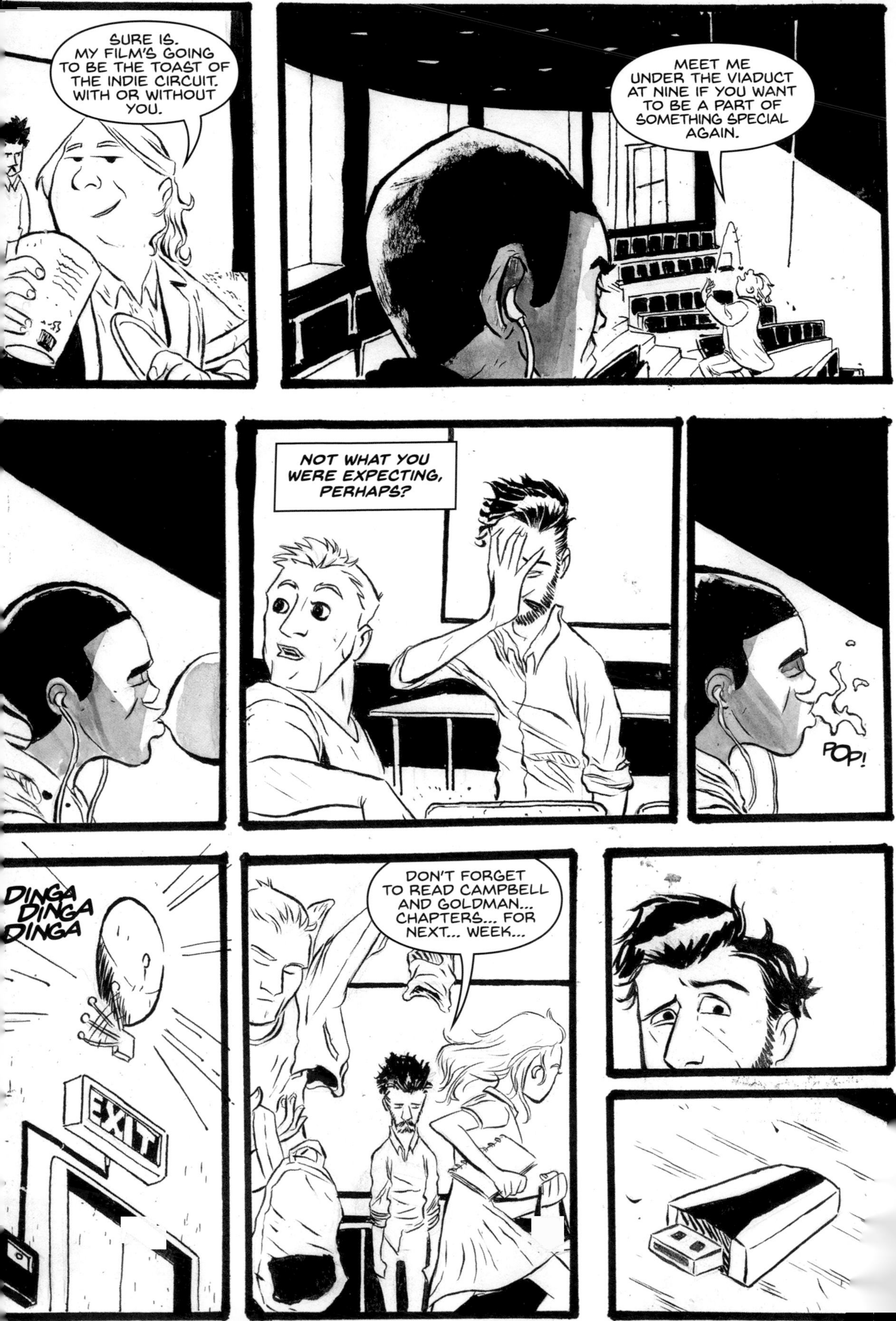
SURE IS. MY FILM'S GOING TO BE THE TOAST OF THE INDIE CIRCUIT. WITH OR WITHOUT YOU.
MEET ME UNDER THE VIADUCT AT NINE IF YOU WANT TO BE A PART OF SOMETHING SPECIAL AGAIN.
NOT WHAT YOU WERE EXPECTING, PERHAPS?
POP!
DINGA DINGA DINGA
EXIT
DON'T FORGET TO READ CAMPBELL AND GOLDMAN... CHAPTERS... FOR NEXT... WEEK...

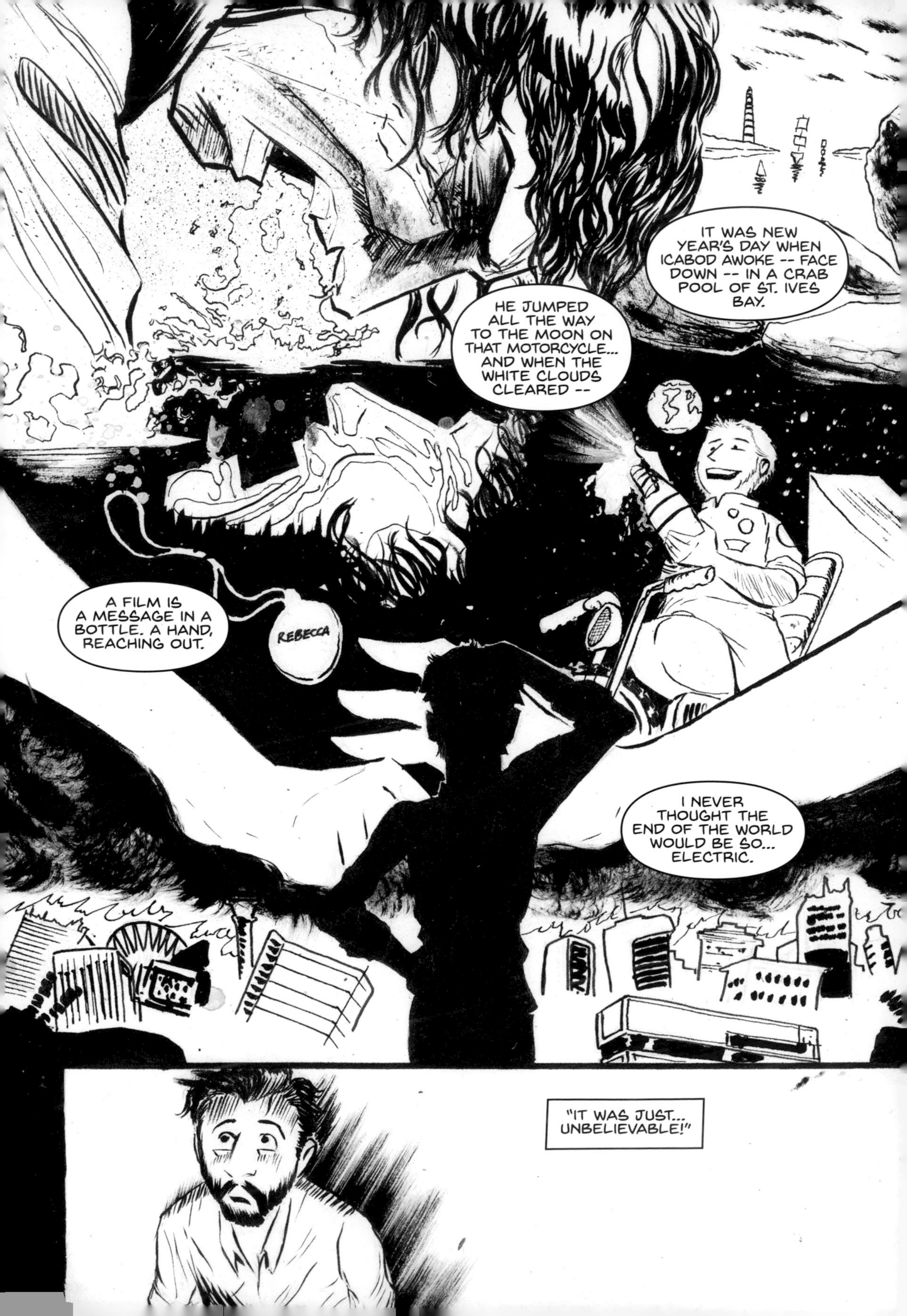
IT WAS NEW YEAR'S DAY WHEN ICABOD AWOKE -- FACE DOWN -- IN A CRAB POOL OF ST. IVES BAY.
HE JUMPED ALL THE WAY TO THE MOON ON THAT MOTORCYCLE... AND WHEN THE WHITE CLOUDS CLEARED --
A FILM IS A MESSAGE IN A BOTTLE. A HAND, REACHING OUT.
REBECCA
I NEVER THOUGHT THE END OF THE WORLD WOULD BE SO... ELECTRIC.
"IT WAS JUST... UNBELIEVABLE!"

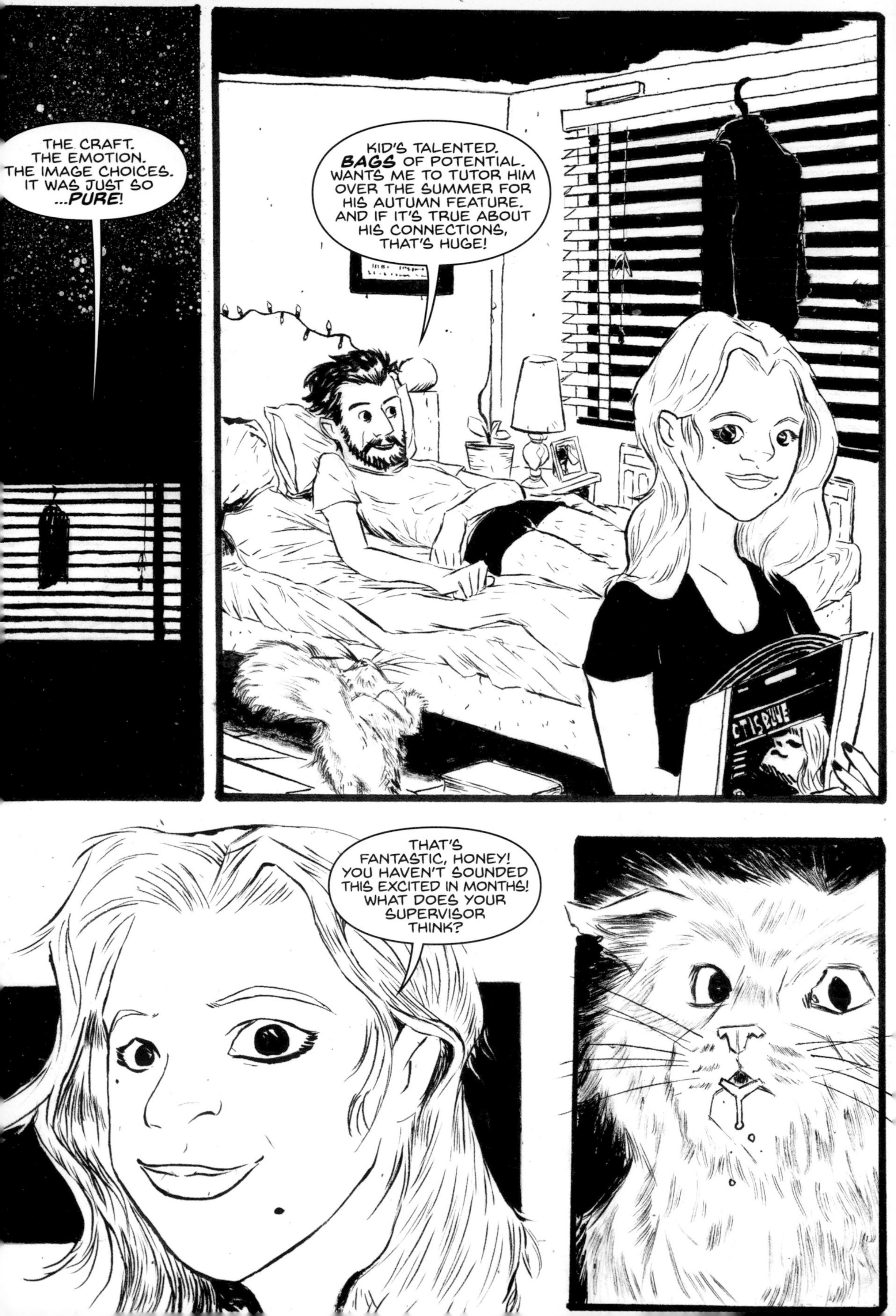
THE CRAFT. THE EMOTION. THE IMAGE CHOICES. IT WAS JUST SO ...*PURE*!
KID'S TALENTED. ***BAGS*** OF POTENTIAL. WANTS ME TO TUTOR HIM OVER THE SUMMER FOR HIS AUTUMN FEATURE. AND IF IT'S TRUE ABOUT HIS CONNECTIONS, THAT'S HUGE!
THAT'S FANTASTIC, HONEY! YOU HAVEN'T SOUNDED THIS EXCITED IN MONTHS! WHAT DOES YOUR SUPERVISOR THINK?

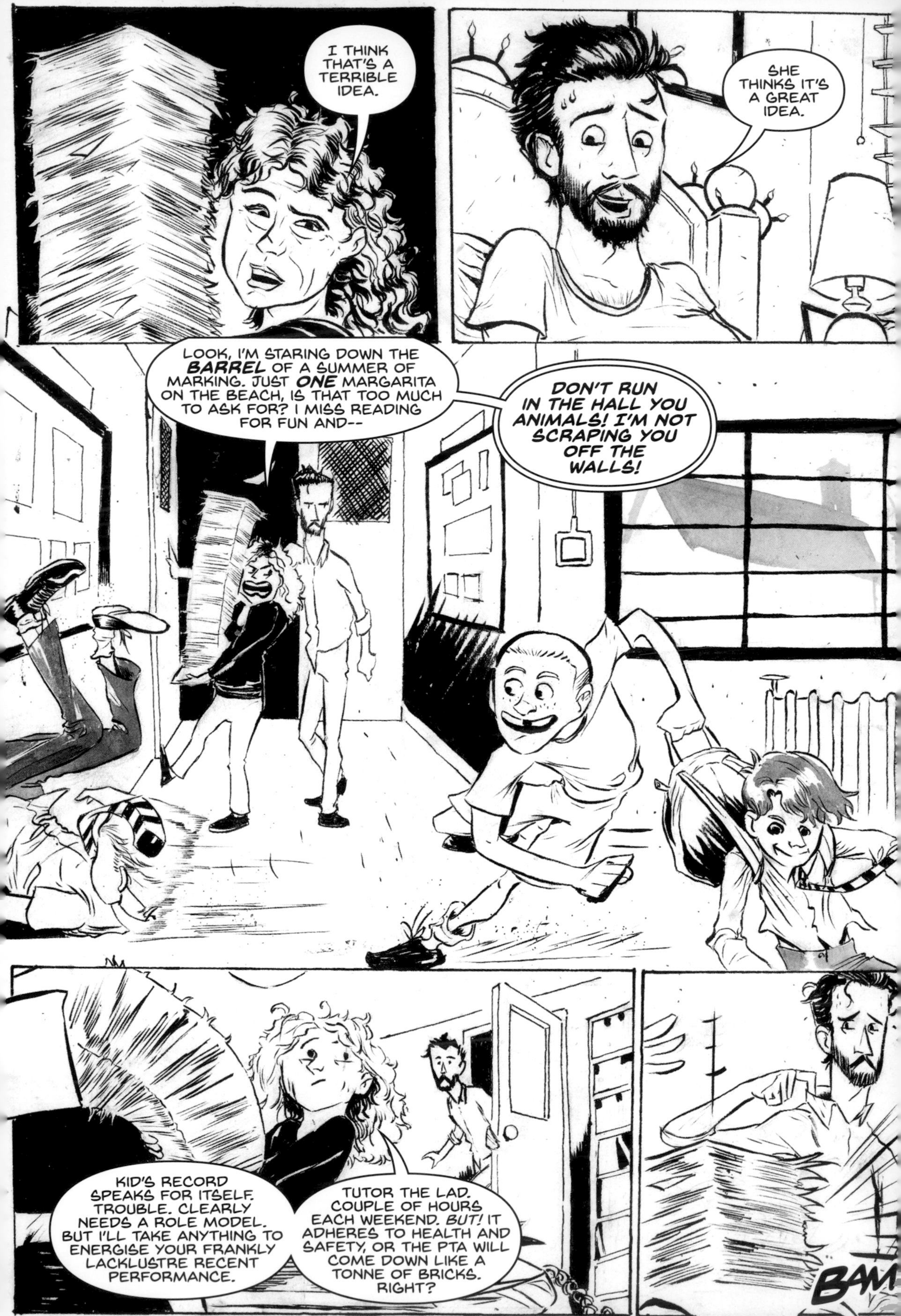
I THINK THAT'S A TERRIBLE IDEA.
SHE THINKS IT'S A GREAT IDEA.
LOOK, I'M STARING DOWN THE **BARREL** OF A SUMMER OF MARKING. JUST ***ONE*** MARGARITA ON THE BEACH, IS THAT TOO MUCH TO ASK FOR? I MISS READING FOR FUN AND--
DON'T RUN IN THE HALL YOU ANIMALS! I'M NOT SCRAPING YOU OFF THE WALLS!
KID'S RECORD SPEAKS FOR ITSELF. TROUBLE. CLEARLY NEEDS A ROLE MODEL. BUT I'LL TAKE ANYTHING TO ENERGISE YOUR FRANKLY LACKLUSTRE RECENT PERFORMANCE.
TUTOR THE LAD. COUPLE OF HOURS EACH WEEKEND. *BUT!* IT ADHERES TO HEALTH AND SAFETY, OR THE PTA WILL COME DOWN LIKE A TONNE OF BRICKS. RIGHT?
BAM

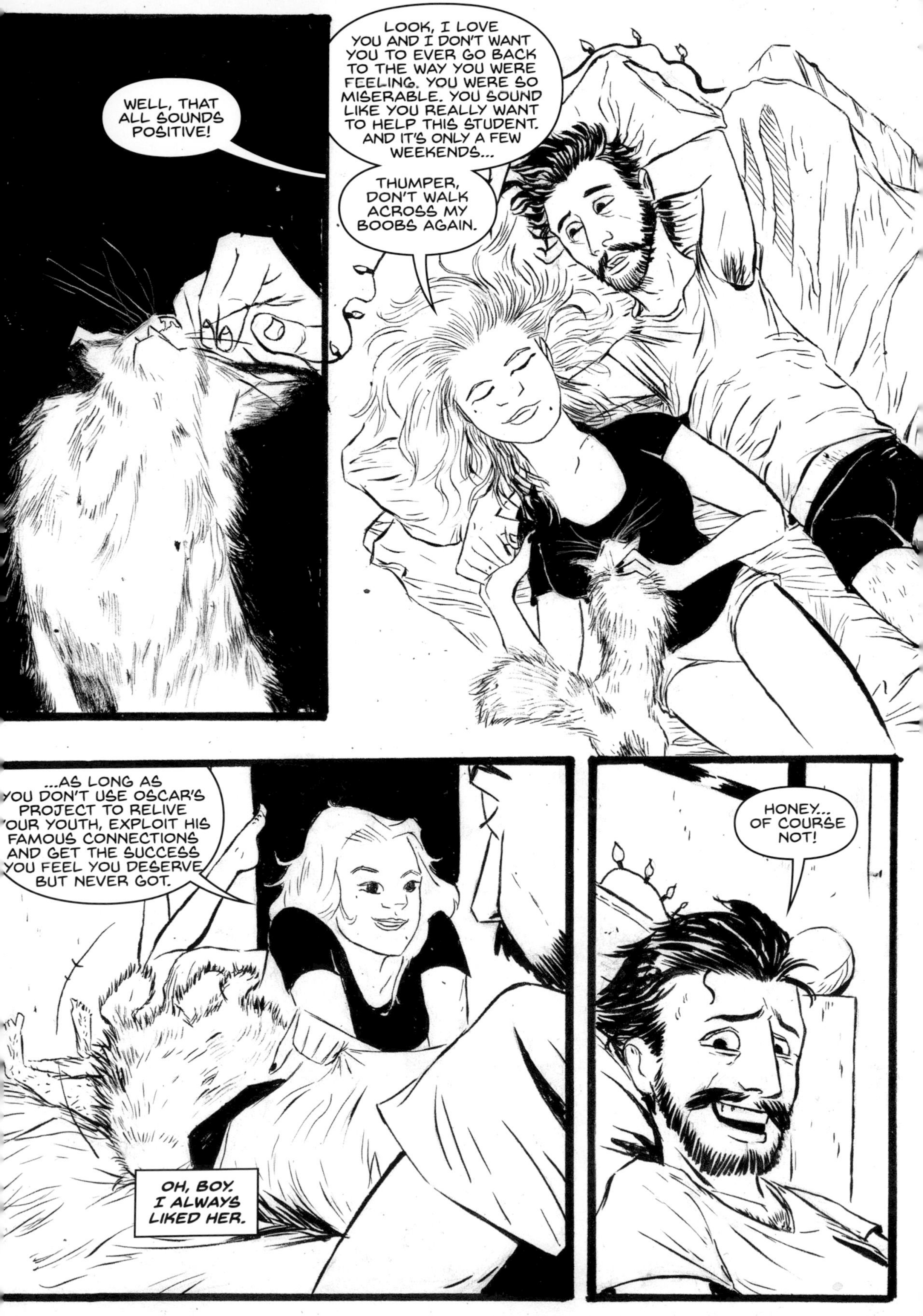
WELL, THAT ALL SOUNDS POSITIVE!
LOOK, I LOVE YOU AND I DON'T WANT YOU TO EVER GO BACK TO THE WAY YOU WERE FEELING. YOU WERE SO MISERABLE. YOU SOUND LIKE YOU REALLY WANT TO HELP THIS STUDENT. AND IT'S ONLY A FEW WEEKENDS...
THUMPER, DON'T WALK ACROSS MY BOOBS AGAIN.
...AS LONG AS YOU DON'T USE OSCAR'S PROJECT TO RELIVE YOUR YOUTH, EXPLOIT HIS FAMOUS CONNECTIONS AND GET THE SUCCESS YOU FEEL YOU DESERVE BUT NEVER GOT.
OH, BOY. I ALWAYS LIKED HER.
HONEY... OF COURSE NOT!

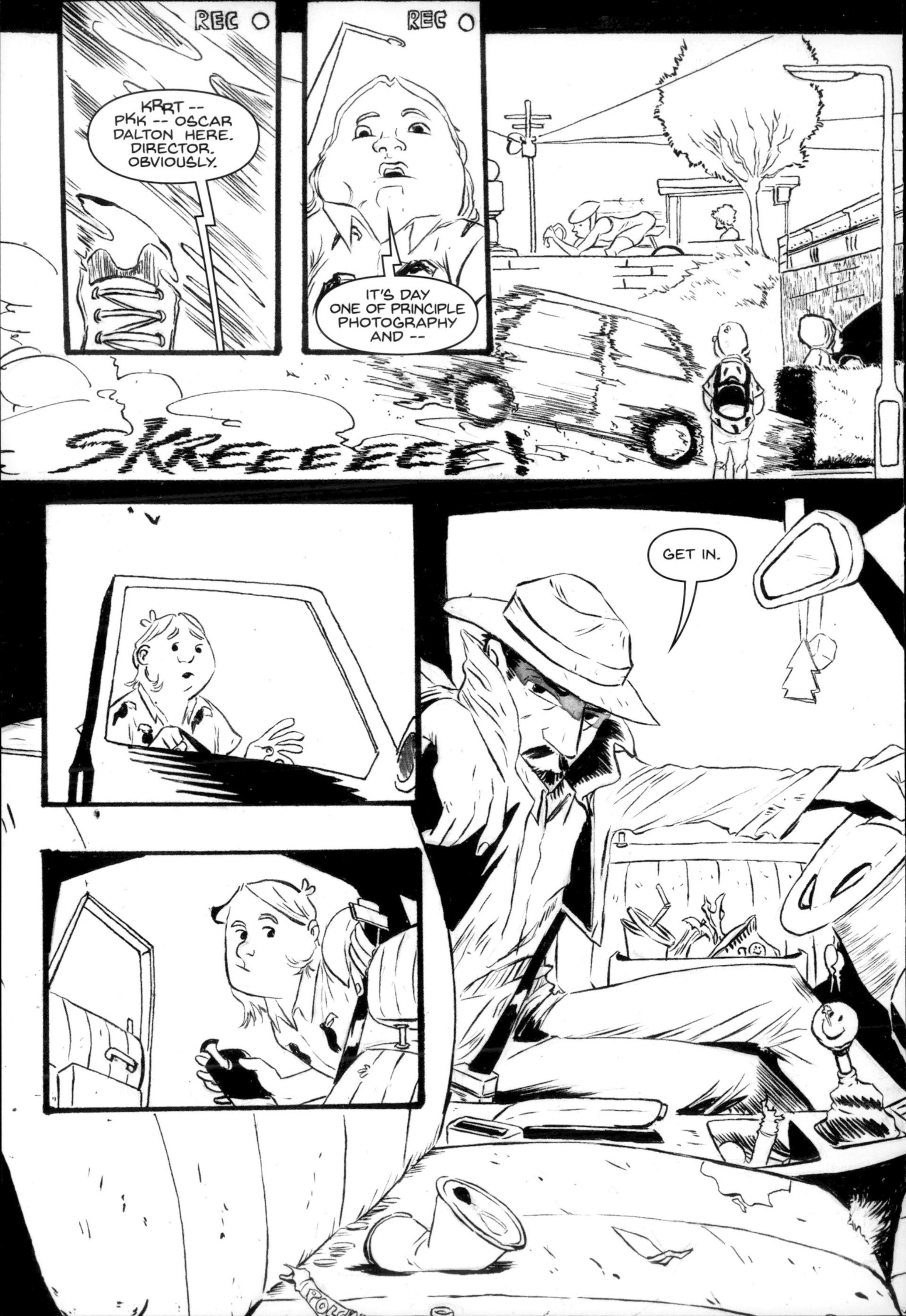

REC
KRRT -- PKK -- OSCAR DALTON HERE. DIRECTOR. OBVIOUSLY.
REC
IT'S DAY ONE OF PRINCIPLE PHOTOGRAPHY AND --
SKREEEEEEE!
GET IN.

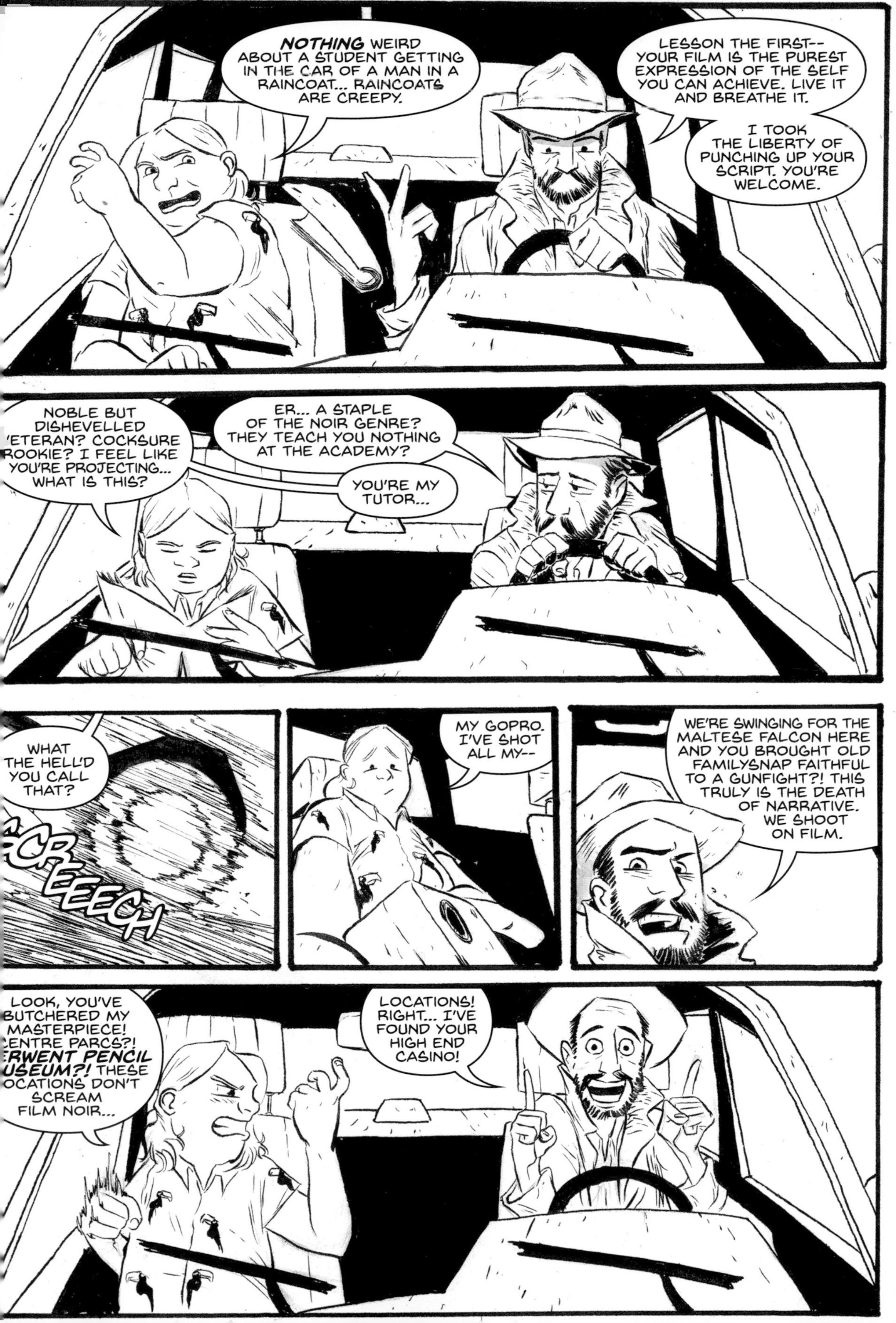

NOTHING WEIRD ABOUT A STUDENT GETTING IN THE CAR OF A MAN IN A RAINCOAT... RAINCOATS ARE CREEPY.
LESSON THE FIRST-- YOUR FILM IS THE PUREST EXPRESSION OF THE SELF YOU CAN ACHIEVE. LIVE IT AND BREATHE IT.
I TOOK THE LIBERTY OF PUNCHING UP YOUR SCRIPT. YOU'RE WELCOME.
NOBLE BUT DISHEVELLED 'ETERAN? COCKSURE ROOKIE? I FEEL LIKE YOU'RE PROJECTING... WHAT IS THIS?
ER... A STAPLE OF THE NOIR GENRE? THEY TEACH YOU NOTHING AT THE ACADEMY?
YOU'RE MY TUTOR...
WHAT THE HELL'D YOU CALL THAT?
CREEECH
MY GOPRO. I'VE SHOT ALL MY--
WE'RE SWINGING FOR THE MALTESE FALCON HERE AND YOU BROUGHT OLD FAMILYSNAP FAITHFUL TO A GUNFIGHT?! THIS TRULY IS THE DEATH OF NARRATIVE. WE SHOOT ON FILM.
LOOK, YOU'VE BUTCHERED MY MASTERPIECE! CENTRE PARCS?! ERWENT PENCIL USEUM?! THESE OCATIONS DON'T SCREAM FILM NOIR...
LOCATIONS! RIGHT... I'VE FOUND YOUR HIGH END CASINO!

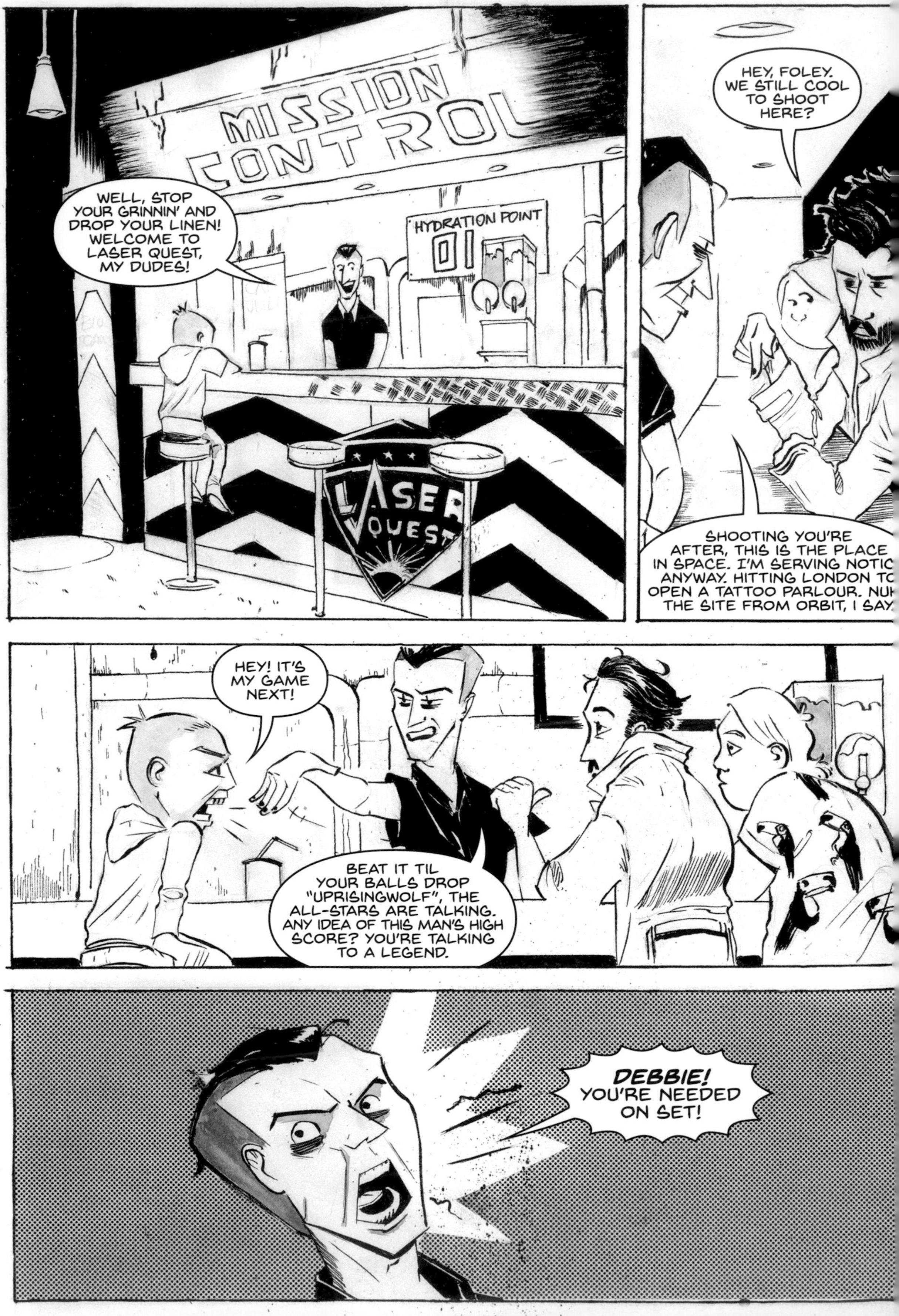
MISSION CONTROL
WELL, STOP YOUR GRINNIN' AND DROP YOUR LINEN! WELCOME TO LASER QUEST, MY DUDES!
HYDRATION POINT 01
LASER QUEST
HEY, FOLEY. WE STILL COOL TO SHOOT HERE?
SHOOTING YOU'RE AFTER, THIS IS THE PLACE IN SPACE. I'M SERVING NOTIC ANYWAY. HITTING LONDON TO OPEN A TATTOO PARLOUR. NUK THE SITE FROM ORBIT, I SAY.
HEY! IT'S MY GAME NEXT!
BEAT IT TIL YOUR BALLS DROP "UPRISINGWOLF", THE ALL-STARS ARE TALKING. ANY IDEA OF THIS MAN'S HIGH SCORE? YOU'RE TALKING TO A LEGEND.
DEBBIE! YOU'RE NEEDED ON SET!

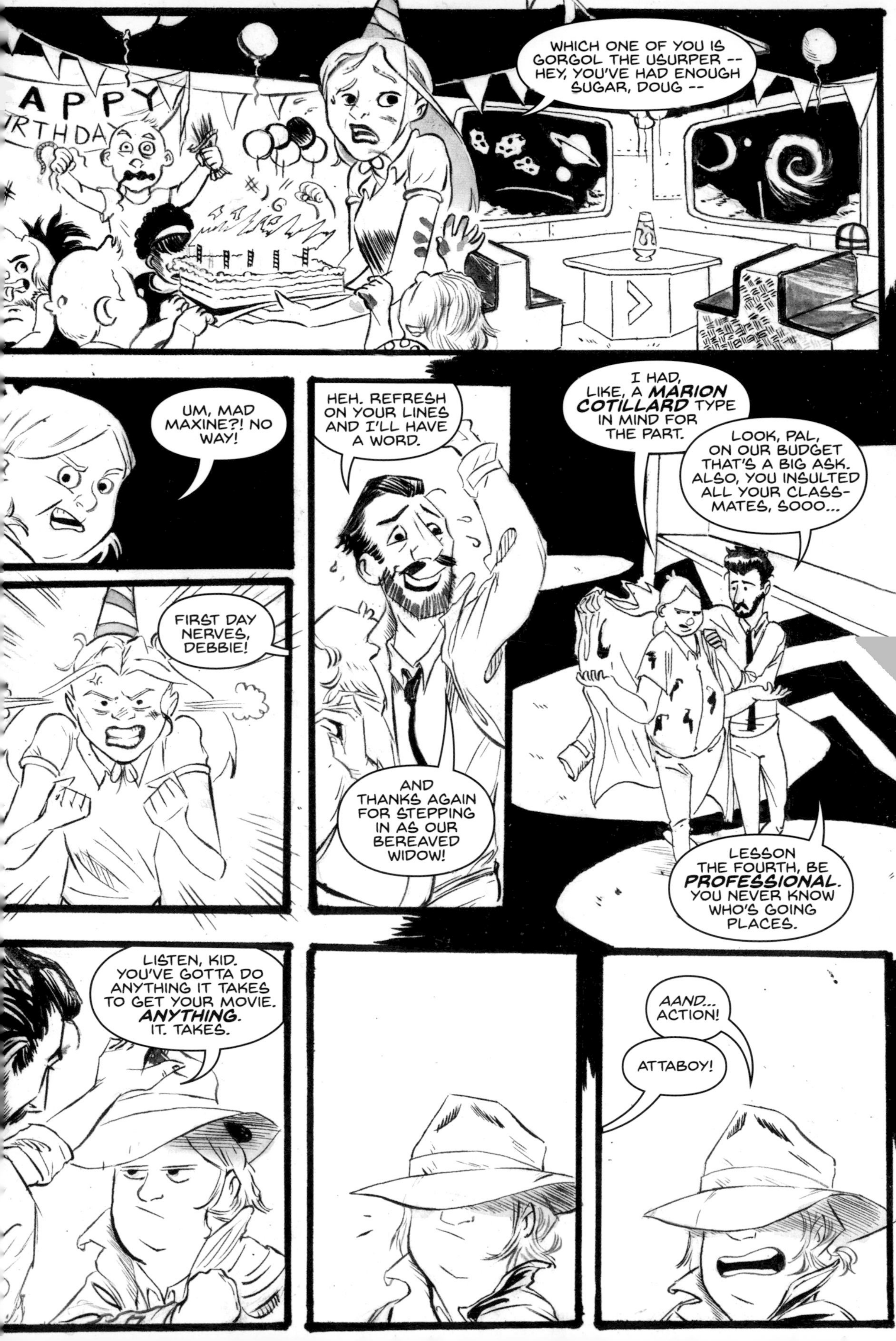
APPY
RTHDA
WHICH ONE OF YOU IS GORGOL THE USURPER -- HEY, YOU'VE HAD ENOUGH SUGAR, DOUG --
UM, MAD MAXINE?! NO WAY!
FIRST DAY NERVES, DEBBIE!
HEH. REFRESH ON YOUR LINES AND I'LL HAVE A WORD.
AND THANKS AGAIN FOR STEPPING IN AS OUR BEREAVED WIDOW!
I HAD, LIKE, A MARION COTILLARD TYPE IN MIND FOR THE PART.
LOOK, PAL, ON OUR BUDGET THAT'S A BIG ASK. ALSO, YOU INSULTED ALL YOUR CLASS-MATES, SOOO...
LESSON THE FOURTH, BE PROFESSIONAL. YOU NEVER KNOW WHO'S GOING PLACES.
LISTEN, KID. YOU'VE GOTTA DO ANYTHING IT TAKES TO GET YOUR MOVIE. ANYTHING. IT. TAKES.
AAND... ACTION!
ATTABOY!

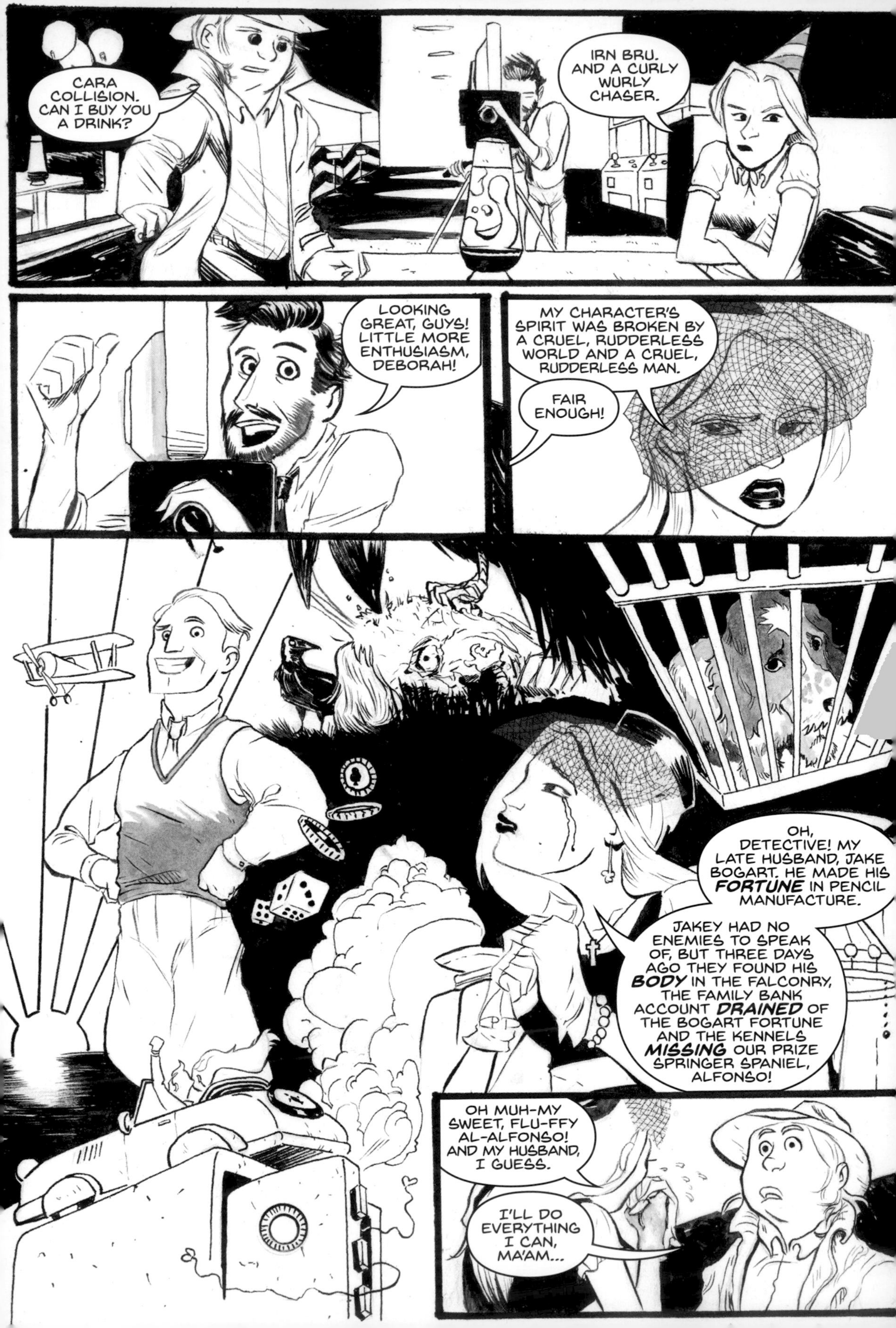
CARA COLLISION. CAN I BUY YOU A DRINK?
IRN BRU. AND A CURLY WURLY CHASER.
LOOKING GREAT, GUYS! LITTLE MORE ENTHUSIASM, DEBORAH!
MY CHARACTER'S SPIRIT WAS BROKEN BY A CRUEL, RUDDERLESS WORLD AND A CRUEL, RUDDERLESS MAN.
FAIR ENOUGH!
OH, DETECTIVE! MY LATE HUSBAND, JAKE BOGART. HE MADE HIS FORTUNE IN PENCIL MANUFACTURE.
JAKEY HAD NO ENEMIES TO SPEAK OF, BUT THREE DAYS AGO THEY FOUND HIS BODY IN THE FALCONRY, THE FAMILY BANK ACCOUNT DRAINED OF THE BOGART FORTUNE AND THE KENNELS MISSING OUR PRIZE SPRINGER SPANIEL, ALFONSO!
OH MUH-MY SWEET, FLU-FFY AL-ALFONSO! AND MY HUSBAND, I GUESS.
I'LL DO EVERYTHING I CAN, MA'AM...

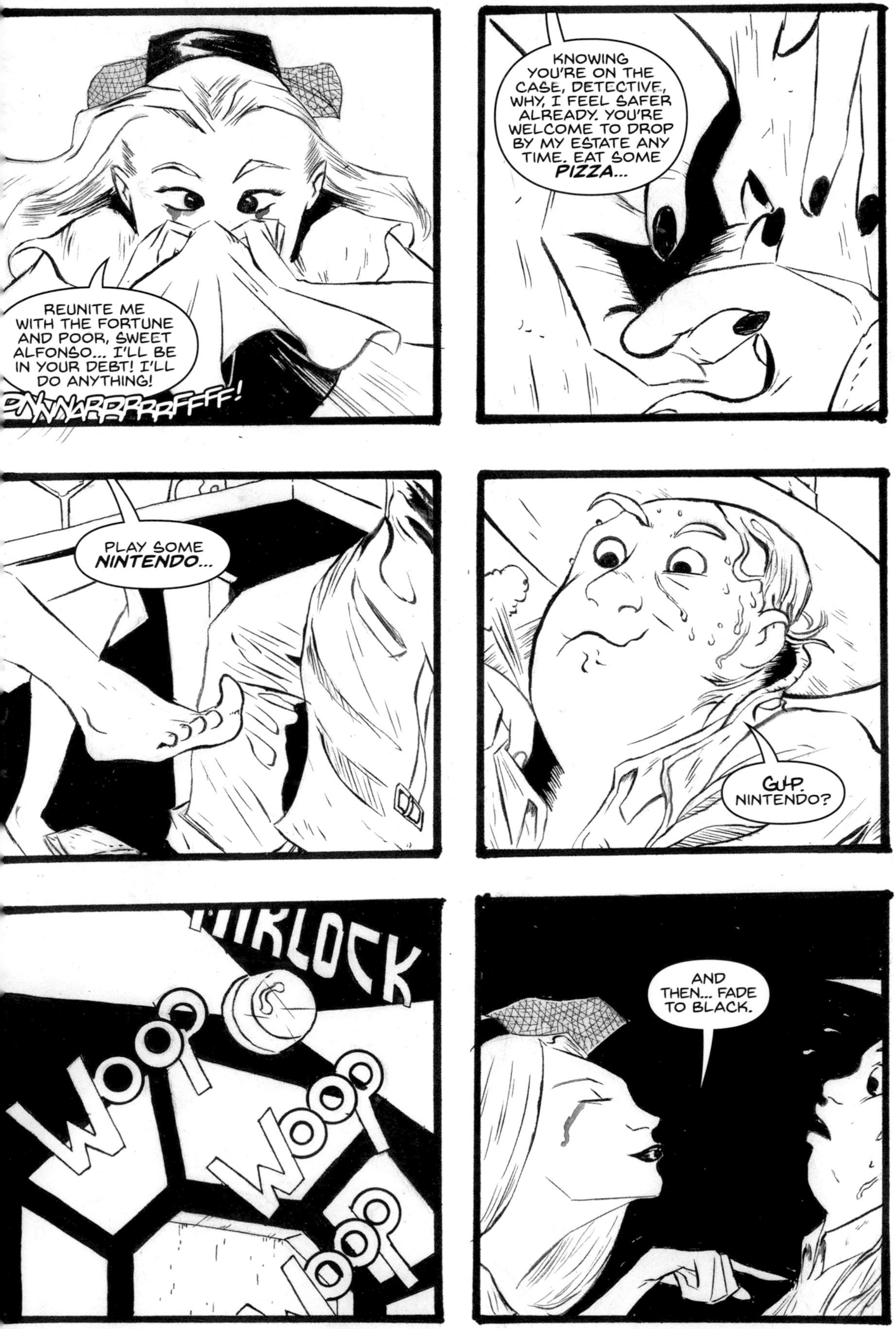
REUNITE ME WITH THE FORTUNE AND POOR, SWEET ALFONSO... I'LL BE IN YOUR DEBT! I'LL DO ANYTHING!
KNOWING YOU'RE ON THE CASE, DETECTIVE, WHY, I FEEL SAFER ALREADY. YOU'RE WELCOME TO DROP BY MY ESTATE ANY TIME. EAT SOME **PIZZA...**
PLAY SOME **NINTENDO...**
GULP. NINTENDO?
WOOP
WOOP
WOOP
AND THEN... FADE TO BLACK.

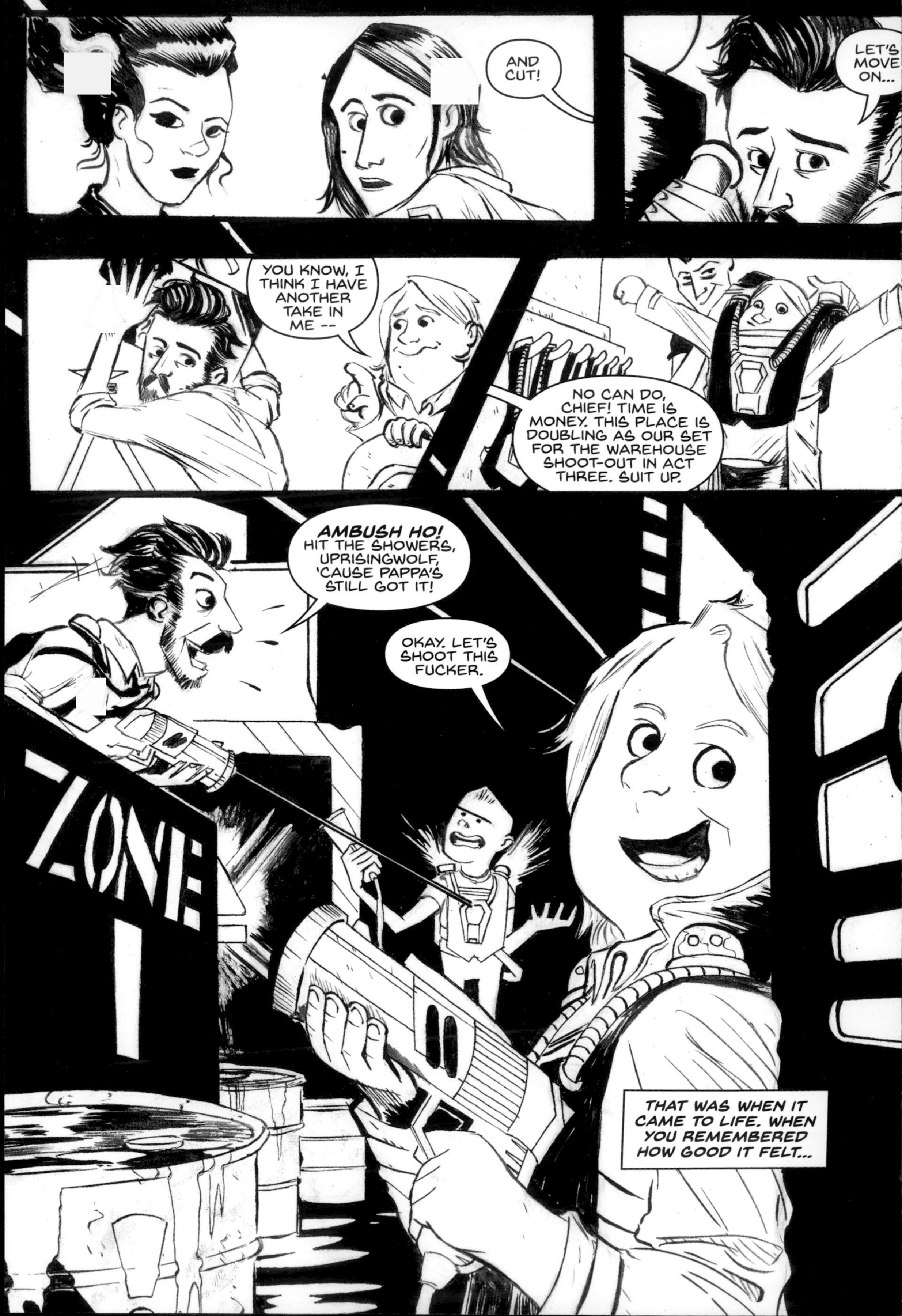
AND CUT!
LET'S MOVE ON...
YOU KNOW, I THINK I HAVE ANOTHER TAKE IN ME --
NO CAN DO, CHIEF! TIME IS MONEY. THIS PLACE IS DOUBLING AS OUR SET FOR THE WAREHOUSE SHOOT-OUT IN ACT THREE. SUIT UP.
AMBUSH HO! HIT THE SHOWERS, UPRISINGWOLF, 'CAUSE PAPPA'S STILL GOT IT!
OKAY. LET'S SHOOT THIS FUCKER.
ZONE 1
THAT WAS WHEN IT CAME TO LIFE. WHEN YOU REMEMBERED HOW GOOD IT FELT...

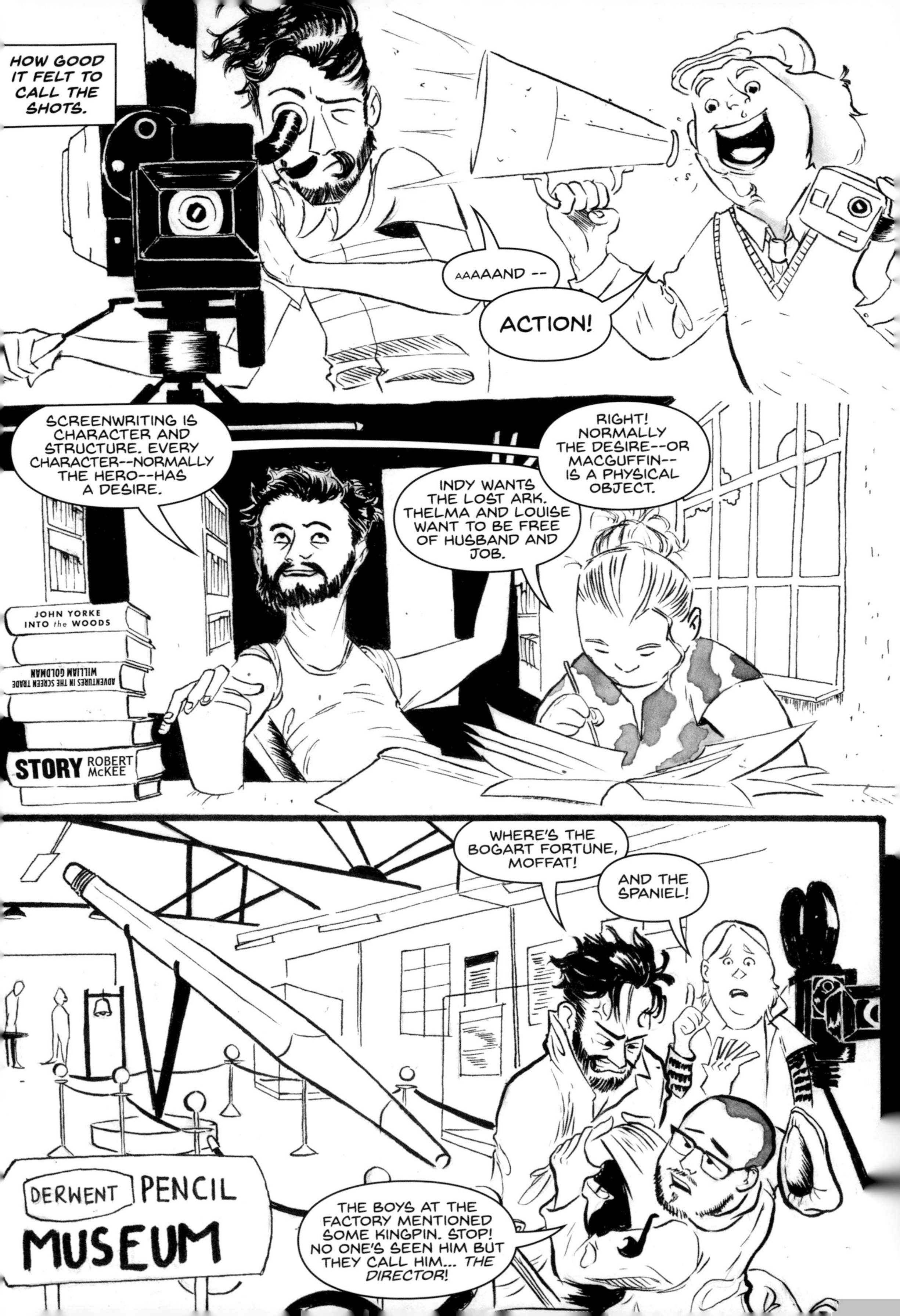
HOW GOOD IT FELT TO CALL THE SHOTS.
AAAAAND --
ACTION!
SCREENWRITING IS CHARACTER AND STRUCTURE. EVERY CHARACTER--NORMALLY THE HERO--HAS A DESIRE.
RIGHT! NORMALLY THE DESIRE--OR MACGUFFIN--IS A PHYSICAL OBJECT.
INDY WANTS THE LOST ARK. THELMA AND LOUISE WANT TO BE FREE OF HUSBAND AND JOB.
JOHN YORKE INTO the WOODS
ADVENTURES IN THE SCREEN TRADE WILLIAM GOLDMAN
STORY ROBERT McKEE
WHERE'S THE BOGART FORTUNE, MOFFAT!
AND THE SPANIEL!
DERWENT PENCIL MUSEUM
THE BOYS AT THE FACTORY MENTIONED SOME KINGPIN. STOP! NO ONE'S SEEN HIM BUT THEY CALL HIM... THE DIRECTOR!

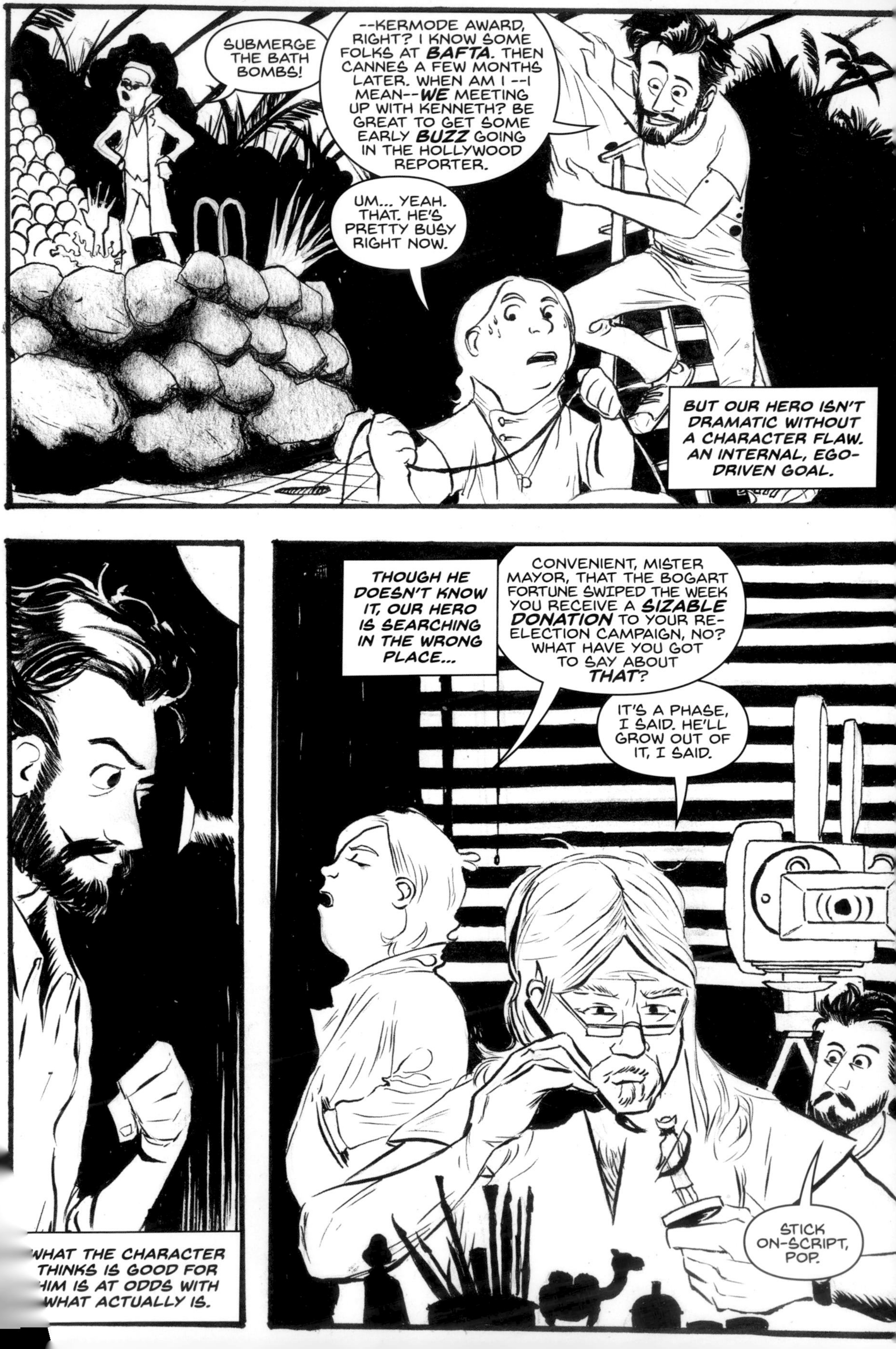
SUBMERGE THE BATH BOMBS!
--KERMODE AWARD, RIGHT? I KNOW SOME FOLKS AT BAFTA. THEN CANNES A FEW MONTHS LATER. WHEN AM I --I MEAN--WE MEETING UP WITH KENNETH? BE GREAT TO GET SOME EARLY BUZZ GOING IN THE HOLLYWOOD REPORTER.
UM... YEAH. THAT. HE'S PRETTY BUSY RIGHT NOW.
BUT OUR HERO ISN'T DRAMATIC WITHOUT A CHARACTER FLAW. AN INTERNAL, EGO-DRIVEN GOAL.
WHAT THE CHARACTER THINKS IS GOOD FOR HIM IS AT ODDS WITH WHAT ACTUALLY IS.
THOUGH HE DOESN'T KNOW IT, OUR HERO IS SEARCHING IN THE WRONG PLACE...
CONVENIENT, MISTER MAYOR, THAT THE BOGART FORTUNE SWIPED THE WEEK YOU RECEIVE A SIZABLE DONATION TO YOUR RE-ELECTION CAMPAIGN, NO? WHAT HAVE YOU GOT TO SAY ABOUT THAT?
IT'S A PHASE, I SAID. HE'LL GROW OUT OF IT, I SAID.
STICK ON-SCRIPT, POP.

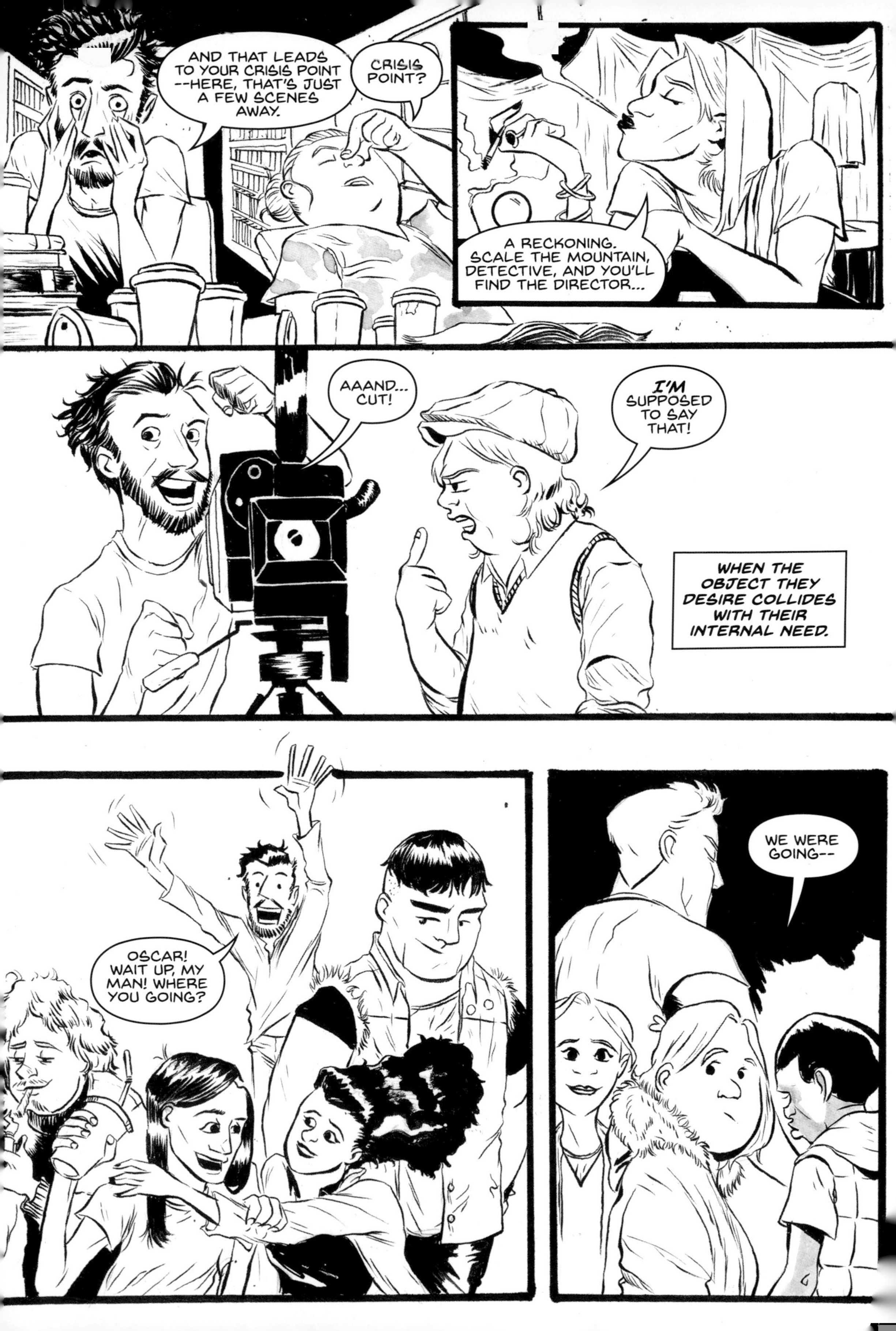
AND THAT LEADS TO YOUR CRISIS POINT --HERE, THAT'S JUST A FEW SCENES AWAY.
CRISIS POINT?
A RECKONING. SCALE THE MOUNTAIN, DETECTIVE, AND YOU'LL FIND THE DIRECTOR...
AAAND... CUT!
I'M SUPPOSED TO SAY THAT!
WHEN THE OBJECT THEY DESIRE COLLIDES WITH THEIR INTERNAL NEED.
OSCAR! WAIT UP, MY MAN! WHERE YOU GOING?
WE WERE GOING--

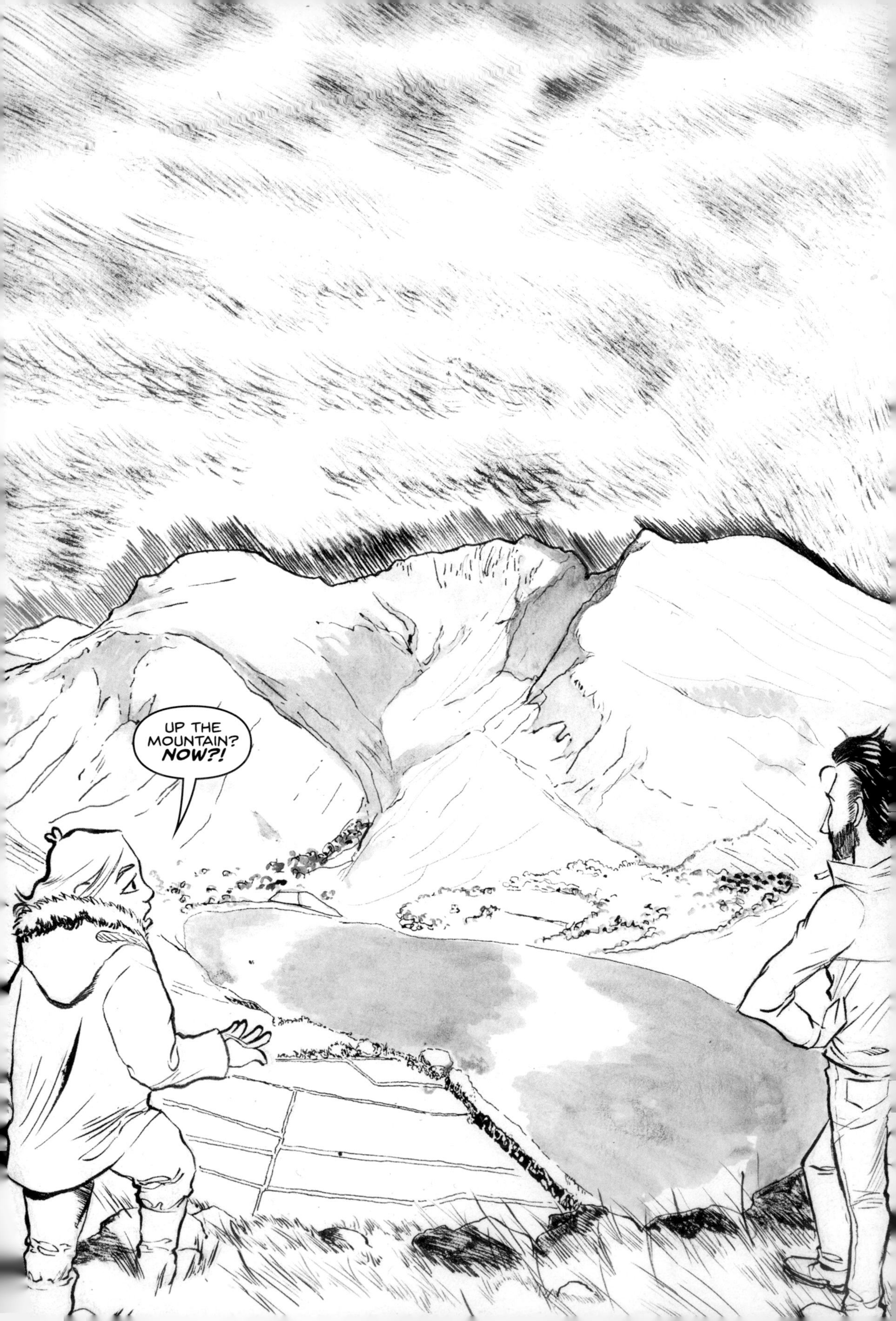
UP THE MOUNTAIN? NOW?!

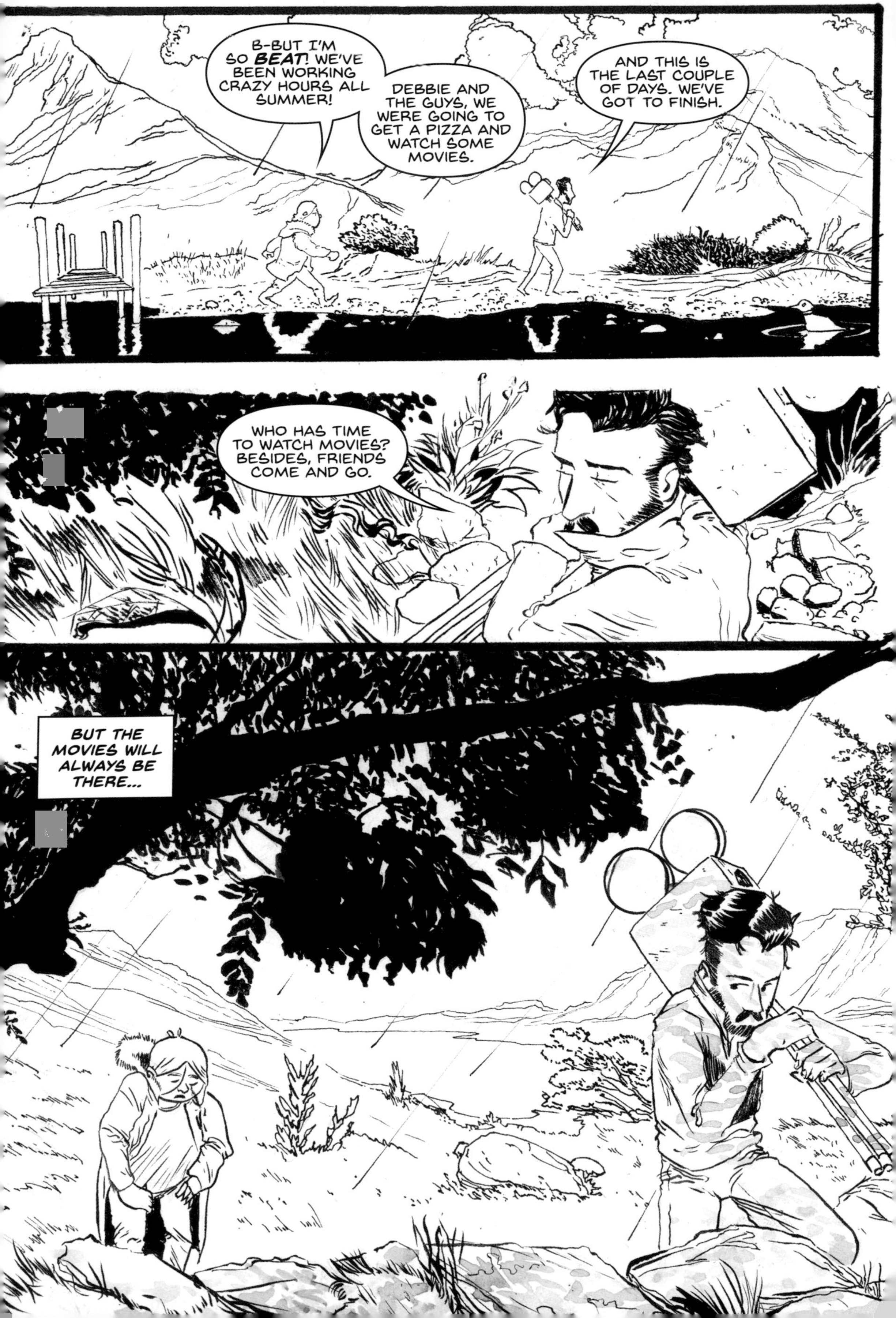
B-BUT I'M SO BEAT! WE'VE BEEN WORKING CRAZY HOURS ALL SUMMER!
DEBBIE AND THE GUYS, WE WERE GOING TO GET A PIZZA AND WATCH SOME MOVIES.
AND THIS IS THE LAST COUPLE OF DAYS. WE'VE GOT TO FINISH.
WHO HAS TIME TO WATCH MOVIES? BESIDES, FRIENDS COME AND GO.
BUT THE MOVIES WILL ALWAYS BE THERE...

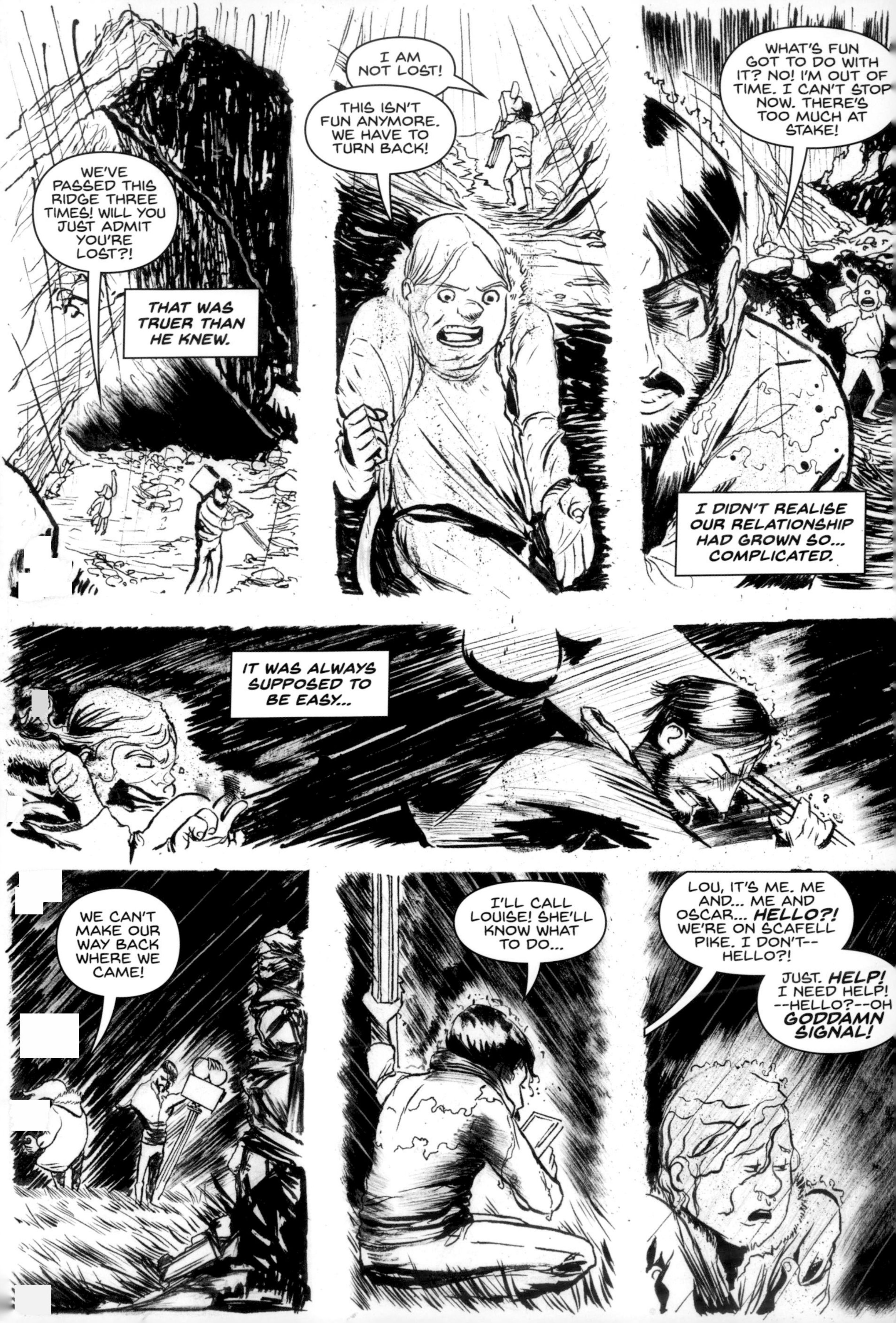
WE'VE PASSED THIS RIDGE THREE TIMES! WILL YOU JUST ADMIT YOU'RE LOST?!
THAT WAS TRUER THAN HE KNEW.
I AM NOT LOST!
THIS ISN'T FUN ANYMORE. WE HAVE TO TURN BACK!
WHAT'S FUN GOT TO DO WITH IT? NO! I'M OUT OF TIME. I CAN'T STOP NOW. THERE'S TOO MUCH AT STAKE!
I DIDN'T REALISE OUR RELATIONSHIP HAD GROWN SO... COMPLICATED.
IT WAS ALWAYS SUPPOSED TO BE EASY...
WE CAN'T MAKE OUR WAY BACK WHERE WE CAME!
I'LL CALL LOUISE! SHE'LL KNOW WHAT TO DO...
LOU, IT'S ME. ME AND... ME AND OSCAR... HELLO?! WE'RE ON SCAFELL PIKE. I DON'T-- HELLO?!
JUST. HELP! I NEED HELP! --HELLO?--OH GODDAMN SIGNAL!

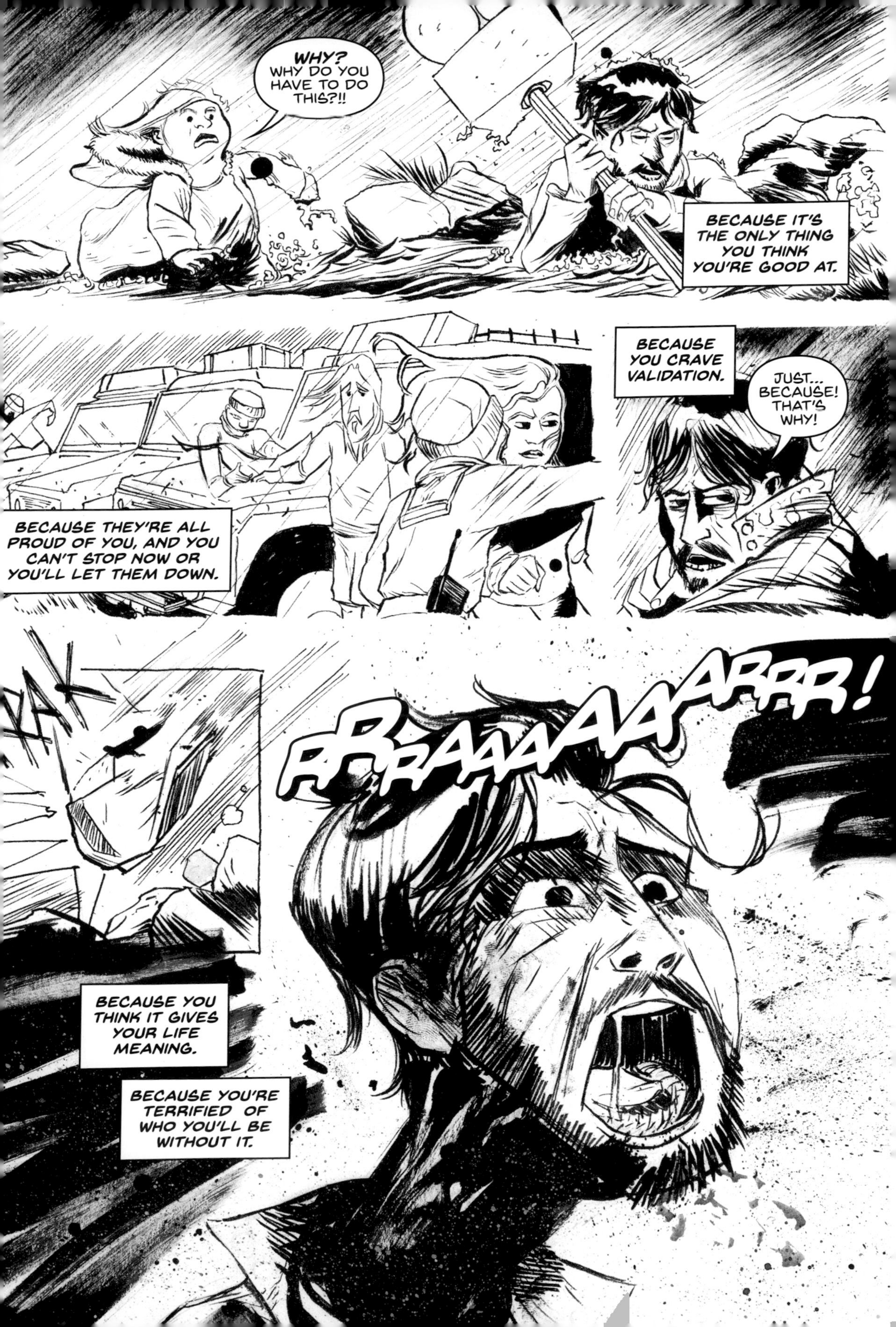
WHY? WHY DO YOU HAVE TO DO THIS?!!
BECAUSE IT'S THE ONLY THING YOU THINK YOU'RE GOOD AT.
BECAUSE THEY'RE ALL PROUD OF YOU, AND YOU CAN'T STOP NOW OR YOU'LL LET THEM DOWN.
BECAUSE YOU CRAVE VALIDATION.
JUST... BECAUSE! THAT'S WHY!
RRRAAAAAAARRRR!
BECAUSE YOU THINK IT GIVES YOUR LIFE MEANING.
BECAUSE YOU'RE TERRIFIED OF WHO YOU'LL BE WITHOUT IT.

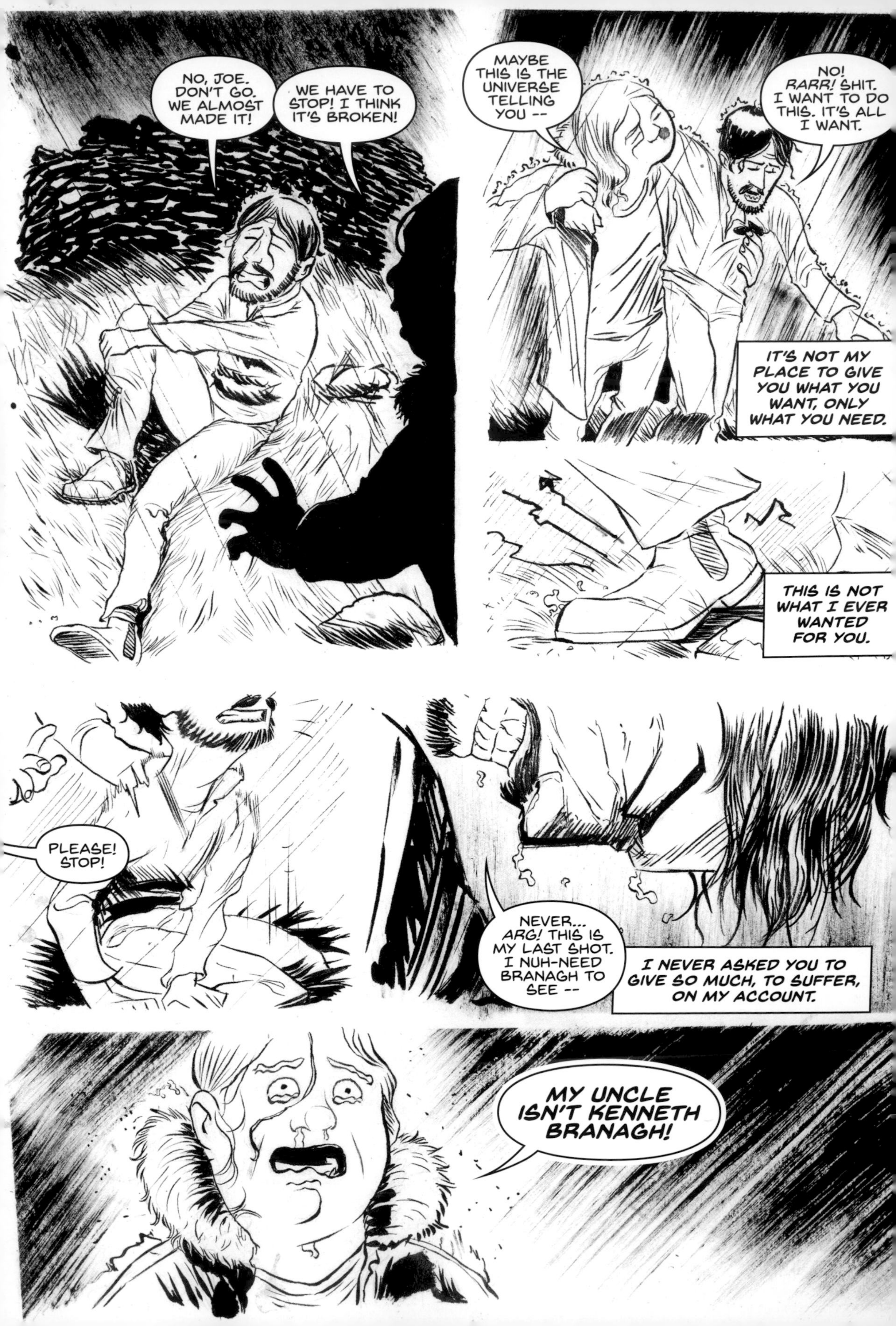
NO, JOE. DON'T GO. WE ALMOST MADE IT!
WE HAVE TO STOP! I THINK IT'S BROKEN!
MAYBE THIS IS THE UNIVERSE TELLING YOU --
NO! RARR! SHIT. I WANT TO DO THIS. IT'S ALL I WANT.
IT'S NOT MY PLACE TO GIVE YOU WHAT YOU WANT, ONLY WHAT YOU NEED.
THIS IS NOT WHAT I EVER WANTED FOR YOU.
PLEASE! STOP!
NEVER... ARG! THIS IS MY LAST SHOT. I NUH-NEED BRANAGH TO SEE --
I NEVER ASKED YOU TO GIVE SO MUCH, TO SUFFER, ON MY ACCOUNT.
MY UNCLE ISN'T KENNETH BRANAGH!

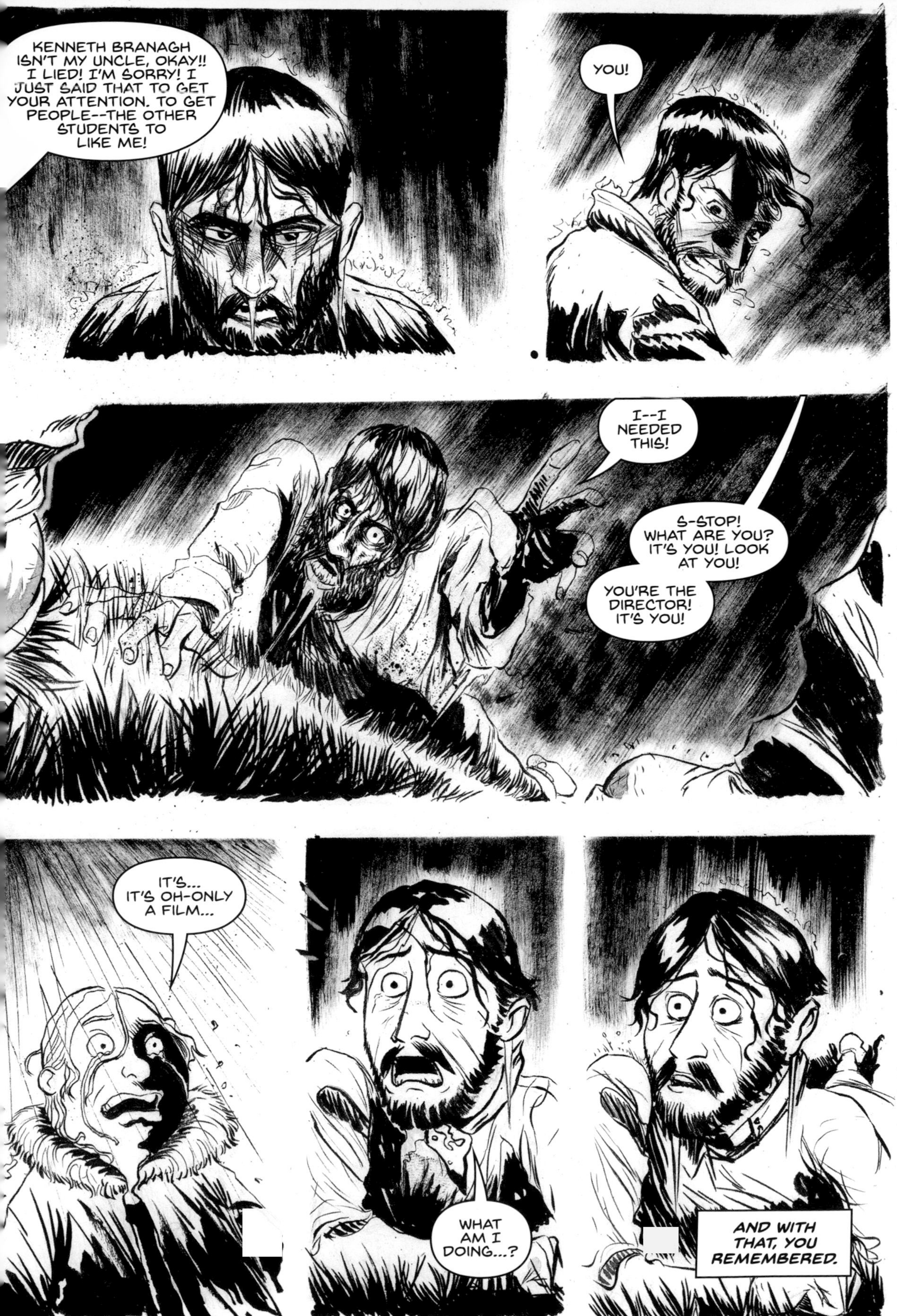
KENNETH BRANAGH ISN'T MY UNCLE, OKAY!! I LIED! I'M SORRY! I JUST SAID THAT TO GET YOUR ATTENTION. TO GET PEOPLE--THE OTHER STUDENTS TO LIKE ME!
YOU!
I--I NEEDED THIS!
S-STOP! WHAT ARE YOU? IT'S YOU! LOOK AT YOU!
YOU'RE THE DIRECTOR! IT'S YOU!
IT'S... IT'S OH-ONLY A FILM...
WHAT AM I DOING...?
AND WITH THAT, YOU REMEMBERED.

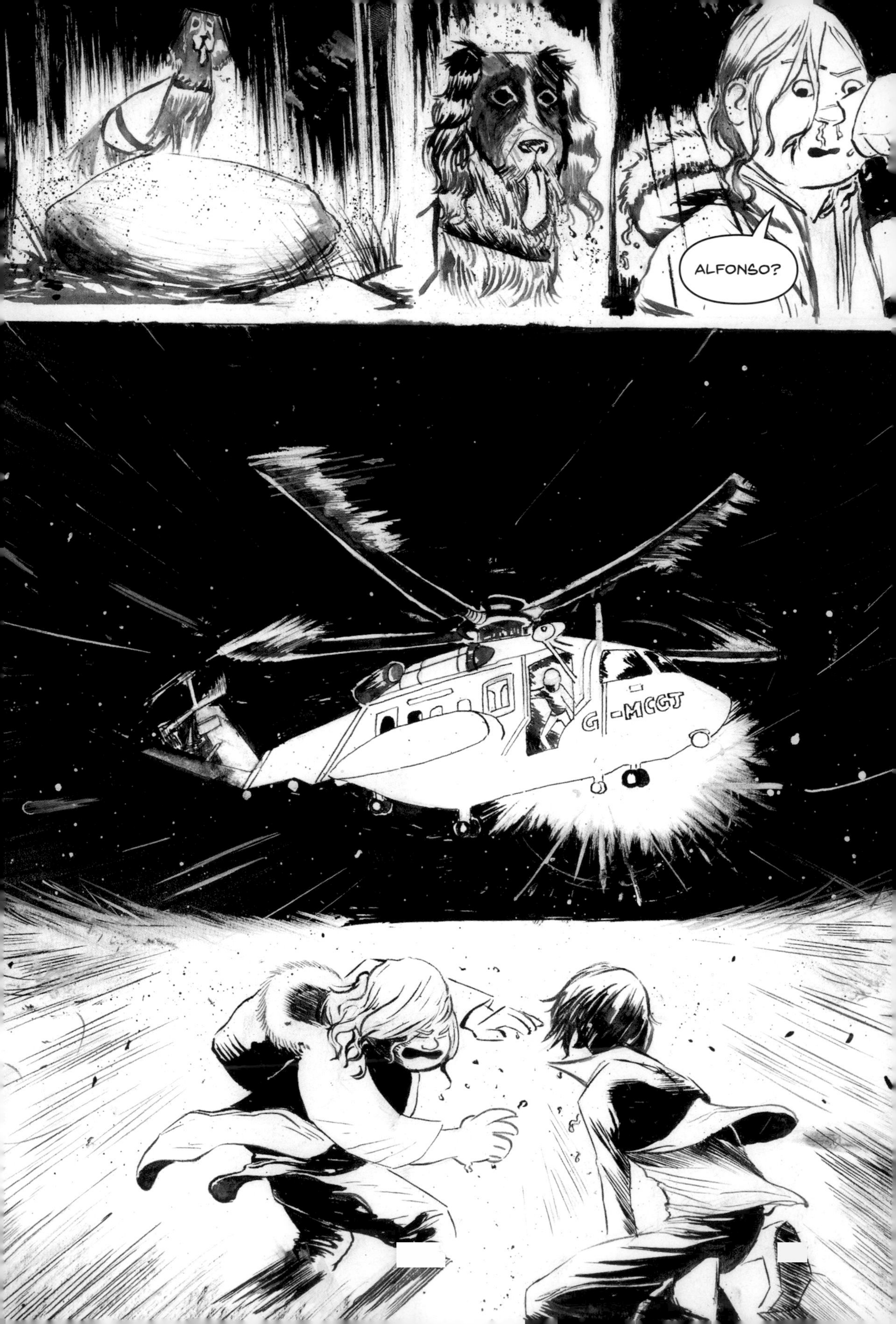
ALFONSO?
G-MCGT

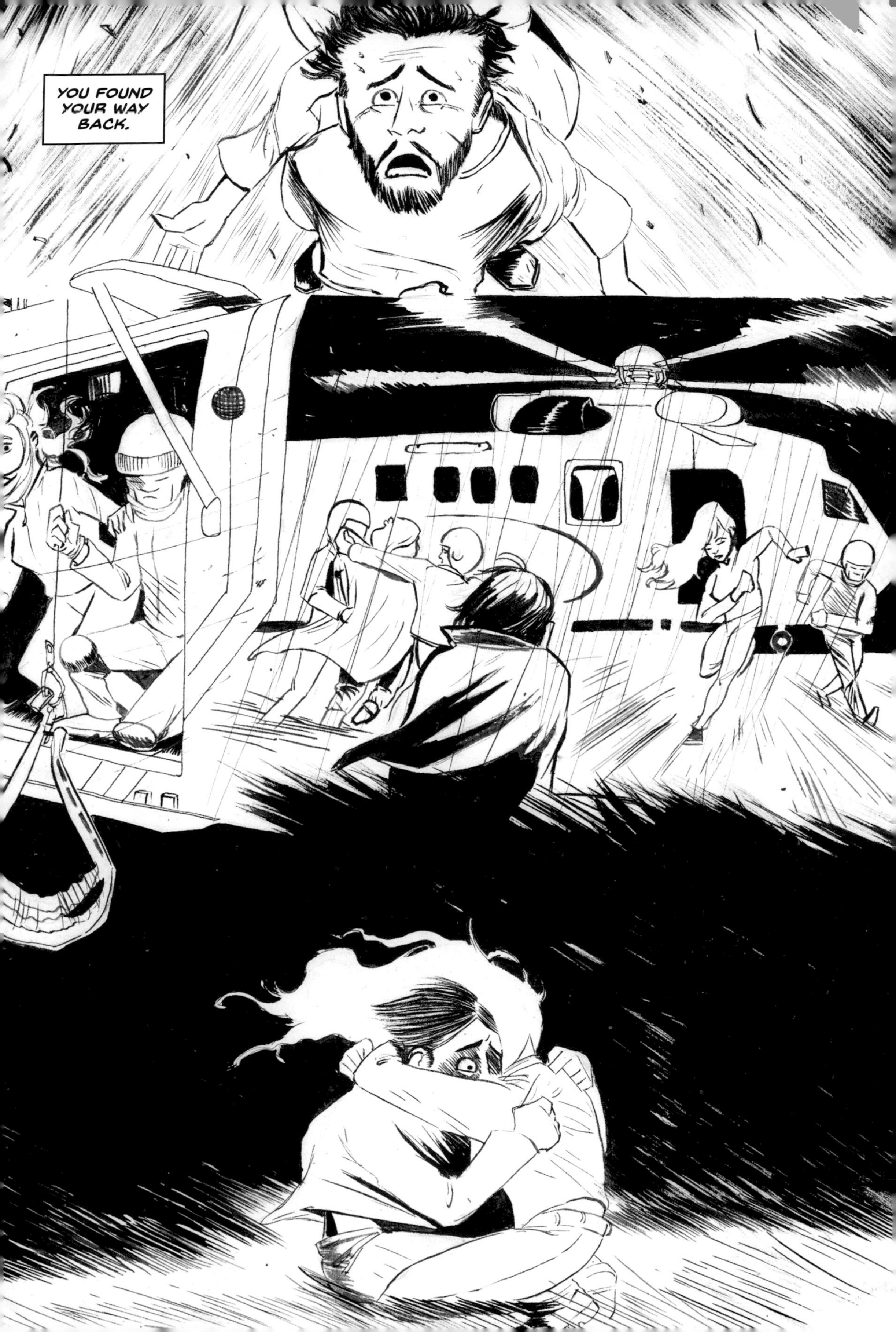
YOU FOUND YOUR WAY BACK.

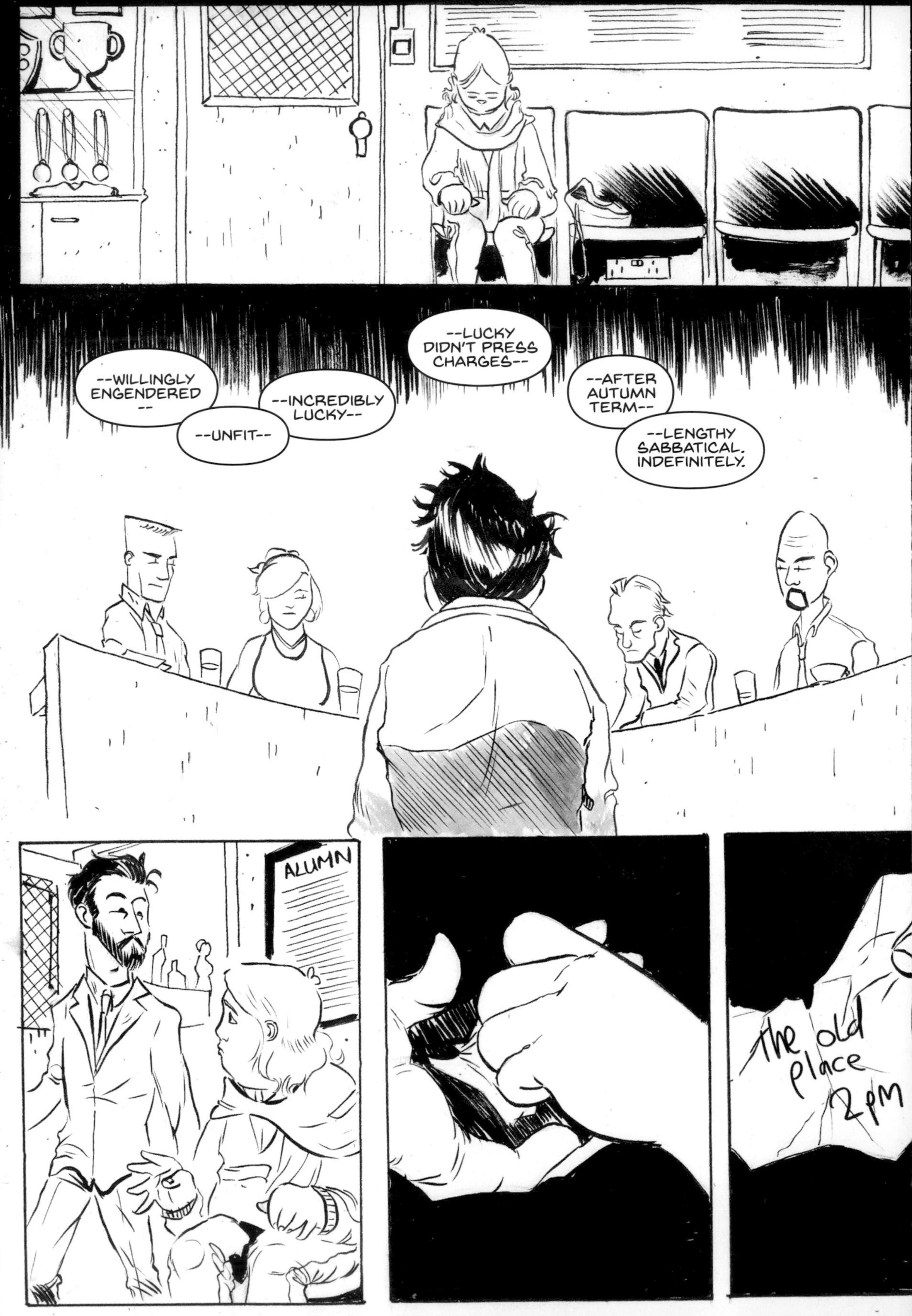
--WILLINGLY ENGENDERED --
--UNFIT--
--INCREDIBLY LUCKY--
--LUCKY DIDN'T PRESS CHARGES--
--AFTER AUTUMN TERM--
--LENGTHY SABBATICAL. INDEFINITELY.
ALUMN
the old place 2pM

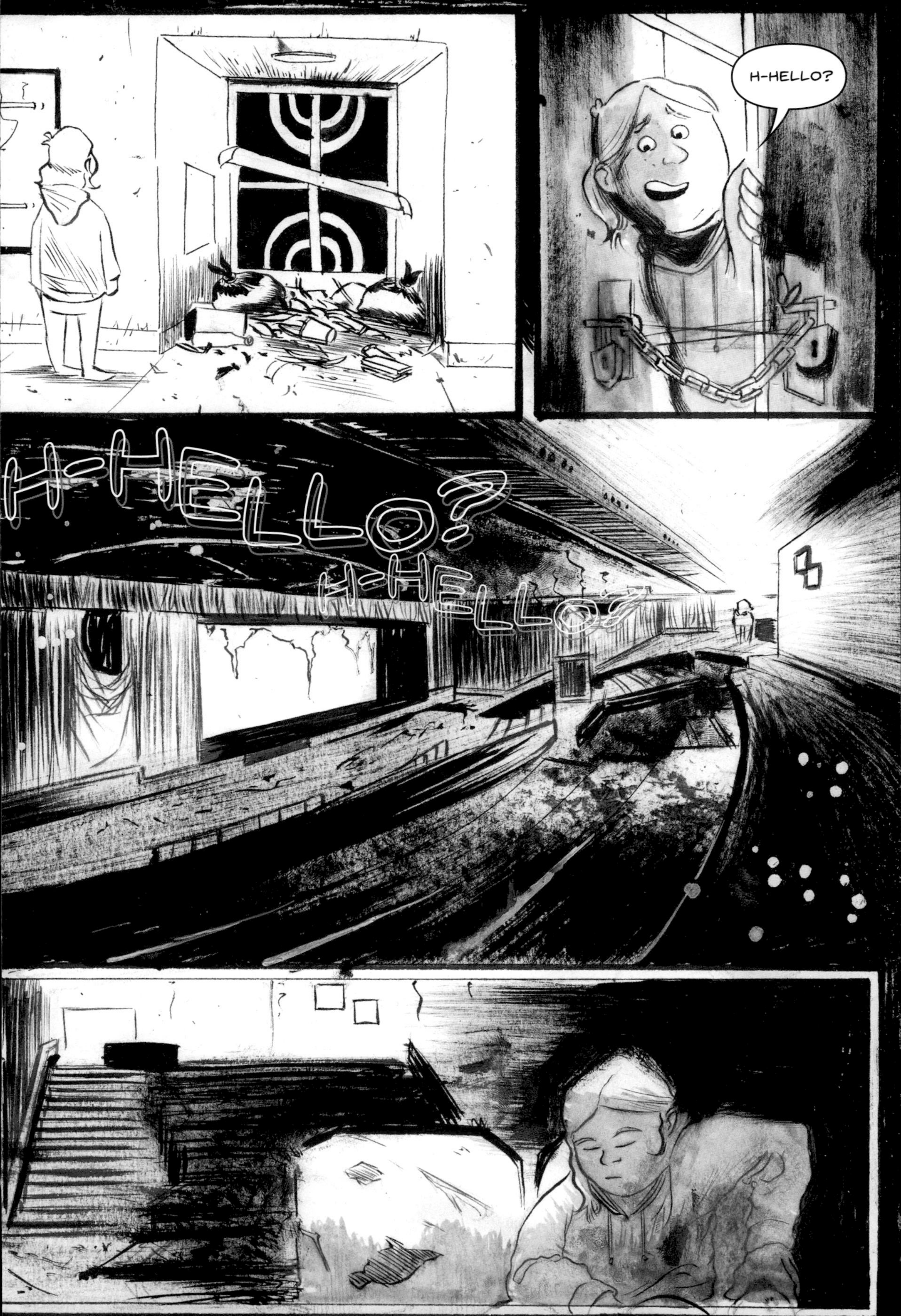
H-HELLO?
H-HELLO?
H-HELLO?

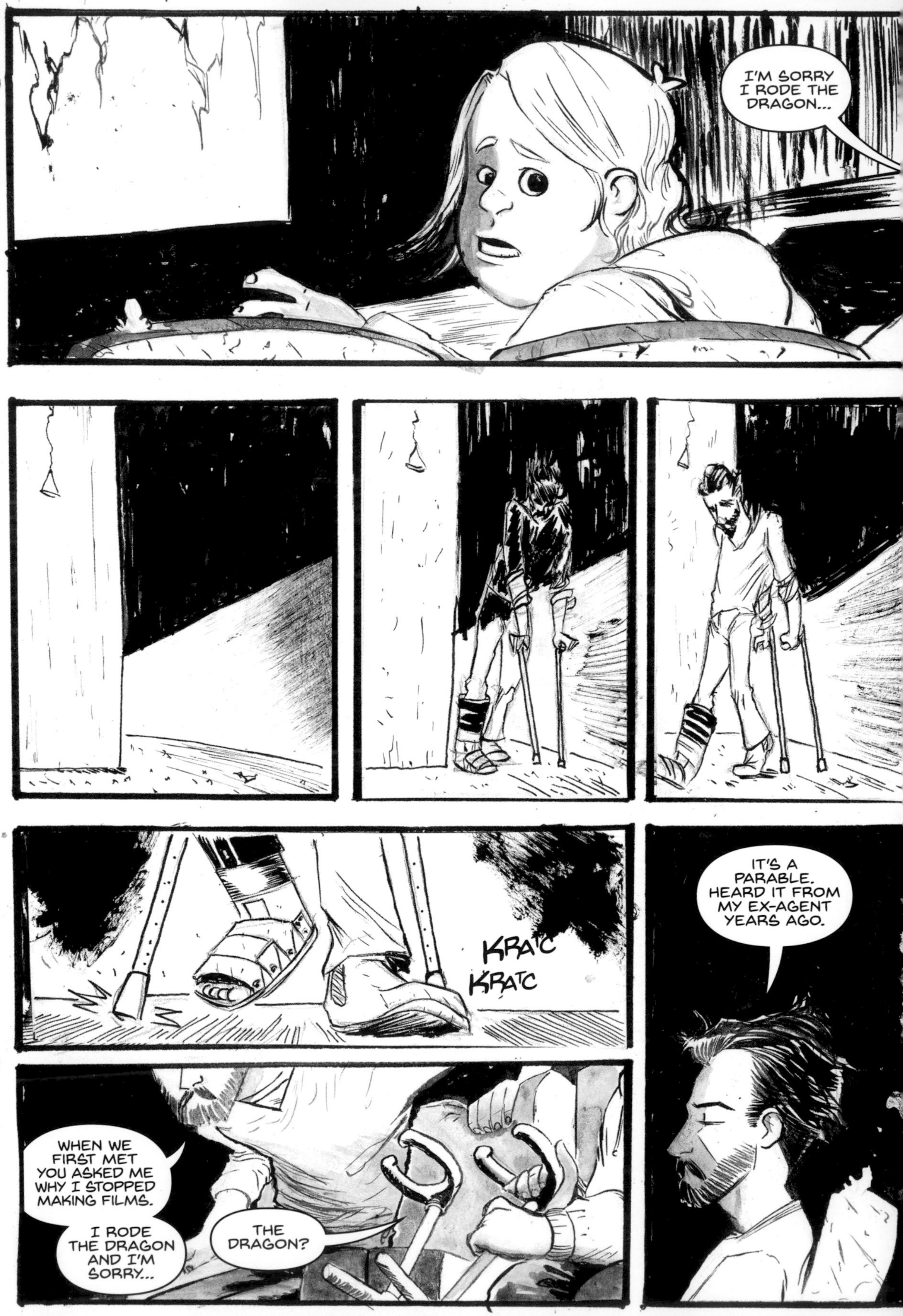
I'M SORRY I RODE THE DRAGON...
KRATC
KRATC
IT'S A PARABLE. HEARD IT FROM MY EX-AGENT YEARS AGO.
WHEN WE FIRST MET YOU ASKED ME WHY I STOPPED MAKING FILMS.
I RODE THE DRAGON AND I'M SORRY...
THE DRAGON?

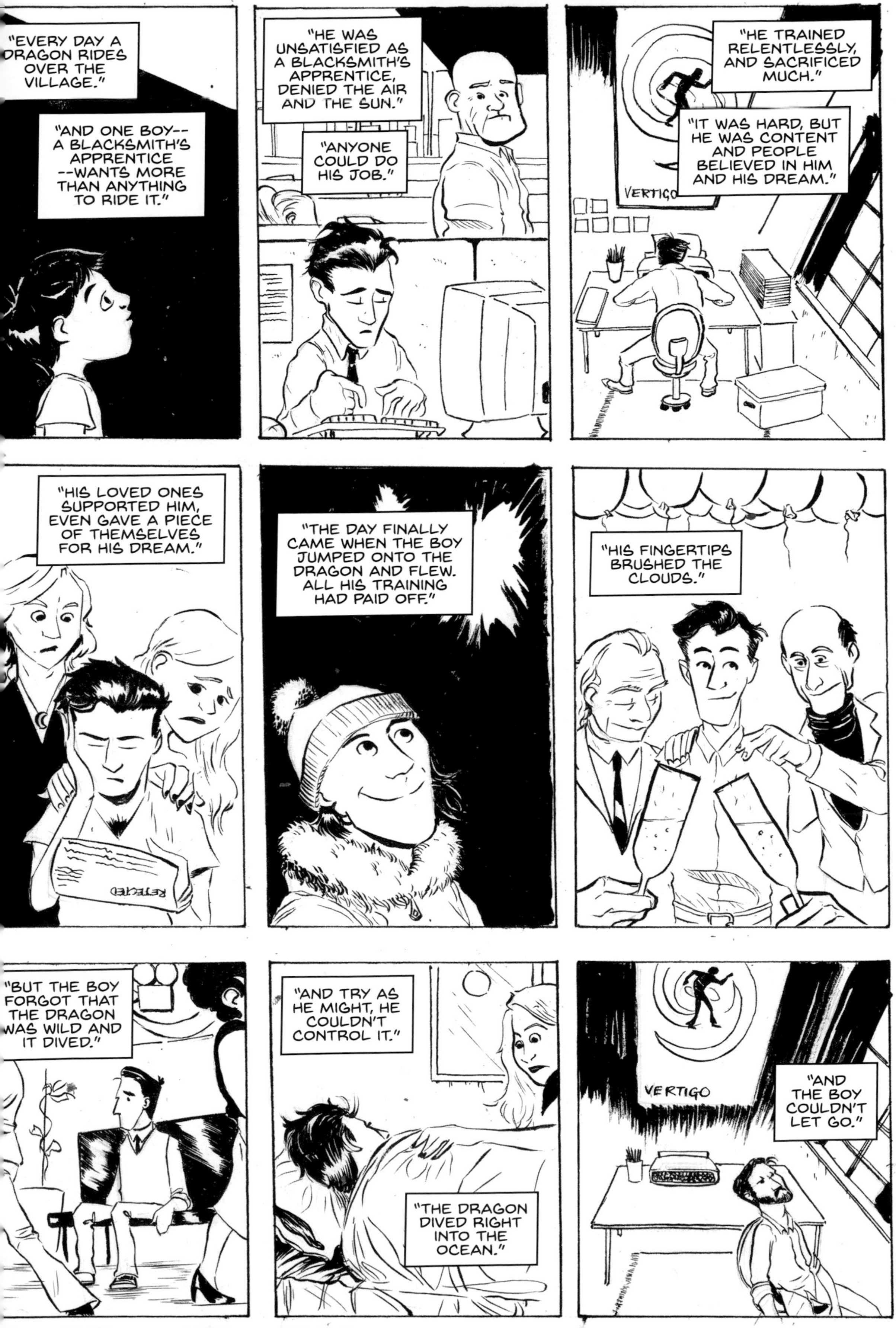
"EVERY DAY A DRAGON RIDES OVER THE VILLAGE."
"AND ONE BOY-- A BLACKSMITH'S APPRENTICE --WANTS MORE THAN ANYTHING TO RIDE IT."
"HE WAS UNSATISFIED AS A BLACKSMITH'S APPRENTICE, DENIED THE AIR AND THE SUN."
"ANYONE COULD DO HIS JOB."
"HE TRAINED RELENTLESSLY, AND SACRIFICED MUCH."
"IT WAS HARD, BUT HE WAS CONTENT AND PEOPLE BELIEVED IN HIM AND HIS DREAM."
VERTIGO
"HIS LOVED ONES SUPPORTED HIM, EVEN GAVE A PIECE OF THEMSELVES FOR HIS DREAM."
REJECTED
"THE DAY FINALLY CAME WHEN THE BOY JUMPED ONTO THE DRAGON AND FLEW. ALL HIS TRAINING HAD PAID OFF."
"HIS FINGERTIPS BRUSHED THE CLOUDS."
"BUT THE BOY FORGOT THAT THE DRAGON WAS WILD AND IT DIVED."
"AND TRY AS HE MIGHT, HE COULDN'T CONTROL IT."
"THE DRAGON DIVED RIGHT INTO THE OCEAN."
VERTIGO
"AND THE BOY COULDN'T LET GO."

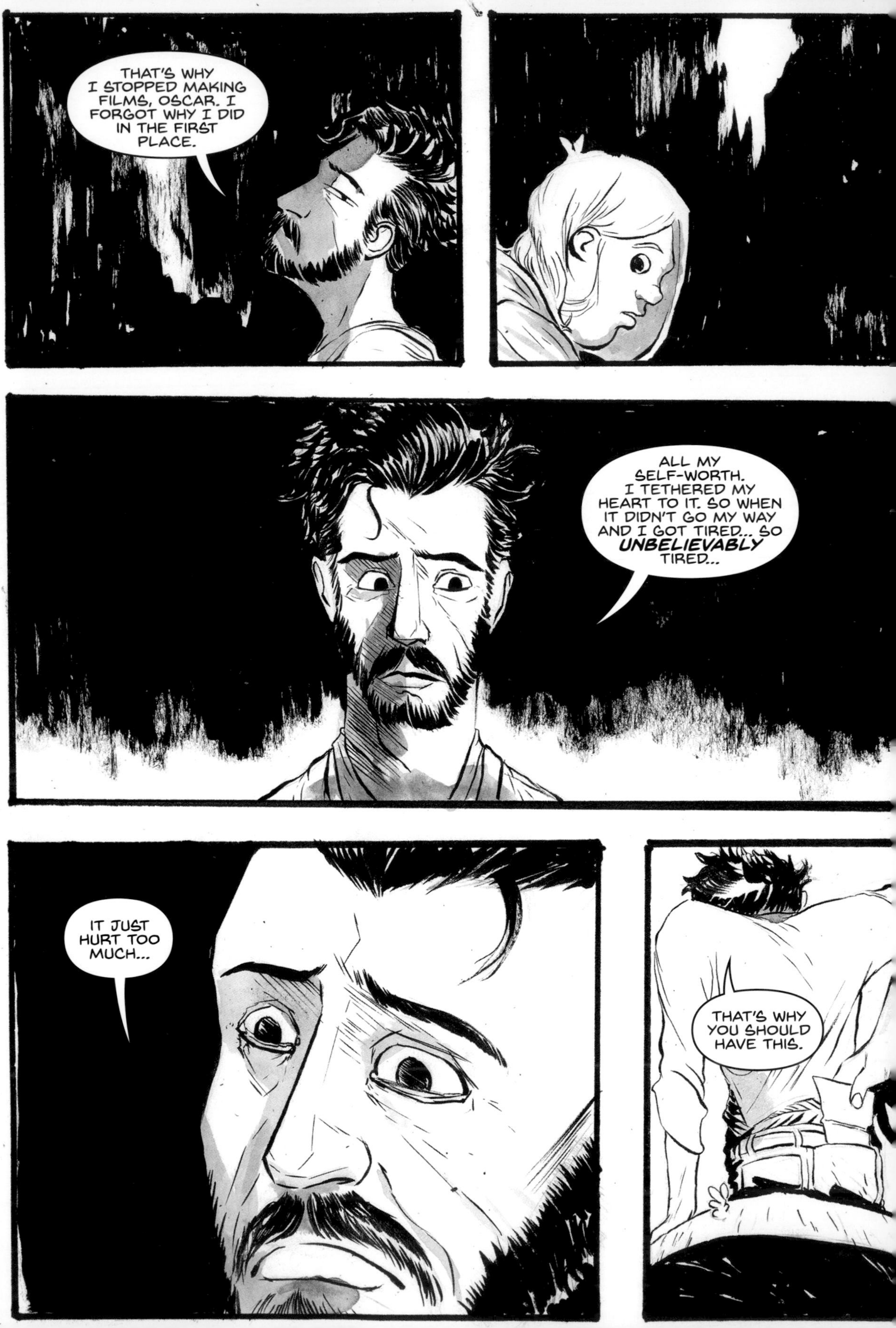
THAT'S WHY I STOPPED MAKING FILMS, OSCAR. I FORGOT WHY I DID IN THE FIRST PLACE.
ALL MY SELF-WORTH. I TETHERED MY HEART TO IT. SO WHEN IT DIDN'T GO MY WAY AND I GOT TIRED... SO UNBELIEVABLY TIRED...
IT JUST HURT TOO MUCH...
THAT'S WHY YOU SHOULD HAVE THIS.

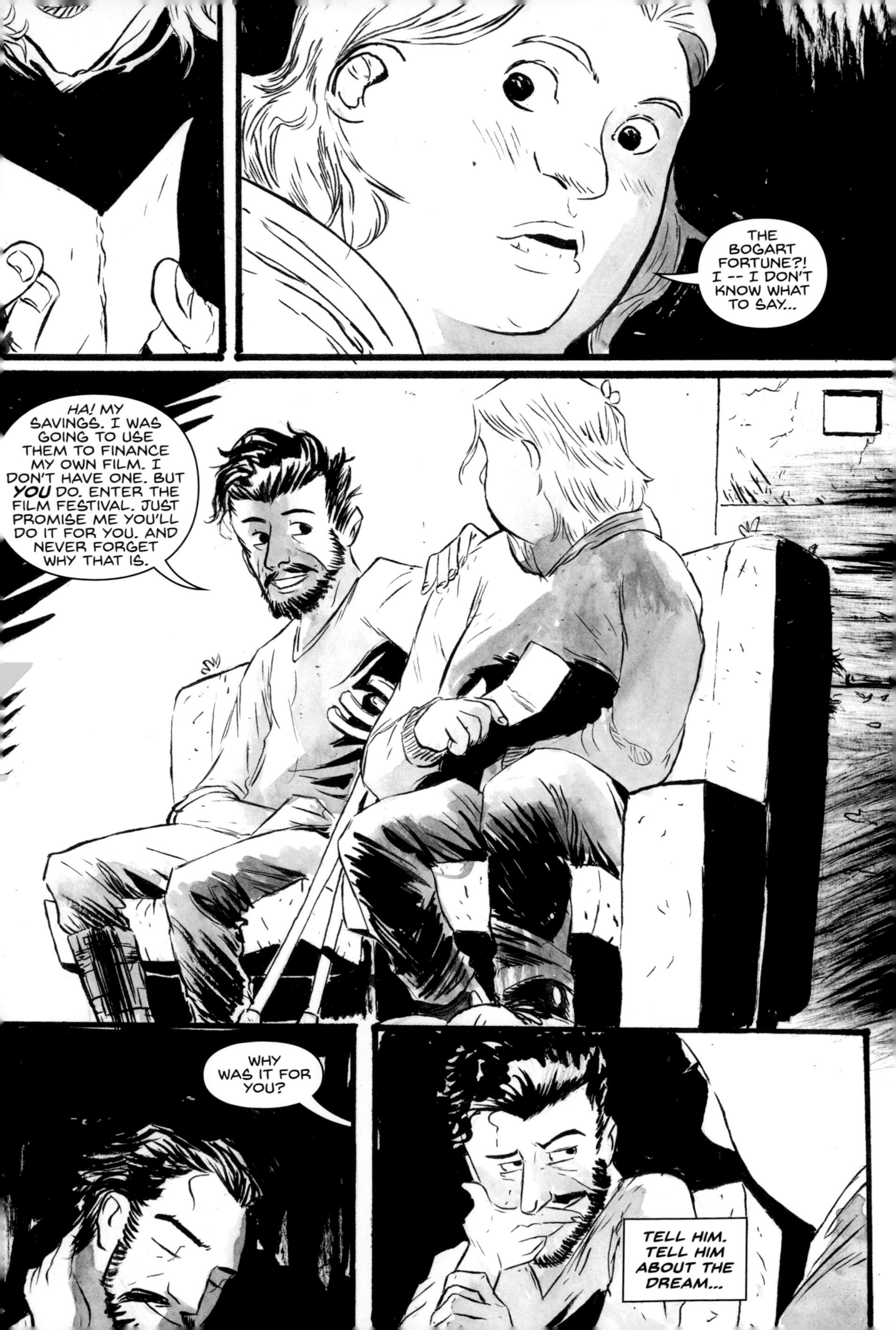
THE BOGART FORTUNE?! I -- I DON'T KNOW WHAT TO SAY...
HA! MY SAVINGS. I WAS GOING TO USE THEM TO FINANCE MY OWN FILM. I DON'T HAVE ONE. BUT YOU DO. ENTER THE FILM FESTIVAL. JUST PROMISE ME YOU'LL DO IT FOR YOU. AND NEVER FORGET WHY THAT IS.
WHY WAS IT FOR YOU?
TELL HIM. TELL HIM ABOUT THE DREAM...

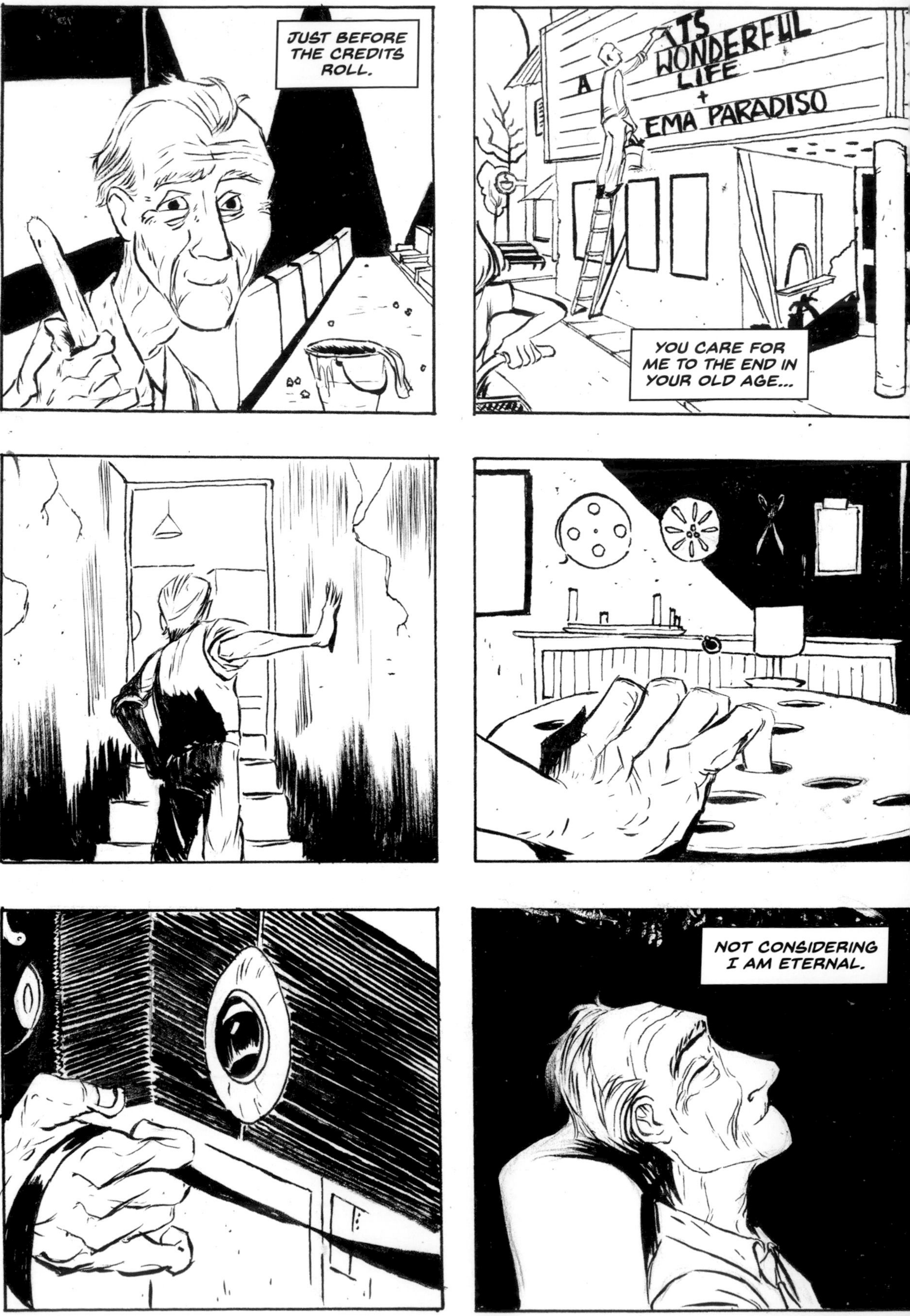
JUST BEFORE THE CREDITS ROLL.
A
WONDERFUL
LIFE
+
PARADISO
YOU CARE FOR ME TO THE END IN YOUR OLD AGE...
NOT CONSIDERING I AM ETERNAL.

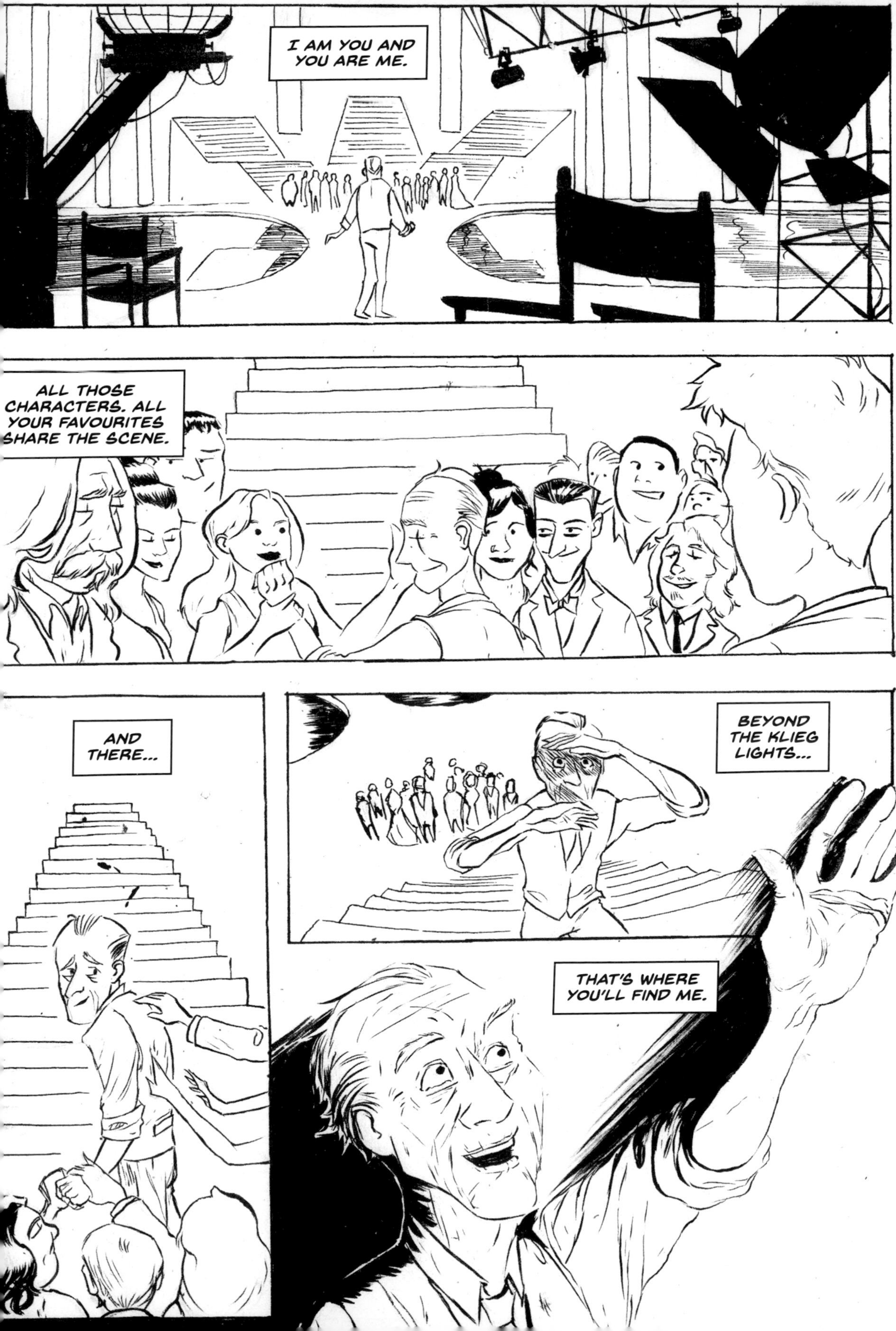

I AM YOU AND YOU ARE ME.
ALL THOSE CHARACTERS. ALL YOUR FAVOURITES SHARE THE SCENE.
AND THERE...
BEYOND THE KLIEG LIGHTS...
THAT'S WHERE YOU'LL FIND ME.

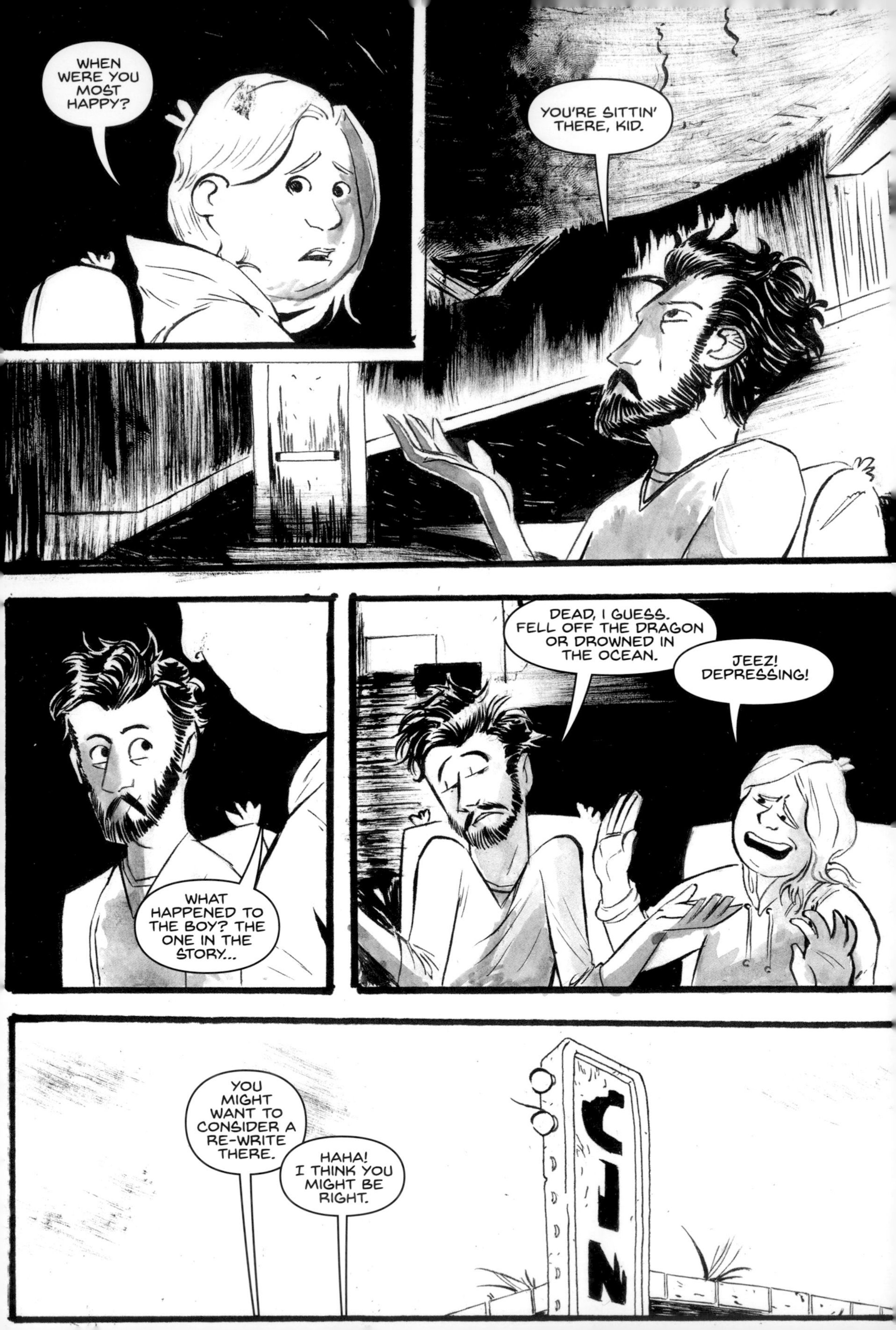
WHEN WERE YOU MOST HAPPY?
YOU'RE SITTIN' THERE, KID.
WHAT HAPPENED TO THE BOY? THE ONE IN THE STORY...
DEAD, I GUESS. FELL OFF THE DRAGON OR DROWNED IN THE OCEAN.
JEEZ! DEPRESSING!
YOU MIGHT WANT TO CONSIDER A RE-WRITE THERE.
HAHA! I THINK YOU MIGHT BE RIGHT.

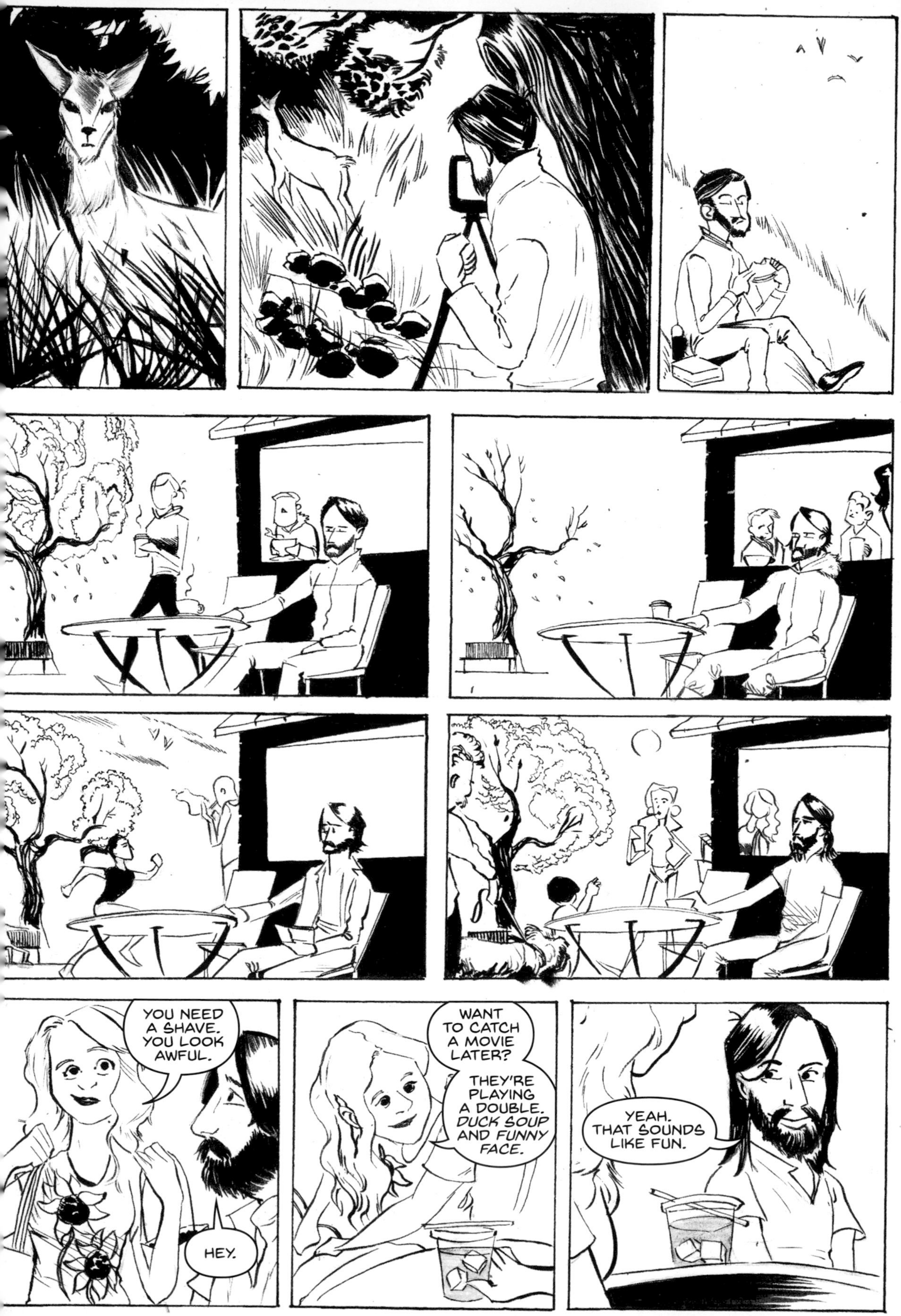
YOU NEED A SHAVE. YOU LOOK AWFUL.
HEY.
WANT TO CATCH A MOVIE LATER?
THEY'RE PLAYING A DOUBLE. *DUCK SOUP* AND *FUNNY FACE*.
YEAH. THAT SOUNDS LIKE FUN.

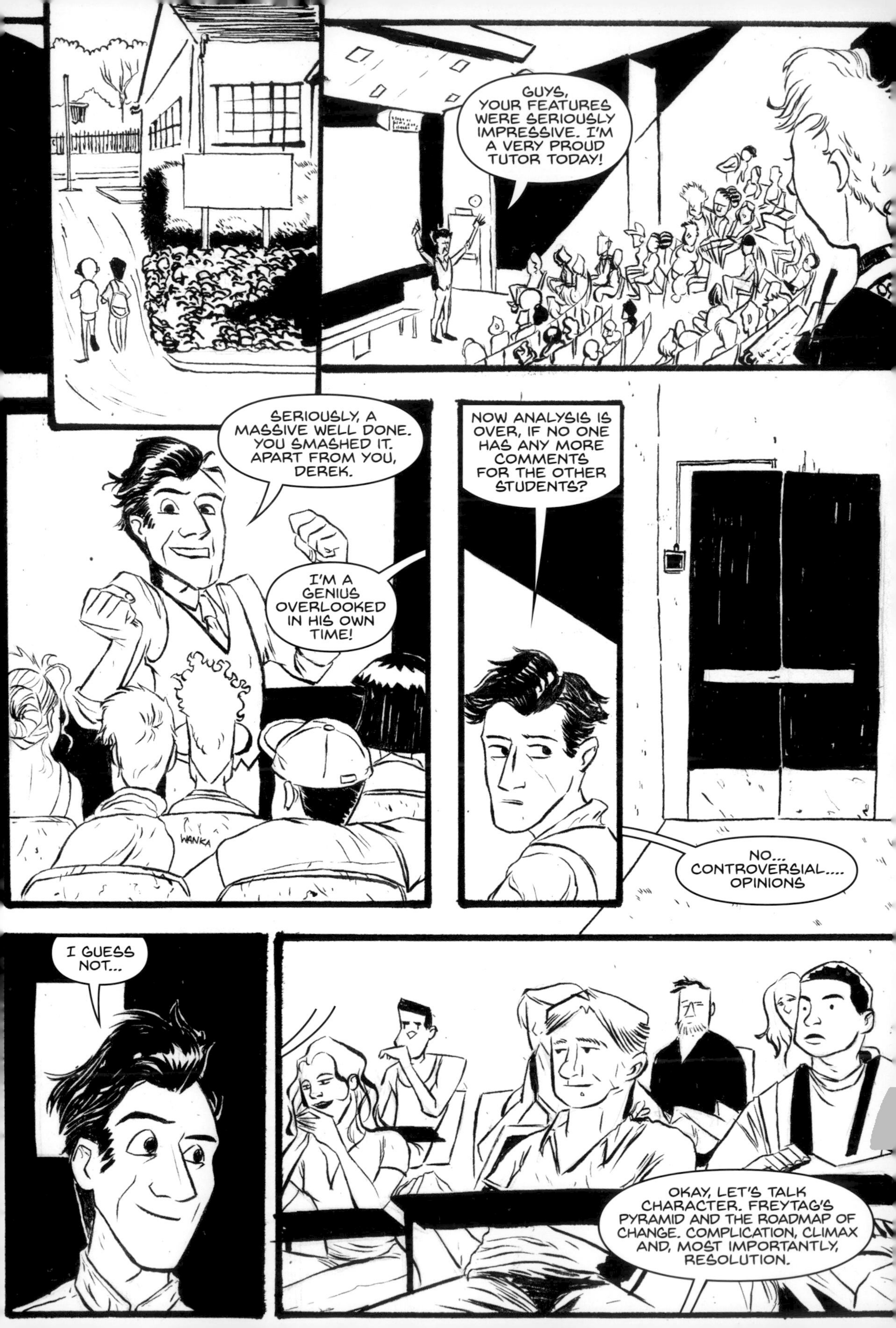
GUYS, YOUR FEATURES WERE SERIOUSLY IMPRESSIVE. I'M A VERY PROUD TUTOR TODAY!
SERIOUSLY, A MASSIVE WELL DONE. YOU SMASHED IT. APART FROM YOU, DEREK.
I'M A GENIUS OVERLOOKED IN HIS OWN TIME!
WANKA
NOW ANALYSIS IS OVER, IF NO ONE HAS ANY MORE COMMENTS FOR THE OTHER STUDENTS?
NO... CONTROVERSIAL.... OPINIONS
I GUESS NOT...
OKAY, LET'S TALK CHARACTER. FREYTAG'S PYRAMID AND THE ROADMAP OF CHANGE. COMPLICATION, CLIMAX AND, MOST IMPORTANTLY, RESOLUTION.

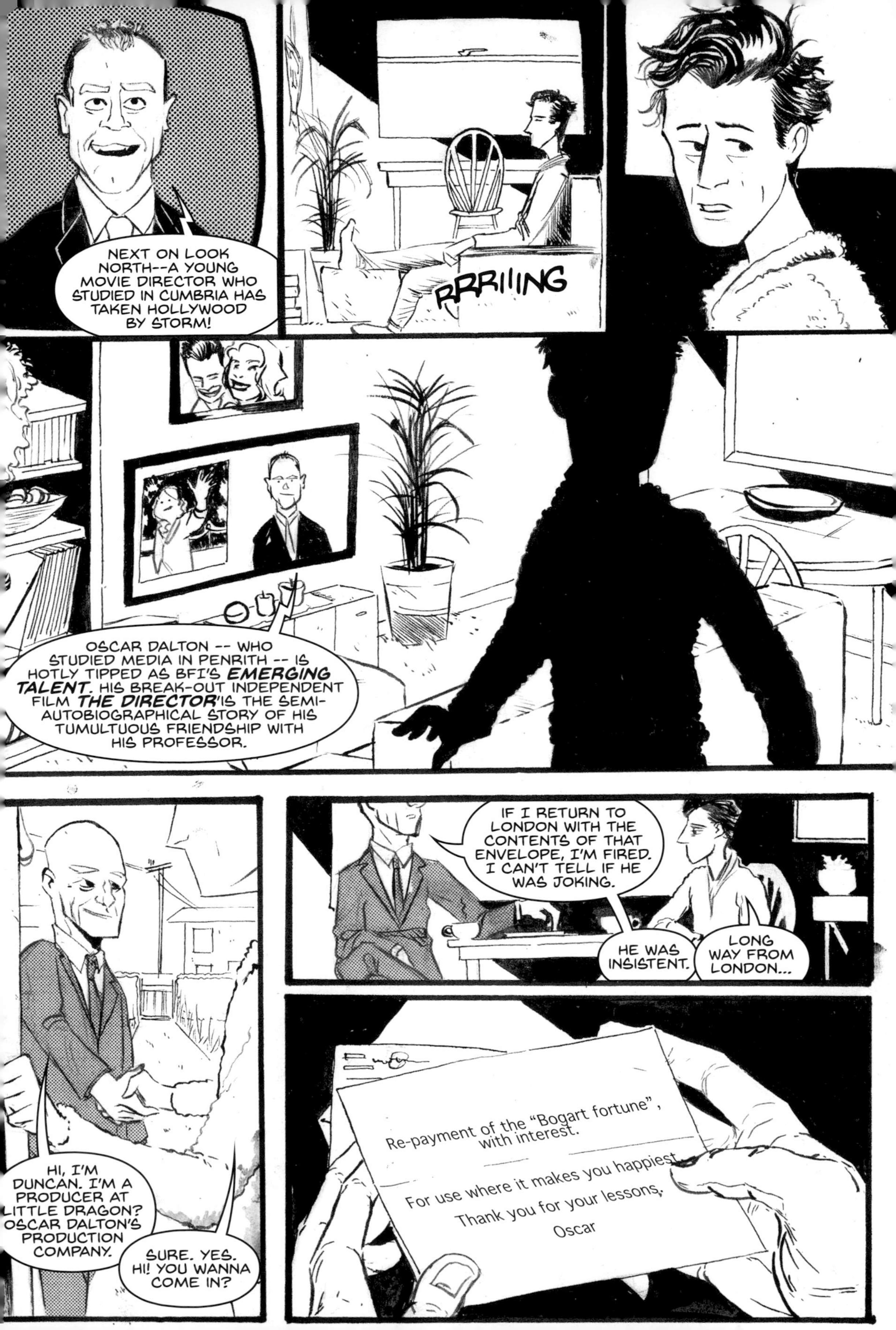
NEXT ON LOOK NORTH--A YOUNG MOVIE DIRECTOR WHO STUDIED IN CUMBRIA HAS TAKEN HOLLYWOOD BY STORM!
RRRIIING
OSCAR DALTON -- WHO STUDIED MEDIA IN PENRITH -- IS HOTLY TIPPED AS BFI'S **EMERGING TALENT**. HIS BREAK-OUT INDEPENDENT FILM ***THE DIRECTOR***'S THE SEMI-AUTOBIOGRAPHICAL STORY OF HIS TUMULTUOUS FRIENDSHIP WITH HIS PROFESSOR.
HI, I'M DUNCAN. I'M A PRODUCER AT LITTLE DRAGON? OSCAR DALTON'S PRODUCTION COMPANY.
SURE. YES. HI! YOU WANNA COME IN?
IF I RETURN TO LONDON WITH THE CONTENTS OF THAT ENVELOPE, I'M FIRED. I CAN'T TELL IF HE WAS JOKING.
HE WAS INSISTENT.
LONG WAY FROM LONDON...
Re-payment of the "Bogart fortune", with interest.
For use where it makes you happiest.
Thank you for your lessons,
Oscar

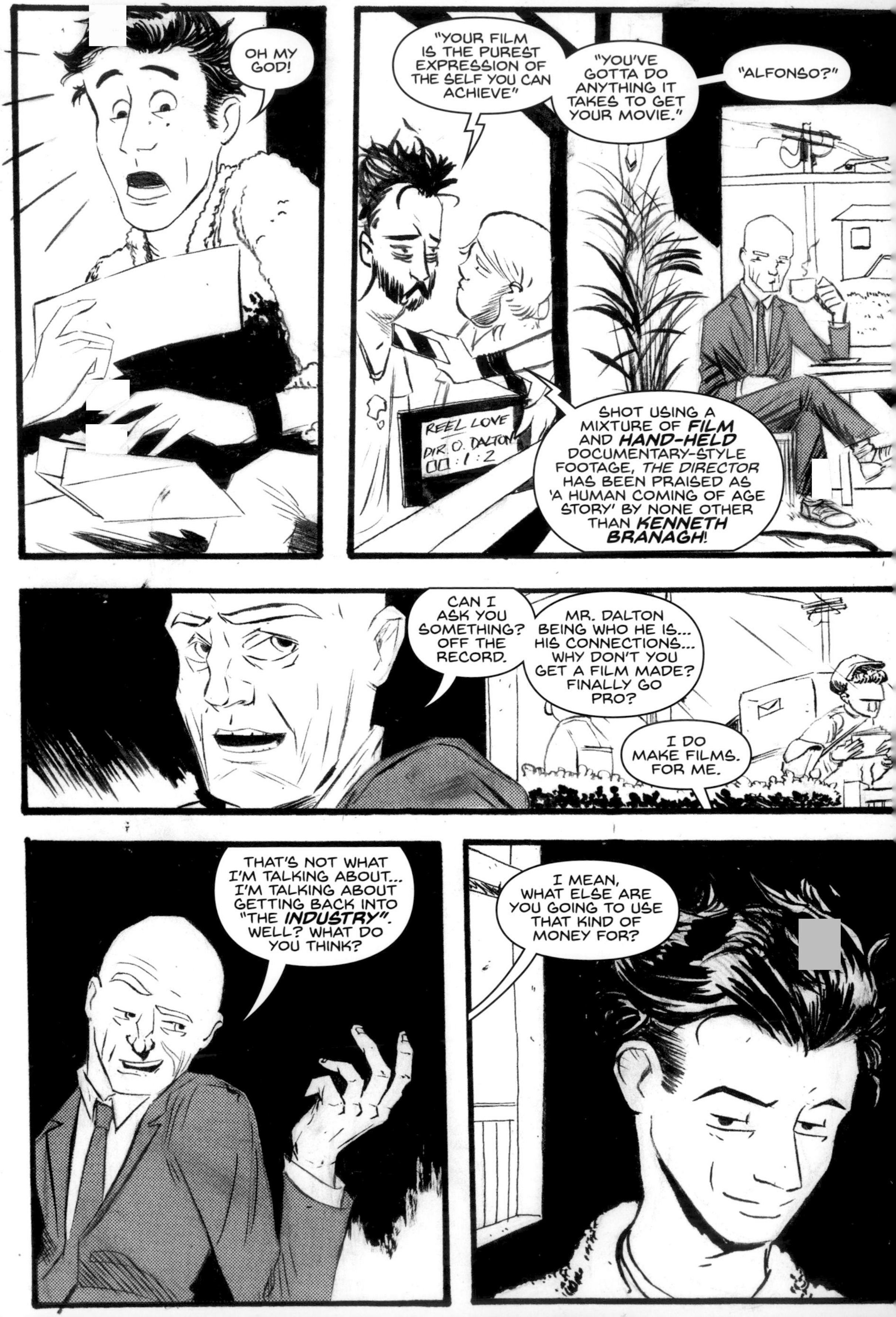
OH MY GOD!
"YOUR FILM IS THE PUREST EXPRESSION OF THE SELF YOU CAN ACHIEVE"
"YOU'VE GOTTA DO ANYTHING IT TAKES TO GET YOUR MOVIE."
"ALFONSO?"
REEL LOVE
DIR. O. DALTON
SHOT USING A MIXTURE OF FILM AND HAND-HELD DOCUMENTARY-STYLE FOOTAGE, THE DIRECTOR HAS BEEN PRAISED AS 'A HUMAN COMING OF AGE STORY' BY NONE OTHER THAN KENNETH BRANAGH!
CAN I ASK YOU SOMETHING? OFF THE RECORD.
MR. DALTON BEING WHO HE IS... HIS CONNECTIONS... WHY DON'T YOU GET A FILM MADE? FINALLY GO PRO?
I DO MAKE FILMS. FOR ME.
THAT'S NOT WHAT I'M TALKING ABOUT... I'M TALKING ABOUT GETTING BACK INTO "THE INDUSTRY". WELL? WHAT DO YOU THINK?
I MEAN, WHAT ELSE ARE YOU GOING TO USE THAT KIND OF MONEY FOR?

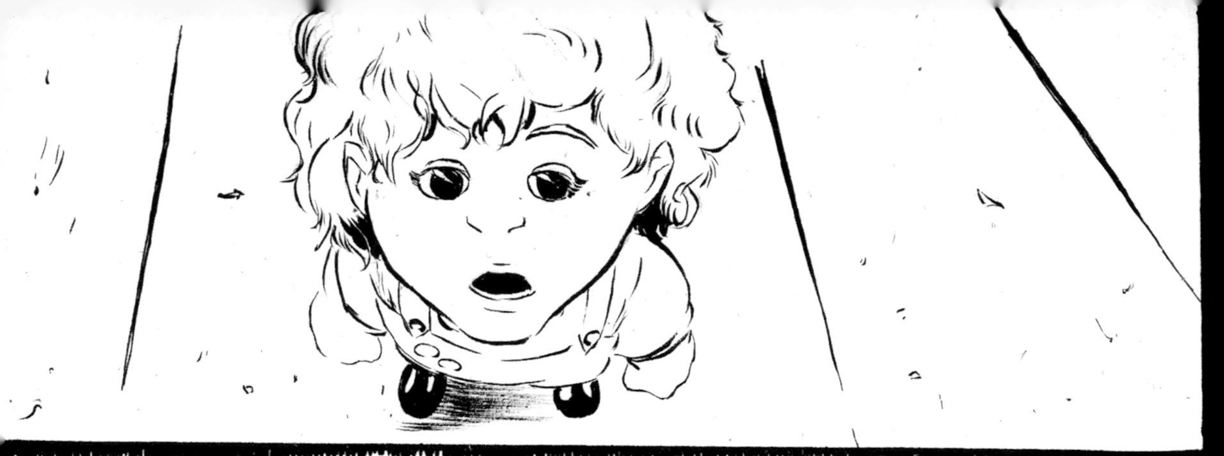

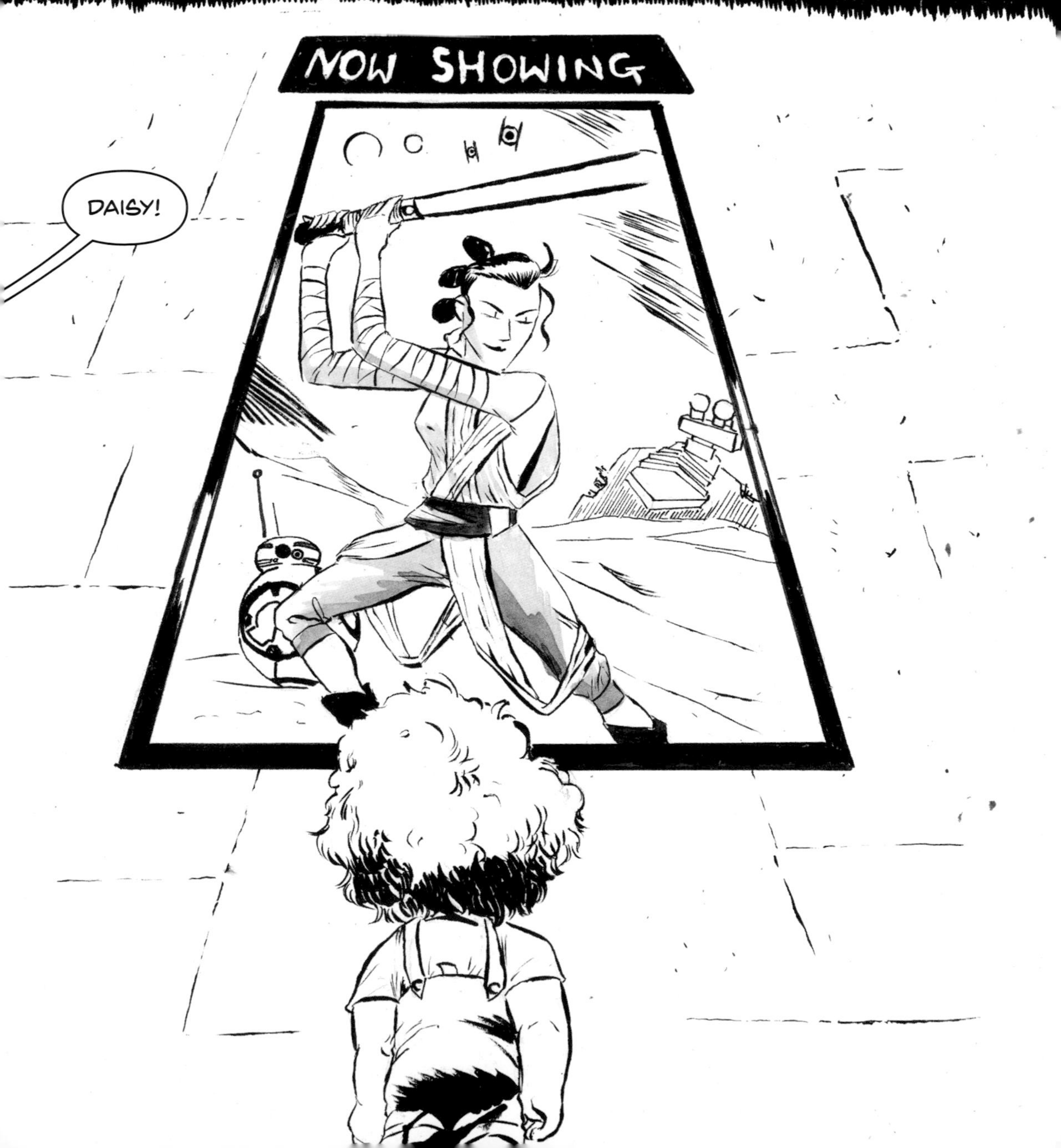
NOW SHOWING
DAISY!

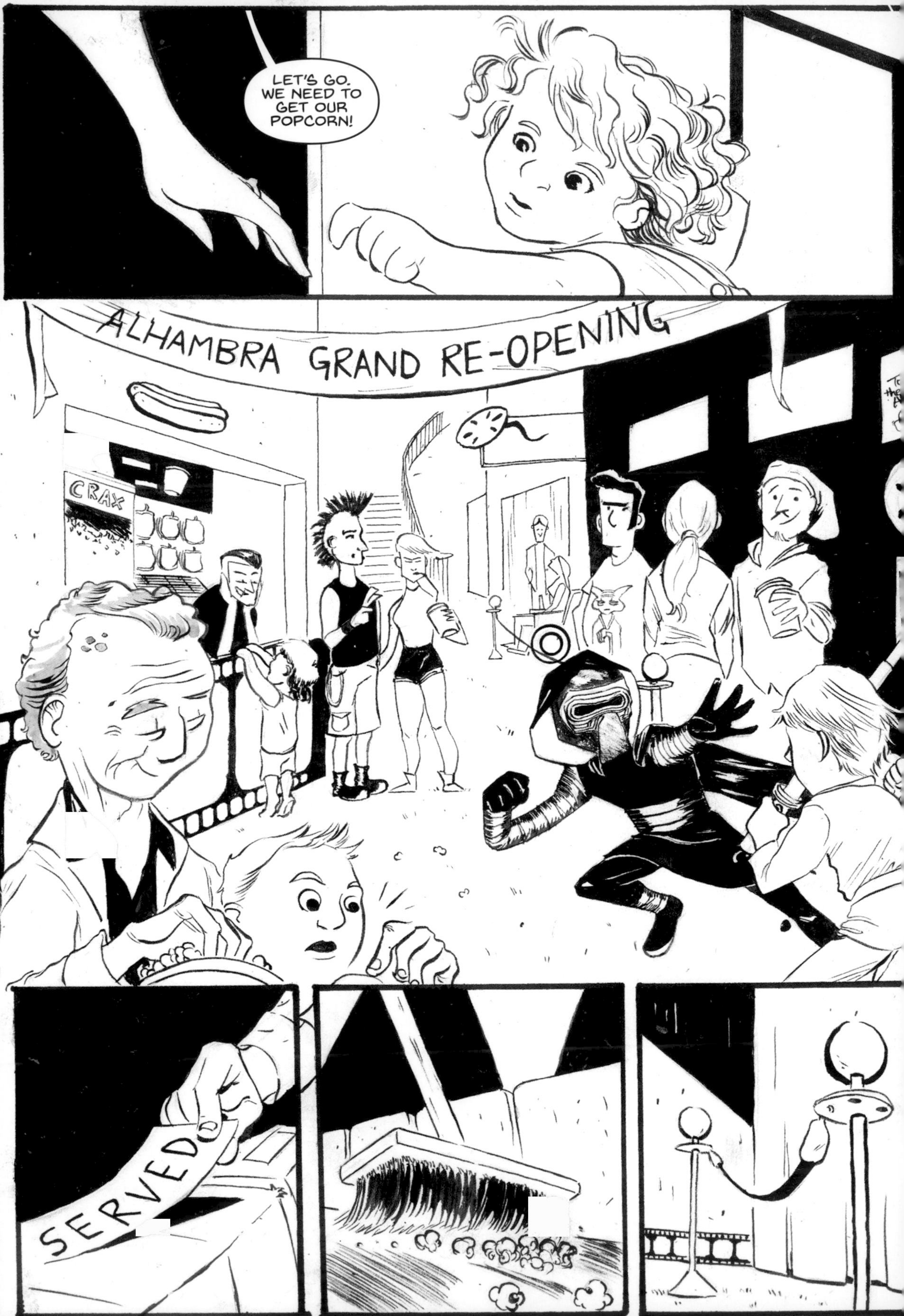
LET'S GO. WE NEED TO GET OUR POPCORN!
ALHAMBRA GRAND RE-OPENING
CRAX
SERVED

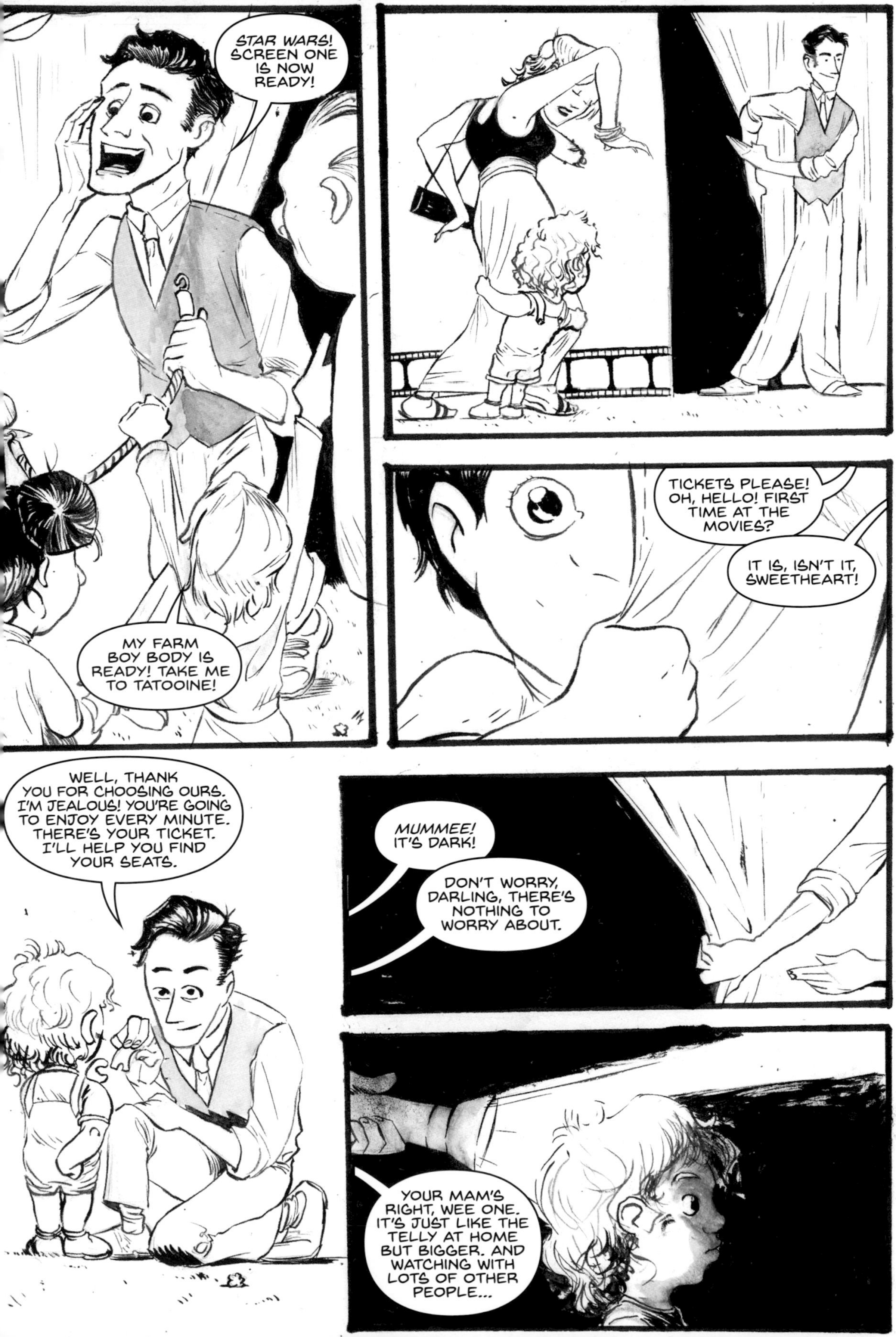
STAR WARS! SCREEN ONE IS NOW READY!
MY FARM BOY BODY IS READY! TAKE ME TO TATOOINE!
TICKETS PLEASE! OH, HELLO! FIRST TIME AT THE MOVIES?
IT IS, ISN'T IT, SWEETHEART!
WELL, THANK YOU FOR CHOOSING OURS. I'M JEALOUS! YOU'RE GOING TO ENJOY EVERY MINUTE. THERE'S YOUR TICKET. I'LL HELP YOU FIND YOUR SEATS.
MUMMEE! IT'S DARK!
DON'T WORRY, DARLING, THERE'S NOTHING TO WORRY ABOUT.
YOUR MAM'S RIGHT, WEE ONE. IT'S JUST LIKE THE TELLY AT HOME BUT BIGGER. AND WATCHING WITH LOTS OF OTHER PEOPLE...

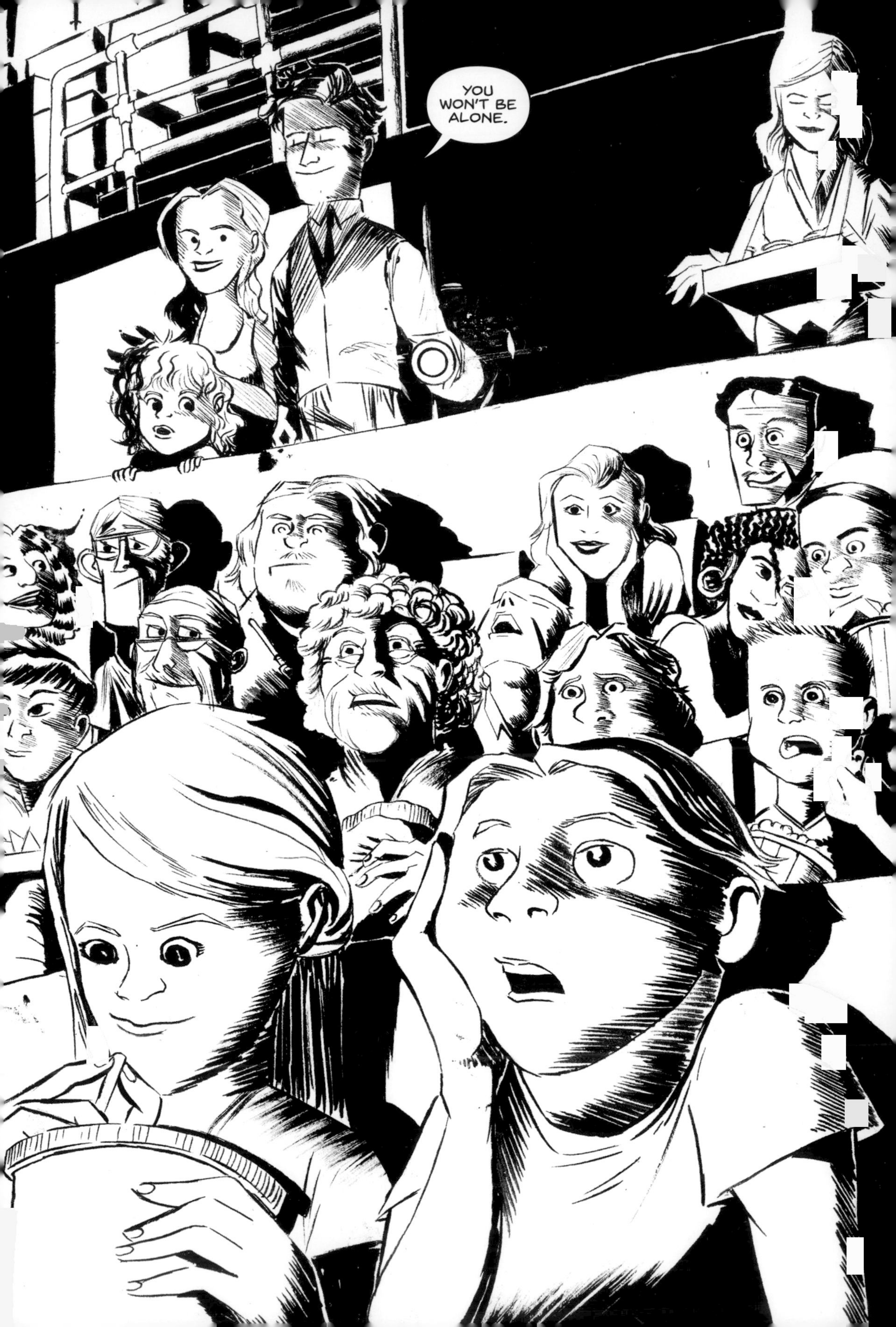
YOU WON'T BE ALONE.

Acknowledgments

Reel Love began when I returned to my hometown after a period of years away. It was a hard time to find work and I moved between jobs, eventually working for the local family-run cinema I had grown up visiting. After work one night, I drove around the empty roads of the Eden valley listening to Bruce Springsteen, thinking about where I had been since leaving home and where I wanted to go next. Absently, I drew the first pages of *Reel Love* that night, with no real idea of what I was making.

Thanks to my family, who not only cultivated a household which valued and nurtured creativity of all kinds, but who also remain selfless with their time, patience and collective willpower. They have been essential in cheerleading me down this track.

Thanks to my editor Lizzie Kaye for having faith in the book and electing to champion my voice, as well as the Unbound team for helping us cross the finish line. Thanks to Pye Parr for his outstanding work in lettering.

My thanks to the Prince Charles and Genesis Cinemas in London for their assistance in promotion. Thanks also to Alan Towers and the team at the Lonsdale cinema in Penrith, upon which this book is loosely based.

Thanks to Tommy at the Imagination Station in Carlisle and Karl Asaa at Orbital Comics, both of whom happily stocked my self-published comics long before a legitimate publisher came calling. The success I've managed is due to both the UK small press and global crowdfunding communities, and I would not be in the position I'm in now without the support of many friends and strangers. My heartfelt appreciation goes to them.

My thanks to Julie Tait and the Lakes International Comic Art Festival, along with the Arts Council of England for their assistance in getting this book made.

Thanks to Doug Cowie and the Royal Holloway University of London Creative Writing program for doing their best to expand my limited writing horizons.

I'm also indebted to the various artists I've been lucky enough to collaborate with over the years. John Pearson, Mark Penman and Conor Boyle in particular have inspired me to be a practising artist, and I'm grateful for their aid, generous mentoring and crucial assistance. Surrounding yourself in talent is key to progress, and I quite simply wouldn't be doing this without watching them do it better.

Thanks to Oliver Pickles for reading drafts and keeping me in Jaffa cakes in the run up to completion.

My thanks to Jeff Smith, Jeff Lemire, Frank Quitely and countless other comic industry professionals who have dispensed advice and encouragement.

Perhaps the greatest contributor to this book existing beyond my brain is Colin Bell who, when it was nothing more than a few tentative and raw pages, recognised the book's value when I didn't consider it more than therapy. For his decision to letter and self-publish the first chapter (and for his good humour) I'm extremely grateful.

Thanks to Max Deacon, my longest-serving proofreader. Max never fails to get to the heart of what I'm trying to achieve in my work, and suggests adjustments I can't - or sometimes refuse - to see, but which inevitably improve the whole. His years of support and friendship have been a gift.

Finally, thanks to Louise Richardson for her constant warmth and understanding. Be it the early hours or the last minute, she freely imparts the perspective and humour I often lack and for which I'm deeply grateful.

Reel Love was drawn by hand in Cumbria, London and Oxford using Winsor & Newton brushes and Indian ink. I was taught the rudiments of drawing by Margaret, my grandmother on my mother's side, and by Ernest, my grandfather on my father's side. Though he didn't live to see this debut, he recognised something deeper among a careless carousel of childhood interests. Humouring the latest New Thing – be it the tuneless music I concocted, the uncoordinated football or the self-conscious acting – he told me, "I still think you could make it as a cartoonist." Looks like he was right.

Owen Michael Johnson, Oxford, 2018.

Owen Michael Johnson is a writer and cartoonist from Kirkoswald in the Lake District. His comic book writing has garnered two British Comic Award nominations for *Raygun Roads* (2013) with INDIO! and *Beast Wagon* (2015) with John Pearson. *Reel Love* is his debut graphic novel as writer and artist. He has promoted comics for Titan and *2000 AD*. Owen currently lives in Oxford.

Supporters

Unbound is a new kind of publishing house. Our books are funded directly by readers. This was a very popular idea during the late eighteenth and early nineteenth centuries. Now we have revived it for the internet age. It allows authors to write the books they really want to write and readers to support the books they would most like to see published.

The names listed below are of readers who have pledged their support and made this book happen.

If you'd like to join them, visit **www.unbound.com**.

Finn
G-Man (Comics Anonymous)
Ananda Allan
James Atherton
Matt Bainbridge
Robin Barnard
John Beeching
Chris Bennett
Ian Bowkett
Mark Bowsher
Paul Braidford
Nick Brokenshire
John P Carr
Charlie Clarke
Ricky Claydon
GMark Cole
Joe Coleman
Lakes International Comics Festival
James Corcoran
Arts Council
Douglas Cowie
Daniel Cox
David Crompton
Becky D'Anna
Max Deacon
James Dowling
Edward Doyle
Alisha Ebling
Michael Eckett
Joseph England
Jack Fallows
Adam Falp
Jack Firth
Alex Fitch
Caroline Gale
Maria Goodson
Joe Gordon
Hywel Griffith
Paul Groom

Jason Guth

James Hancock

Andrew Harle

Ned Hartley

Claire Heuvingh

David Hitchcock

Jeff Horne

Lee Howes

Steven Ingram

Johari Ismail

Andrew James

Rosie Johnson

Dawn Johnson

Ian Johnson

Paddy Johnston

Candice Karenin

Christopher Keith-Wright

Dan Kieran

Rebecca Knight

Lukas Kraina

Ute Liersch

Robert Lilley (Bristol)

Garry Mac

Cairn Macfarland

Xander Mackenzie

Colin Mathieson

Craig Mattinson

John Mitchinson

Paul Moore

Carlo Navato

Sha Nazir

Monty Nero

Ryan O'Sullivan

Max Olesker

Sam Oliver-Watts

G Ortego

Sally Osborn

Scott Pack

Alex Paknadel

Heather Palmer

Mark Penman

Oliver Pickles

Michael Plasom-Scott

Justin Pollard

Dan Pratt

Chris Prendergast

Sharron Preston

Jenna Propst

Henry Quinton-Zorn

Michele Richardson

Steve and Jan Richardson

Louise Richardson

Jennifer Richardson

Jacob Rivera

Lisi Russell
Sam Savage
Martin Simmonds
Thal Sneddon
Matt Soffe
Efthymios Stamos
Martin Stiff
Brian Thompson
Alan Towers
Damian Treece
Angela Turner
Stevie Turner
Ram V
Stephanie Wasek
Steve White
Dan Whitehead
Jason Wilson
Joshua Winning
Dion Winton-Polak
David Wood
Robert Young